Foucault and Theology

Other titles in the Philosophy and Theology series include:

Zizek and Theology, Adam Kotsko
Nietzsche and Theology, Craig Hovey
Girard and Theology, Michael Kirwan
Wittgenstein and Theology, Tim Labron
Hegel and Theology, Martin J. De Nys
Derrida and Theology, Steven Shakespeare
Badiou and Theology, Frederiek Depoortere
Vattimo and Theology, Thomas G. Guarino
Kierkegaard and Theology, Murray Rae
Kant and Theology, Pamela Sue Anderson and Jordan Bell
Adorno and Theology, Christopher Craig Brittain

Foucault and Theology

Jonathan Tran

t&t clark

Published by T&T Clark International
A Continuum Imprint
The Tower Building, 11 York Road, London SE1 7NX
80 Maiden Lane, Suite 704, New York, NY 10038

www.continuumbooks.com

All rights reserved. No part of this publication may be reproduced or transmitted in any form or by any means, electronic or mechanical, including photocopying, recording or any information storage or retrieval system, without permission in writing from the publishers.

© Jonathan Tran, 2011

Jonathan Tran has asserted his right under the Copyright, Designs and Patents Act, 1988, to be identified as the Author of this work.

British Library Cataloguing-in-Publication Data
A catalogue record for this book is available from the British Library.

ISBN 13: 978-0-567-03342-0 (hardback)
ISBN 13: 978-0-567-03343-7 (paperback)

Typeset by Newgen Imaging Systems Pvt Ltd, Chennai, India

For Thierry McEldowney

Contents

Acknowledgments	ix
Introduction	1
1. Witness, not Resistance	3
2. Global Capitalism's Power	7
3. Overview	13

Part 1 Power and Totality

1 Power	17
1. Retheorizing Power	22
2. Biopower	26
3. Power's Ruse	34
4. "Courage to Begin Anew"	39
2 Capitalism, Totality, and Resistance	48
1. "Immanence in Its Simplest Form"	50
2. The Demise of the Nation-State	53
3. Empire	55
4. The Church's New Visibility	61

Part 2 Self-Writing

3 Biography and Biopolitics	67
1. What Is Biography?	69
2. *Salmagundi 97*	73
3. The Modern Self's Biography	76
4. Biography and Absence	82
5. Biography as Theology	86
4 Writing the Self	93
1. Where There Is Power, There Are Selves	97
2. Surfaces of Emergence: For and Against Heidegger	102
3. Confessing the Self	112

5 Self-Care: The Case of Animals — 125
   1. Eating Animals — 130
   2. The Claims of Vegetarianism — 135
   3. Coming to Terms — 139
   4. The Difficulty of Reality — 145
   5. Seeing — 149
   6. Companionship with Animals: Eucharistic Seeing — 153

Postscript — 160

Notes — 163
Index — 207

Acknowledgments

Long before Michel Foucault taught me the work thought brings to bear on itself, my brother Thierry taught me to love thinking, a gift about as endless as one can receive. To him I dedicate this book with greatest affection.

My wife Carrie and I lost two babies to miscarriages as this book was being completed. Mourning those losses has helped me appreciate more fully Carrie's deep grace and the extraordinary gifts that are our other children, Tahlia and David. We can only hope that all my time with Michel Foucault will somehow help us more joyfully join our lives to the gracious gift of God's triune life.

This book could not have been written without consecutive Summer Sabbatical Grants from the Office of the Vice President for Research at Baylor University, a 2009 Baylor University Arts and Humanities Research Development Grant, and subsequent summer travel allowances provided by Dr. Bill Bellinger, Chair of Baylor's Religion Department. Dr. William Storrar of Princeton Theological Seminary provided summer research residency at the Center for Theological Inquiry, Princeton, NJ in summer of 2008, as did Dr. Mark Mann at the Wesleyan Center for 21st Century Thought at Point Loma Nazarene University in summers 2009 and 2010. Moody-Jones Library at Baylor University, especially its staff and highly proficient inter-library loan and delivery services, made research less cumbersome than it could have been. Lindsay Cleveland, K. C. Flynn, and Tyler Grant provided fantastic research assistance in every facet. Stanley Hauerwas, Craig Hovey, Chris Moore, Jenny Howell, and John Wright each read portions of this book and offered invaluable suggestions. Tom Kraft at T&T Clark proved to be an exceedingly responsive and patient editor.

Portions of this book were presented at the Annual Meetings of the Society of Christian Ethics as well as the Institute for

Acknowledgments

Theology, Imagination and the Arts, St Mary's College at the University of St Andrews. Sections of Chapter 1 were previously published as "Transgressing Borders: Genetic Research, Immigration, and Discourses of Sacrifice," *Journal of the Society of Christian Ethics* 28:2 (2008), 97–116; and "The Otherness of Children as a Hint of an Outside: Michel Foucault, Richard Yates, and Karl Barth on Suburban Life," *Theology & Sexuality* 15:2 (2009), 191–211. Respective permissions from Georgetown University Press and Equinox Publishing Ltd© 2009 are much appreciated. Finally, thanks to Penguin Press for permission to use portions of J. M. Coetzee's *Elizabeth Costello* (New York: Penguin, 2004).

Introduction

James Bernauer reports the following exchange between the atheist Michael Foucault and several American academics at the University of California in the spring of 1983, in what would prove to be the final year of Foucault's life. Speaking of the possibility of resistance, Foucault said:

> Despair and hopelessness are one thing; suspicion is another. And if you are suspicious, it is because, of course, you have a certain hope. The problem is to know which kind of hope you have, and which kind of hope it is reasonable to have in order to avoid what I would call not the "pessimistic circle" you speak of, but the political circle which reintroduces in your hopes, and through your hopes, the things you want to avoid by these hopes.

When someone commented that Foucault sounded "very Christian" he replied, "Yes, I have a very strong Christian, Catholic background, and I am not ashamed."[1]

The following serves a single purpose. Michel Foucault offers a profound, if complicated, account of hope at a time when there exists many reasons for despair. I intend to appropriate this account toward Christian ends. While the differences between Foucault's hope and the church's hope are multiple and deep, I will spend little time analyzing those differences, for the simple reason that I find Foucault too interesting to digress much from what he has to say. Throughout this book, I stray from his texts only for the occasional purpose of taking what he says to clarify a few things Christianity has to say. Along the way, I try to offer a fresh analysis of Foucault and from that a fresh analysis of Christianity.

My appropriation consists of two parts. First, I describe this hope by examining Foucault's figuration of power and tease out his conception of resistance implicit to it. Second, I characterize this conception of resistance as freedom and subjectivity most readily articulated in the last stages of Foucault's career. In order to thicken my description of power and show why it might be helpful to Christian faithfulness, in the first part I relate Foucault's ubiquity of power to the totalizing efforts of late capitalism. I believe this demonstrates quite dramatically how Foucault's strange notion of power portends the fate of capitalist societies. This also allows us a glimpse into what remains for contemporary existence and so why Foucault continues to matter for us. To this end, I represent capitalism's totalizing powers through Michael Hardt and Antonio Negri's three-part *Empire* series. Hardt and Negri ably demonstrate the complete nature of power's transformative capabilities as well as reasons for hope within it. Continuing my argument in the second part, I link Foucault's account of freedom and subjectivity, what he calls "self-care," to Christian discipleship. By care for the self Foucault means the self's ability to tell its own story, to both be determined by and determine the meaning of its existence. To this end, I begin the second part by ruminating on biography, juxtaposing a fascinating controversy over a Foucault biography with Foucault's work on self-comportment and self-writing in relationship to the modern self's biography. Next I outline Foucault's complicated conception of the self's constitution in freedom by traveling the distance of Martin Heidegger's deep influence on Foucault. Following, I offer an instance of what Christian self-care might look like by turning to companionship with animals and exemplifying self-care through the autobiographic trope of "saving one's soul" in the context of enveloping capitalist logics of power discussed in the book's first part. I do so by tending to what Stanley Cavell and Cora Diamond have taken as ordinary language philosophy as attention to self and world.

Beyond exegeting Foucault in a certain way, I am concerned here with Christian faithfulness amidst late capitalism. This concern will take form as an in-depth analysis of Foucault's complex notion of subjectivity, power, and resistance. Taking his portrayal of power, my study attempts to describe the current circumstances in which the church finds herself. Foucault once said about Gilles Deleuze that in hindsight we will see the twentieth century as

Introduction

Deleuzian. This book thinks about the world as if Foucauldian, though the sensibilities of this book are not Foucauldian but rather Christian. Being a book about Christianity, this book is not exegetical simply in regards to Foucault's many texts. I will not be seeking here to delineate the corpus and career of Michel Foucault, nor will I be trying to articulate all the ways that corpus and career can be considered "theological." That is a project well worth undertaking and others have had the good sense to pursue it.[2] That is not my aim. My aim is both more modest in terms of Foucault and more ambitious in terms of Foucault and Christianity. Simply, I think Foucault helps Christians think about Christian faithfulness.

1. Witness, not Resistance

While the many differences between Foucault's thought and Christian theology deserve lengthy treatment, one crucial distinction needs to be placed front and center so that the ground can be cleared for the book's larger argument. I state this difference at the beginning and imply it in everything that follows. Foucault thinks the world belongs to power. Christians think the world belongs to God. I initially wanted to subtitle this book "Power, *Resistance*, and Christianity." My good friend John Wright reminded me how ill-conceived "resistance" as a preamble was, namely because it presupposed a state of affairs that posited God as at best interfering on a prior ontological arrangement, that Christians need to "resist" powers before, more immediate than, and superior to God as Father, Son, and Holy Spirit. Within such a framework, the allure of "resistance" would be similar to certain Romanticist strains of Enlightenment thinking that sought to revitalize a world desacralized by Kant. Resistance comes to signal, in this frame, the radical stance of those who hold firm while everyone else caves in. Who wouldn't want to think of themselves, in that line of thought, as "resisting," just as who wouldn't want to be sided with right? Throughout my reading of Foucault in the pages ahead, I presuppose, in contrast, that Christianity does entail resistance, but not in this way. The church's resistance, instead, is internal to a more pervasive disposition: witness. Resistance is only one of multiple forms of witness. Making resistance the church's primary task positions it in a reactive and ancillary posture to the world (that the world is to be resisted as such), always on the defensive, determined by another, only resistant. Rather than resisting, the church seeks to be church and hence help the world, as Stanley Hauerwas famously says, see itself as world. But this only happens, following Hauerwas, if the church is indeed church, such that the world can know itself to be world. And the church *is* church by worship. Against capitalism's demands for complete allegiance, the church's worship of God confronts the world as resistance; this striking difference—that the church would rather worship the crucified and risen Christ than all that money has to offer—Christians call witness. Witness lets the world know there are better things to worship than money. Resistance becomes an important mode of witness within this frame; being church and resisting world go hand in hand, but being church, rather than resisting the world, is the church's first task. It is in this way that we can talk about resistance, as internal and part of the larger vocation of witness. The church is church for herself and *for* the world. This is the kind of action missing if resistance is taken as primary; resistance alone does not seek to convert. Witness seeks to convert the world, if only to its reality, and incarnates all kinds of languages, including resistance, for that purpose. For Christianity, resistance indicates the lengths the church will go to for the sake of the world.

Christians witness to goodness and truthfulness they believe exists before power. Power is no thing on its own. Part of the good news of Christianity is precisely this priority of goodness and truthfulness because Christianity refuses to imagine goodness and truthfulness as somehow competing with evil and falsity. It does not think there is a contest, as if we need to wait and see who prevails. Power is not some *thing* in the world, and certainly not something diametrically opposed and coeval to God. Power axiomatically and ontologically comes after that which it embeds. The goodness and peacability of creation comes first. Power is linked into the relations that constitute the peacable and good creation. This is to claim with the anti-Manichean Foucault that power is not necessarily bad—this book will argue that much

Introduction

power can be directed for good—and that its inducements presume freedom. Still power cannot be allowed to upstage the story.

These issues are more than academic for my previously mentioned friend John, who, along with teaching theology, has for years pastored a multi-congregation church in downtown San Diego. John's church has seven congregations, only one of which speaks English. His church feeds hundreds of homeless and needy people a week. One could say his church is "resisting" the crushing pressures of poverty brought on by global capitalism, but John wouldn't put it that way. Rather, his church witnesses to God's goodness and so cannot help but see capitalism as but a flash within the drama of God's trinitarian life. Instead of capitalism, "the Kingdom of God is at hand; repent and believe the Good News." I have often puzzled at John's fascination with the movement known as Radical Orthodoxy and its assertions of trinitarian peace over against ontological violence. What I've come to understand is how Radical Orthodoxy's version of things re-articulates the biblical narrative into which John emplots the life (and death) of Mid-City Nazarene Church. If he did not have the victory attested by the Gospel's primacy, what could Mid-City be but a meager if admirable mode of resistance? To be sure, Mid-City has had its share of victories, including its weekly distributions to the poor, beautiful modes of Christian discipleship, and a regular presence in San Diego's municipal politics. Still, by standards both inside and outside the church, Mid-City is not much to brag about. Its English-speaking congregation seats a mere 50 people each week, most of whom are idealistic students from John's theology and Bible courses at Point Loma Nazarene University. Its working budget is a pittance compared to the lavish budgets of many American churches. Outside the Nazarenes (no loadstone of Protestant influence), few people have even heard of the church, much less mimic its food distributions, multi-congregational polity, or vibrant modes of faithfulness. One could deem Mid-City "successful" if one were motivated by the rallying cry of "resistance." Accordingly, Mid-City succeeds to the extent that it resists (in the same way that a speed bump slows down) the powers that be. But again, that is not how John would talk about his church.

Resistance language, which the reader will find amply used in the book, fails theologically when it does not begin with the abundant goodness of the Father revealed by the Son made present through the Holy Spirit. The "powers" are not some *thing* that must be defeated in order for God's reign to be restored; rather, the powers have already been made subject to God's eternal reign. John's church witnesses to that reign. When Mid-City feeds people it seeks to make publicly known what is already the case: God, not capitalism, rules. As such, it is capitalism, not Christian communities like Mid-City, that resists through active rebellion a rule that can be *at most* resisted, though not ultimately denied. Mid-City's ministry looks like resistance only if you think capitalism has won, and if Christians think capitalism has won, no amount of resistance will save the church. John's church operates as it does because it believes the world belongs to God, not power. There are things the church and he as pastor "resist"—namely, sin—but such resistance is secondary to a state of affairs such resistance must always presuppose. To put resistance prior to witness is to concede that only resistance remains, that there is nothing left to witness to. Hence in starting, we need to begin with a Christian understanding of power that both allows us to take seriously what Foucault offers without endorsing the ontology it can invite. This is important to John, and should be important to us. It is important for John to know that when he hands out produce to the luckless Cambodian woman, he doesn't understand it as a handout, a concession amidst capitalism's otherwise dominance. Rather, he understands it as sharing in what he and Mid-City have been given a share of, God's giving of his own body that makes capitalistic notions of property, scarcity, and competition literal privations of the good. Such bodily sharing is not charity; or, it is charity of a different kind, charity between God and his people, which Mid-City and the luckless together share in by their sharing with one another. This is not resistance but simply what one does when Jesus is Lord, when the Kingdom has already come, when one believes, amidst the atheistic strictures of capitalism, the Good News. To witness Mid-City's multi-congregational sharing as *worship* is to see power *as* diffuse and polymorphic as Foucault claims, and to acknowledge that Foucault is wrong about power in at least this basic sense.

Introduction

2. Global Capitalism's Power

I started by saying that this book presumes the Christian church within a particular context, which I named as late capitalism. From what I've already covered, we can qualify that in an important way: this is a book about the church's witness to God's reign in the context of late capitalism. Hence, it takes as seriously the context of late capitalism as it does God's reign. Some might suggest taking capitalism's strident authority as seriously as God's reign a mistake, as if acknowledging the former somehow undermines the latter. However, authority by its nature exists only in its effects. If God's reign does not rule somewhere, it is not authoritative as we normally use the word. This does not mean that God's authority is always visible; indeed, as we will learn from Foucault, power is often most authoritative when unseen or unacknowledged. But it is to insist that God's power is somewhere, even if that somewhere is everywhere. Acknowledging the context of power does not undermine but rather affirms power because such an acknowledgment displays authority as relationally comprised. As powerful as capitalism is, God is more powerful. We are in part shown God's power by way of being shown its rule over capitalism. In this sense, capitalism is made to give testimony to the power of God, made subject to God's authority over history, even a history that includes imprecations like capitalism. In taking seriously the context of capitalism, we take seriously God's reign over capitalism. Indeed, there is no "capitalism" except that which is always already subject to God's subjugation of all things. Describing in detail capitalism's workings describes in detail God's workings.

It is here that Foucault is particularly helpful, for no one has given us a more perspicacious, if controversial, description of power. Foucault was able to do so because he understood power beyond capitalism, or better yet, capitalism in terms of power. Foucault's departure from Marxist theory proved pivotal in this regard because it helped him discern the broader context within which capitalism comes to theoretical prominence. According to Foucault, Marxism failed exactly where it claimed success and hence only spread the ruse of liberation. Like the structuralism Foucault entertained earlier in his career, Marxist theory,

Foucault observed, was unable to account for its own development and in that sense failed to take seriously Kant's transcendental critique as fulfilled in Nietzsche. Both structuralism and Marxism presumed both the ability to observe how power entraps us *and* the ability to escape those trappings. Foucault thought it was precisely this presumption of escape that belied the actuality of power. When Marx narrated the various junctures of historical materialism's turnings (from feudal serfdom to capital to liberation), he did so by smuggling in a rationalist explanation of those turnings, as if Hegel's "self-consciousness" alone enabled epochal shifts in history. This continued the Cartesian dialectic between subject, knowledge, and freedom that could then be deployed to legitimate one's claim to certainty. Politically one need only revisit the bloody history of Marxist revolutions (and the French Revolution as precursor) to see how such certainty played out. What caught Foucault's attention was how a revolutionary Marxism could cast itself as the end of history without any sense of irony, and the proletariat according to the Marxists a self-fashioned Hegelian world-historical figure. Such posturing would not survive the barest of genealogies, and the dogged genealogy Foucault received from Nietzsche guaranteed its theoretical defeat.

Marxism and structuralism did teach Foucault about power. In the same way that its presumption of truthfulness proved its greatest weakness, Marxism's failure proved for Foucault its most valuable lesson. From its posturing, Foucault learned not only why he could not, literally, be a card-carrying Marxist, but more important for his development, about a world where Marxism seemed to inspire such a broad following. What did people see in Marxism? It could not actually be, given the constituencies of twentieth-century French Marxism (affluent, educated, bourgeois and bored), fomented by the material conditions of poverty. So what was it? According to Foucault a certain vision of the self inspired adherence to at least the idea of Marxist revolution as realization of a natural and primordial freedom. In other words, Marxism allowed us to believe, at least for a moment, that freedom spoke of a natural and necessary reality, and if only we believed it, we would have it. Hence, Marxism was but the latest version of what Foucault would later dub "the repressive hypothesis" deployed to legitimate political action. Foucault's brief spell with

Introduction

structuralism helped him see that theoretical critique always needs to accompany political critique (just as theoretical structuralism need always attend social structuralism) otherwise political critique, and purveyors of political critique, will arrive with ready-made political warrants. In order for these warrants to gain traction, an antithesis needed to be foisted against which a freed self would emerge. In *The History of Sexuality*, Foucault caricatured this an urban legend around sexual repression, the supposed Victorian oppression of sexuality that held back a self always clamoring toward expression if not for Victorian oppression. This mythic antithesis gave structure to freedom as that which encumbered an otherwise natural propensity for sexual fulfillment. It was Foucault's genius to demythologize sex and to show exactly what the notion of repression was doing, that is, writing the story of freedom as the story of the self narrated in terms of a dialectic of repression and freedom, which cashed out in a political claim that once oppression could be overcome the self could finally realize itself. As long as it remained oppressed, the self was not truly itself. History became the story of humanity's self-discovery, its emergence from self-incurred tutelage. Like their Hegelian forbearers, purveyors of the repressive hypothesis suggested a rationalistic trigger as that which would awaken the self, as the self came to realize first its bondage and then its eventual road to freedom through revolution. The brilliant ploy could label anything that stood in its way "the oppressor" and hence justify any kind of action against oppression (against the oppressors) in the name of freedom as the very form of history. Again, Foucault's genius was to turn Marxists structuralism on itself and to analyze the story (why people were attracted to it; why some came up with it; how it was useful, etc.), to proffer an alternative explanation of things, to name it myth, to see in its will to truth will to power and both as mobile armies of metaphors. As Paul Veyne said in interpreting Foucault:

> in thinking they are seeking the truth of things, people succeed only in establishing the rules according to which they will be said to be speaking truly or falsely. In this sense, knowledge is not only linked to the powers that be, it is not only a weapon of power, it is not even power at the same time that it is knowledge; knowledge is only

> power, radically, for one can speak truly by virtue of the force of the rules imposed at one time or another by a history whose individuals are at once, and mutually, actors and victims.³

The repressive hypothesis for Foucault did point to some realities regarding sexual normalization, which was not unimportant to Michel Foucault, but more significantly for Foucault, it named the enduring myth of Enlightenment accounts of freedom that he saw streaming through narratives like Marxian historical materialism.

One might ask whether Foucault himself was victim to the ploy. If by rational self-consciousness the oppressed could claim truth by recognizing the myth's ploy, was not Foucault himself positing a certain self-realization to the extent that he could identify by his genius the mythic nature of the repressive hypothesis, and hence a certain kind of truth, by claiming to stand outside the circle, by claiming his transcendental critique more *truthful* than Hegel's, Marx's, and so on? This has certainly been the suggestion of critics of postmodernism, that it cannot account for its own suspicions and the epistemic positions from which postmodernists lay them. We will return to this important question, and its metaphysical implications and whether or not Foucault was quietly endorsing ontology at the same moment he was trying to rid us of it.

Returning to late capitalism, through Foucault's repressive hypothesis, one can begin to come to terms with the vast authority that capitalism is. If there is no primordial state of freedom that becomes oppressed first by feudalism and now by capitalism only to be freed by proletariat uprising, then what is there? Simply, an immanent horizon of power coded to the local effects of power. There is no more "capitalism" than there is "revolution" or any other epochal periodization. These are all habits of speech that help situate one in the world and claim one's telic imposition as truthful and one's political action necessary and even inevitable. Indeed to the extent that these discourses rival one another, one can see how they work, as contrastive self-justifying narratives that vie for one's imaginative allegiance. In other words, we can understand them as competing powers. Capitalism embodies this order

Introduction

of things because it does not presume anything prior or anything after, neither does it forbid anything prior or after, instead understanding each moment as itself internal to an agonistic horizon of play and force.

Better stated, capitalism understands itself as *the* horizon. What makes the logic of capitalism remarkably intelligible through the lens of Foucault's figuration of power, and hence why Foucault's conceptions of power help us understand what Christianity is contending with in capitalism, is that capitalism imagines no end to its enterprise. Capital seeks to lay bare every space as it makes its way forward colonizing everything. There is, for capitalism, nothing sacred, no true realm of alterity that cannot and should not be encroached upon and commodified. To use Naomi Klein's apt metaphor, capitalism is like a crack addict; it cares about nothing other than how and where it can get its next fix.[4]

The analogy to power is not that capital and power are the same thing, though we see their similarities. But more so, Foucault's conception of power helps us comprehend capitalism's dominance. For Foucault, there is no outside to power, no realm where one can escape power and be free of it. We might say as well, along with the economists, there is no outside to global capitalism. This is part of Foucault's point with the repressive hypothesis that posits freedom and the self's revolution from oppression as flight from the dominance of power. Rather, power, as Foucault famously claimed, is everywhere; there is no realm of "great refusal" such that even resistance to power occurs within the terms of power, as counter-power. One does not resist power by refusing it, but rather learning to strategically inhabit power as to offer contrastive power. Hence, in speaking of resistance, Foucault speaks about surveying its workings and redirecting its energies. This way of thinking is markedly different than the Hegelian dialectic that presumes primordial freedom as the basis for an eventual and even guaranteed freedom. Moreover, Foucault's way of understanding power helps one avoid the self-righteousness of telic notions of freedom that issue in self-justifying political assertions. The connection to capitalism is the recognition that there is no getting out of capitalism, that any resistance to be had to its dominative operations will be had within its relations. By its very definition, capitalism refuses sacred spaces cordoned from its stratagems;

indeed, within its rationale, capitalism covets most that in short supply and so hungers after sacred space, to make it its own, or someone's own. Within the capitalist social imaginary, like Foucault's conception of power, there is no outside, nothing beyond reach, nowhere one can hide or protect or go beyond the reaches of capitalism. Those who resist capitalism, like those who resist power, and claim great refusal to its operations must be infected, from Foucault's perspective, by some strain of the repressive hypothesis. From his vantage then, those who recognize capitalism's power are better off surveying its workings and looking for life within it. Again, like Foucault's conception of power, this does not mean there can be no resistance to capitalism, but simply that those who would resist will have to find ways within the terms given.

The most immediate way Christianity resists capitalism is by resisting this narrative and the suggestion that no space can remain untouched, for doxologically Father, Son, and Holy Spirit identifies for the church that which cannot be possessed, owned, or encroached upon. This is what I meant earlier when I said Christians believe the world belongs to God; it belongs not to capitalism, even if capitalism would like to claim as much, even if much Christianity today looks like it belongs to capitalism. And if the world belongs to God then the story the church tells about the world must begin by acknowledging that capitalism's narrative of dominance is but another of its ploys to own everything. And God's world will not be owned by anything other than God. But how the church speaks of the world belonging to God really matters if she is to speak well of God in that world. And here a full-bodied description of capitalist workings is internal to theological speech because by such descriptions can the church more fully describe who God is, especially the God who though not determined by anything in the world like capitalism, gave himself over to a world that idolatrously supposed just that. By mining the depths of the capitalist myth can the church come to understand the power of Christian practices like asceticism as witness to God's authority and power amidst the consuming claims of capitalism. It will be my contention that Foucault's conception of power helps us *see* this. Foucault's philosophy does not make possible Christian witness, but it can make Christian witness slightly more visible.

Introduction

3. Overview

Hence this book will utilize Foucault's conceptions of power and resistance to undertake a Christian appraisal of the world in which we find ourselves. This will first entail getting clear about Foucault. Rather than delineating his entire corpus, and that corpus in relation to Christian theology, I will turn to the latter half of Foucault's career, with intermittent remarks about what paves its way. I am particularly interested in the period during which he published three of his major works and the lectures and interviews he gave during this timeframe: *Archaeology of Knowledge*, *Discipline and Punish*, and the trilogy on sexuality and self-care. From *Archaeology* forward, Foucault can be seen to be moving beyond his structuralist inheritance while simultaneously still trying to come to terms with Heidegger, who influences his early career. In Foucault's work, Heidegger is apparent in both what and how the young Foucault writes. Heidegger's phenomenological analysis proves fruitful for Foucault's initial philosophical work, and particularly in his conception of knowledge and language. By the time we come to his speculative *Archaeology*, Foucault has culled from Heidegger what he wanted, while turning to more acute, and explicitly post-structuralist, expositions. It is at this point that one sees Foucault both retain notions of phenomenology's emergent self while speaking of that emergence within a novel concept that comes to be known as biopower. These two developments occur in tandem for Foucault and it is more correct to speak of one trajectory: the self's emergence amidst power. Biopower comes to mean for Foucault society's birthing of selves in the image of society. Outlining how this works, which encompasses the whole of Foucault's intellectual career, will be the most hypothetical aspect of my argument because it utilizes a heuristic device (the influence of Heidegger on Foucault's thought) in order to explicate what Foucault means by "surfaces of emergence." In speaking of Foucault in relation to Heidegger, I do not evidence the history of that influence as much as I presume it in order to show how for Foucault the self that comes about through this process finds its precursor in pre-modern, and surprisingly, Christian sources.

Late in his career, Foucault turns to the early church fathers, especially the ascetical Christians as a counterweight to modern self-conceptions he found increasingly untenable. Foucault saw the volumes that comprise the published *History of Sexuality* series as leading into a fourth culminating volume about Christianity. This is a surprising move for those with superficial familiarity of Foucault's legend, but not for those apprised of his unique intellectual creativity. The early Christian self that Foucault both discovers and invents will be one I will configure as an alternative to the selves offered in late capitalism, that is a self given to self-giving rather than self-possession. This will be less akin to recent *ressourcements* trends in theology and more like an attempt to follow Foucault from late modernity to early Christianity and back again. Returning to the ancients will only help us late moderns if we learn how to recoup those sources for modern uses. This is what we find Foucault in the last years of his career trying to do, and what I will try to do here. It would be entirely overstated to suggest that this book tries to get at what Foucault would have gotten to had he lived longer. This book seeks only to present one option he might have chosen.

Part 1
Power and Totality

Basically I have done nothing else for several months but try to provide you with a commentary on these texts on grains and scarcity, which, through some detours, was always the issue.
—Michel Foucault

I think we live at a point of extreme darkness and extreme brightness. Extreme darkness, because we really do not know which direction the light would come. Extreme brightness, because we ought to have the courage to begin anew.
—Michel Foucault

Chapter 1
Power

I am an agent, but also a plant.
—Martha Nussbaum

One of Michel Foucault's great contributions to modern intellectual thought was his relentless need to unsettle the many arrangements that found entire grammars of existence, scuttling our vocabularies of meaning and unveiling the concomitant brutalities that make possible our linguistic worlds. In this way Foucault came to us the unwelcome observer and chronicler of our many pretentions. While Nietzsche shattered with philosophical hammers, Foucault cut with a fine scalpel, slicing into the everyday and revealing a metastasizing pathos gripping modern existence. After all, we late moderns tend to interpret our lives and the worlds we've created in the best possible light, assuming that the terrors endemic in our schools, medical practices, prisons, and knowledges anything but terrible. The few willing to pony up quickly retreat under the justification of benevolence so readily deployed to underwrite presumptions of goodness. Foucault's gift to us is an unwillingness to let go of that which we want to let go. For those who look upon the mad, the uneducated, and the unproductive as ones to be rounded up and shipped off, Foucault stands in the way. Those too willing to excuse the violations of the medical examination under exculpatory chimera of health will find their rationalizations stripped naked as Foucault lays bare the clinical gaze. Foucault shows how convenient it is for us to lampoon Hellenistic love for boys while lionizing our own sexual practices "manifest destiny" after much incurred minority. Foucault will doggedly track down the stink of objectivity and our presumptions that we are right about all these things simply because of where we stand, that is, nowhere in particular; Foucault understood that universality could only be asserted while standing in *it*, that is, in the world. In these things and more, Foucault could not find it in himself to let things go and so we can assign a kind of ethics to the character of his work.[1]

In the last years of his life, Foucault summarized his work thus, "I have tried to show how we have indirectly constituted ourselves through the exclusion of others."[2] This dynamic between self-constitution and exclusion helps bridge two seemingly distinct phases of Foucault's career, that is, his conceptions of power and his later work regarding subjectivity, agency, and "care for the self." In his mind, at least in those last years, these two were related insofar as constitution of selfhood required speech, practices, and conceptualizations that individuated some to the exclusion of others. The self came to be by way of delimitation: reason in relation to madness, health in relation to illness, order to disorder, normality to abnormality, sexuality in relation to perversion, and so on. Since "the self" was not a substance but only a nominal way of speaking of persons in relation to others, then its density could only be achieved by increasingly dense demarcations.[3] Hence, in describing one of his basic categories, Foucault writes, "the *episteme* is not *a sort of grand underlying theory*, it is a space of *dispersion*, it is an *open and doubtless indefinitely describable field of relationships.*"[4] Selfhood may not have substance of its own, but the semblance of substantiality could be gained by contradistinction. For example, in his annual Collège de France lectures given in 1974–1975 (the same timeframe that saw the publication of *Discipline and Punish*) Foucault elaborates the emergence of a new discourse called "expert medico-legal testimony." Through "positive technologies of power" this mode of speech coupled medical and judicial language to conceive a new kind of person: the abnormal. Foucault shows how the separate legal and psychiatric discourses that preceded the nineteenth century paralleled a historic separation between madness and criminality (one could be insane or one could be criminal, but one could not be both because there was no language—and hence no culpability—that could speak of both simultaneously). However, during the nineteenth century we see developed a new speech form that creates a doublet conjoining two hitherto discreet discourses. This doublet produces a new category of person—and hence a new kind of self—which psychiatric diagnosis could animate through certain invocations of social order. In this frame, criminal psychiatry *created* social deviance as a basis of personality. Around this new discourse arose all kinds of novel characters and practices: the expert witness, the pervert, inventorying one's personal history onto which a seminal criminality could be mapped as social abnormality, so on and so forth. The emergence of this new personhood fit within and helped to multiply networks of discourses about abnormality in every field, in turn marshalling society toward the production of normality as a ballast against this emerging "danger to society." In turn, these new organs of normalization further substantiated this new personage, which "was formed in correlation with a set of institutions of control and a series of mechanisms of surveillance and distribution."[5] Such instances of Foucault's work—perhaps what he is most known for—are these contradistinctions whereby the disciplinary features of "power" work to secure personhood. Such instances also demonstrate the basic scheme of Foucault's method, through his various periods and emphases: "I start with the theoretical and methodological decision that consists in saying: Let's suppose that universals don't exist. And then I put the question to history and historians: How can you write history if you do not accept a priori the existence of things like the state, society, the sovereign, and subjects?"[6]

Unless one understands the quasi-metaphysical features of his notion of self-constitution, one will miss what power *does* within Foucault's corpus, or more precisely by what processes power ensues. Power is reared not to encumber or tear down some*thing*. Nor is power the stratagem of certain ones "in power." Indeed, Foucault begins by disabusing us of the illusion that *someone* or *something* is there. He starts with the assumption of nothing and investigates how we generate the semblance of something through habits of speech. His investigations do not postulate the *non*-existence of self, world, or God (even though he may have very well believed their non-existence); again, "Let's suppose that *universals* don't exist," "universals" implicating postulates about existence *and* non-existence. Power, therefore, is dense insofar as it guards empty space, an absence that takes on the sense of presence as the effect of disciplinarity. Because readings of Foucault have tended to focus on disciplinarity qua disciplinarity, we have often missed what is central for him, namely the self that must be so constituted, and hence have largely mistaken Foucault to be a theorist of power.

Such interpreters will be surprised to hear Foucault saying, "I hardly ever use the word 'power' and if I do sometimes, it is always a short cut to the expression I always use: the relationships of power."[7] For Foucault, power was not finally the point. It was only a means of speaking of something more paramount to his concerns (again surprising to those who believed him to be concerned chiefly with oppression): "My role . . . is to show people that they are much freer than they feel, that people accept as truth, as evidence, some themes which have been built up at a certain moment during history, and that this so-called evidence can be criticized and destroyed."[8] Playing that role for Foucault meant refusing to accept declarations of truth that warranted limitations on freedom, or the dictates of freedom as domination given within the terms of late modernity. Helping people see freedom was not for Foucault unrelated to the material conditions of their lives, much of which was ensnared in domination. But neither was his goal to give domination the last word.

> One must observe also that there cannot be relations of power unless the subjects are free . . . Even though the relation of power may be completely unbalanced or when one can truly say that he has "all power" over the other, a power can only be exercised over another to the extent that the latter still has the possibility of committing suicide, of jumping out of the window or of killing the other. That means that in the relations of power, there is necessarily the possibility of resistance, for if there were no possibility of resistance—of violent resistance, of escape, of ruse, of strategies that reverse the situation—there would be no relations of power.[9]

That Foucault counted suicide or killing as expressions of freedom should remove any doubt that Foucault took quite seriously power's domination (I relate suicide to Christian self-giving in the final chapter). Still, if in reading Foucault we only see domination, if forms of coercion were all Foucault had to offer us, then by his own lights he failed us. Foucault hoped that we might see domination and then find ways for freedom to unfold within domination, and even over against it. Foucault suspected that people had acclimated to the dominative conditions that surrounded them, and part of that acclimation was an unwillingness to come to terms with and admit such domination. And yet without such admittance one would be fated to domination. If one could see, then one could strive after the polyvalent modes of freedom and expression within domination. Reading Foucault as only chronicling our many bondages misses the forest for the trees; his real interests lie in showing us the ways we are free. His efforts toward this end follow his attempt to press against what he called "the idea of the universal necessities of human existence," that how things are is not how they have to be. In order to do so, Foucault relied on Nietzschean genealogy applied to our most basic habits, presumptions, and discourses.[10] To the question, "What is the relationship of normalization and the concept of man as the center of knowledge?" Foucault answered, "Through these different practices—psychological, medical, penitential, educational—a certain idea or model of humanity was developed, and now this idea has become normative, self-evident, and is supposed to be universal."[11] If he can show us that the present is at best assemblages of habits, presumptions, and discourses, then we might see nothing is destined by natural necessity (i.e., it had to be that way) but are only cleavages of subjective knowledges— "blocks of historical knowledges that were present in the functional and systemic ensembles"[12]—and if he can bring to the fore alternative habits, presumptions, and discourses, then he can, most importantly, demonstrate that the way things are is simply one way they could have gone. If we can assemble ourselves around alternatives then we can make alternative presents. This is why he labeled his historical chronologies, "histories of the present."

Unpacking Foucault's conception of self-constitution or what he came to call "self-care" will take up the second and larger portion of this book, especially since I think (and have thus far argued) self-care becomes his ultimate and final project. There I will attend to Foucault's attempt to refigure the self in ways that are less exclusionary and better able to offer a multiplicity of options such that less exclusions need be deployed. Propping the self as reasoned, healthy, and normal required us to discipline those deemed by those terms mad, ill, and abnormal. If we could conceptualize selfhood in increasingly diverse ways then the respective exclusions necessary for the self's constitutions could be made to compete, in turn fructifying greater production of selves, which was Foucault's real hope. Again, I will turn to those diverse selves in the second part of the book. Before doing so, I need to delineate in this first part Foucault's understanding of power. I do so in this current chapter by articulating power as positive and productive, in the ways I have been discussing regarding the production of selves through power, and also how such productivity occurs by modes of domination, surveillance, and order. In the next chapter, I attempt to demonstrate what Foucault means by the ubiquity of power by speaking of domination and freedom within late capitalism.

1. Retheorizing Power

Undercutting what he considered the standard conception of power, Foucault stated,

> I do not mean in any way to minimize the importance and effectiveness of State power. I simply feel that excessive insistence on its playing an exclusive role leads to the risk of overlooking all the mechanisms and effects of power which don't pass directly via the State apparatus, yet often sustain the State more effectively than its own institutions, enlarging and maximizing its effectiveness.[13]

Foucault's conception of power restates power in three significant ways. First, according to Foucault, power in its most potent form does not repress individual freedom as implied by the various psychological, economic, or even sexual complaints. Within the classic liberal conceptions of power since Locke and Hobbes, we have tended to think about power as negative and associated it with the coercive organs of the monarchy or nation-state. Such a conception relies on a concomitant account of freedom as unrestrained will or desire; in this case power is that which impedes will or desire. In contrast, power in Foucault's understanding is less about impeding and more about inculcating subjects into certain modalities of life. In discussing the circumscribing power of modern sexuality, he says, "If power takes hold on the body, it isn't through its having first to be interiorised in people's consciousness. There is a network or circuit of biopower, or somato-power, which acts as the formative matrix of sexuality itself as the historical and cultural phenomenon within which we seem at once to recognize and lose ourselves."[14] Power is less about prohibiting individuals from doing what they want and more about getting them to do things while believing they want them. Thus, power here is less about repressing certain tendencies and more about habituating relations within local patterns, habits, and ways of speaking, less (for example) about economic oppression on the part of owners of capital against the proletariat and more about how citizens of capitalist societies constantly labor toward productivity, and less (as another example) about concealing "natural" visceral tendencies and more about disciplining bodies into peculiar though ostensibly normal practices. Foucault's histories (which he termed archaeologies to the extent that he was attempting to chronicle the *discontinuities* between the accidents of time rather than the *foisted continuities* of Enlightenment notions of history as continuous and contiguous) tell the stories of power's ability to discipline bodies, communities, and societies into performances scripted to mental sanity, sexual normality, medical healthiness, legal uprightness, and public education.[15]

Secondly, power is not centralized. According to Foucault,

> I would say that we should direct our researches on the nature of power not towards the juridical edifice of sovereignty, the State apparatuses and the ideologies which accompany them, but towards domination and the material operators of power, toward forms of subjection and the inflections and utilizations of their localised systems, and toward strategic apparatuses. We must eschew the model of Leviathan in the study of power. We must escape from the limited field of juridical sovereignty and State institutions, and instead base our analysis of power on the study of techniques and tactics of domination.[16]

Power certainly can be centralized and some of Foucault's work hints of a panoptical imaging of power wielding its potency as an all-seeing eye. Yet this conception of power tends toward the mythical, myths in turn colonized by power. Foucault argues that power as centralized finds its genesis and expression in political theories inhabiting monarchical orders, whether literally in classical feudal economies or figuratively in the European nation-state's imperialistic agendas. However, modern industrialization disseminated power toward increased diffusion and saturation or what he calls power's "capillary" operations, where no individual, community, or society is free from the ever-present self-directed "gaze" of power, and its ubiquitous and incessant effects. In other words, no "center" holds power while immune to its inducements. The idea of centralized power no matter how monstrous its applications works within a certain constellation. Power makes use of that idea because it is less unsettling than power as not centralized. *As centralized*, power is particular, finite, and fixed; one need only cut off the king's head, a difficult though identifiable task. Centralized power, unlike capillary power, is vulnerable just to the extent that it is located spatially and distended temporally—it cannot go anywhere and it will not endure forever; its vulnerability exists in its centralization whereas capillary power is everywhere to the extent that it is nowhere. For Foucault's capillary power, there is no Big Brother (or Big Capitalist) that can be targeted or blamed, no Central Committee to whom we might direct our protests and vitriol. Rather since capillary power disciplines each of us into its performances, we become the watchers, enforcers and executioners in the ever-present unfolding of power.

Third, power is not agential or sovereign in the standard sense; it does not have intent; power is not someone nor is it exclusively vested in the hands of somebody:

> Let us not, therefore, ask why certain people want to dominate, what they seek, what is their overall strategy. Let us ask, instead, how things work at the level of on-going subjugation, at the level of those continuous and uninterrupted processes which subject our bodies, govern our gestures, dictate our behaviours etc. In other words, rather than ask ourselves how the sovereign appears to us in his

lofty isolation, we should try to discover how it is that
subjects are gradually, progressively, really and materially
constituted through a multiplicity of organisms, forces,
energies, materials, desires, thoughts etc. We should try to
grasp subjection in its material instance as a constitution of
subjects.[17]

Power is not the product of intent.[18] It is simply there. Yet this is not to say that power does not have its purposes or that power does not serve agendas. Because power operates as a general, unspecified and unmanned apparatus, it can be readily appropriated toward any number of ends. The nation-state does not own the multifarious veins of power, does not control the way power controls, and is certainly not invulnerable to the totalizing nature of power, for the ubiquity of power means exactly that nothing stands outside (this will become more apparent in the following chapter where I discuss the nation-state as subservient to global capitalism). There is no "outside" beyond the operations of power. One does not rebel by going beyond the reaches of power since such a "beyond" sounds nonsensical to Foucault. Instead resistance ensues when new assemblages appropriate and redirect power for their own purposes. Centralizing bureaucracies as well as those who rebel against them can each find power's diffuse reach useful for their respective goals. For example, governments do not create the cultural form of patriotism but will definitely use those potencies for their purposes. Multinational corporations did not invent normalization but normalization does incidentally prove an effective social infrastructure for marketing corporate products. Since power is neither intentional nor centralized, power flows in every direction—coercion, repression, creation, resistance, and on and on. As power can be directed so it can be redirected. "There are no relations of power without resistances; the latter are all the more real and effective because they are formed right at the point where relations of power are exercised; resistance to power does not have to come from elsewhere to be real, nor is it inexorably frustrated through being the compatriot of power."[19] The torrents of power can be aimed against the nation-state and patriotism can be configured to undermine, as well as uphold, regimes. Multinational corporations not only seek access to power's organization but are themselves subject to power and vulnerable to processes of normalization—themselves, like nation-states, part of a vast global "society of normalisation."[20]

2. Biopower

In *Discipline and Punish* Foucault begins his well-known discussion of "panopticism" by describing a state of emergency. Plague has set in and death has invaded the world. Suddenly everything shuts down, including cherished notions about life: "the closing of the town and its outlying districts, a prohibition to leave the town on pain of death, the killing of all stray animals."[21] The various communities that once mediated the individual's relationship with the state have become infectious hot zones that need to be disciplined. Everyone now lives alone, receiving direction, rations, and news of the world through the most basic conveyances. As fear grows, people fortify: one survives by keeping others out. "It is a segmented, immobile, frozen space. Each individual is fixed in his place. And, if he moves, he does so at the risk of his life, contagion or punishment." In place of community, one bows to the gaze, social surveillance "alert everywhere" as "inspection functions ceaselessly." Whereas the citizen would normally reject "the penetration of regulation into even the smallest details of everyday life" he now willingly submits since nothing less than survival is at stake: "Everyone locked up in his cage, everyone at his window, answering to his name and showing himself when asked—it is the great review of the living and the dead."[22]

States of emergency begin to find "contagions" at every juncture and time itself marks impending doom. Publics marshal forces and suspend previously inalienable rights, for "against an extraordinary evil, power is mobilized."[23] This conscription demonstrates the great benefit of having already constructed a disciplinary society because the structures of control are already in place, the infrastructures necessary to survive need only be activated in a fuller sense, "to a whole series of 'carceral' mechanisms which seem distinct enough—since they are intended to alleviate pain, to cure, to comfort—but which all attend, like the prison, to exercise a power of normalization."[24] Such modes of life over time habituate citizens as the ubiquitous presence of power entails capillary formations "to induce ... a state of conscious and permanent visibility that assures the automatic functioning of power ... creating and sustaining a power relation independent of the person who exercises it."[25] Power settles at the level of depth, transforming desire so that states of exception become something of a choice and those who resist represent threats to the whole, since exceptionalism demands an all-or-nothing commitment. When Foucault strangely refers to panopticism as "democratic," he means that submission to the powers has become not only necessary but attractive as we learn to love order, homogeneity, and certainty, coming to be at home with terror because it saves us from terror.[26] Foucault compares this positive account of power to power's exclusionary role (which Foucault granted much greater emphasis in his earlier work, specifically *Madness and Civilization*) exemplified through leprosy in contrast to the plague: "The reaction to leprosy is a negative reaction; it is a reaction of rejection, exclusion and so on. The reaction to plague is a positive reaction on inclusion, observation, the formation of knowledge and the multiplication of effects of power."[27] Ironically, whereas those in the quarantined plague town are watched, sequestered, numbered, and thus individualized, those in the leper colony can do whatever they please; left to their own devices after having been rejected and cast out by society, they are no longer subject to society's individuation. The healthy society requires unremitting maintenance, the "healthy," constant production. In their own way, the unhealthy are free as long as they remain outside the city gates.

According to Foucault, states of exception must be liturgically nurtured by "the haunting memory of 'contagions,'"[28] and herein lay the fates of "the criminal," "the insane," "the sexual deviant," "the diseased," "the immigrant," "the malformed," "the racially ambiguous," and "the hermaphrodite," ultimately consigning all strangers, familiar or otherwise, criminal or not, to scare quotes. One begins to see the discursive logic of late modernity's "rituals of exclusion,"[29] practices now routinized by the spectacle of the other: "This surveillance is based on a system of permanent registration ... the role of each of the inhabitants present ... is laid down, one by one ... this document bears 'the name, age, sex of everyone'... Everything that may be observed during the course of the visits... is noted down and transmitted."[30]

Capitalism enters this epic drama on the backside of the nation's teleological myths of civilization defined by plague-like alternatives—e.g., the social contract staves off a Hobbesian primal state of nature: the nation as the cure for the infectious wars of religion. Foucault speaks about the "political dream" of "the plague as a form," which extends indefinitely the state of exception: "rulers dreamt of the state of plague."[31] Here capital colonizes fears generated by the political dream of plague as "an exhaustive, unobstructed power that is completely transparent in its object and exercised to the full" and crafts a total society where "each actor is alone, perfectly individualized and constantly visible... arrang[ing] spatial unities that make it possible to see constantly and to recognize immediately," where "visibility is a trap."[32] Space now becomes "location of bodies in space, of distribution of individuals in relation to one another, or hierarchical organization, of disposition of centres and channels of power, of definition of the instruments and modes of intervention of power."[33] Elsewhere Foucault writes about the ability of the gaze to exact bodily confession or the loquacity of sexuality to articulate "normality."[34] The intransigence of emergency requires power "be given the instrument of permanent, exhaustive, omnipresent surveillance, capable of making all visible, as long as it could remain invisible. It had to be like a faceless gaze that transformed the whole social body into a field of perception."[35]

Foucault was concerned with how the political dream of the plague institutionalized emergency situations. Here we can talk about two moments, the transition to permanency vis-à-vis games of truth, and the play of such games within permanent plague societies. Whether plague names an eventuality of history that gets colonized by games of truth or only mythologies to begin with matters less than the dexterity of power to colonize either. For example, whether "scarcity" (*la disette*) identifies an actual state of affairs diagnosed and addressed by Malthusian economics or more readily the theoretical scaffold upon which modern capitalist competition can produce demand is less important than its working mechanisms. In fact though we might trace its origins to actual food shortages during the seventeenth and eighteenth centuries, the present reality of scarcity as a notion exists very much as what Foucault calls a political dream "focused on a possible event, an event that *could* take place, and which one tries to prevent before it becomes a reality."[36] Especially given Foucault's brand of nominalism, distinctions like actual versus mythical become less important. The plague gains permanency through processes of discursive productivity where absence is secured by its opposites, guarded by blocked subjective knowledges that cohere toward the semblance of solidity. Foucault states, "We have to produce the truth in the same way, really, that we have to produce wealth" and in relation to actual production of things into the world "we have to produce the truth in order to produce wealth" because the actual production of wealth relies on the semantic production of mythologized truths.[37] The political dream of the plague involves similar discursive formations, the construction of placeholders able to name any emergency necessary for the justification of systemic correlates. That is the genius of the plague; it cannot be seen either in form or in reality. It can only be spoken of and its effects only narrated. The development of microbiology's empiricism does nothing to undermine such speech or narratives; actually, microbiology comes into existence within them, and hence can only support their regimes of truth. The transition from plague to panopticon mirrors the instillation of the plague's dream into the psyche of individuals as it takes up residence within the infrastructures of society, indeed often determining both the need and production of such individuals and infrastructures. The efficacy of the panopticon follows the genius of the plague, the production of invisible truths that galvanize entire social orders: invisible plagues and invisible surveillance; that which drives us and those who watch us exist primarily, but not exclusively, in our minds, or more precisely, in our speech. The material implementation of control and surveillance, their institution, finds little resistance as their *raison d'être* settles in the same place from which they arise. Each one becomes proponent and apologist. We defend their reasons as we defend society, coming to eventuate their rationale with society as such. Power both produces such societies and sustains them.

The society that must be defended can only be defended by being constantly reproduced. Its standing infrastructures, which endure as bygone artifacts of predecessor cultures, need to be reactivated by being granted new meaning and hence purpose. They lack meaning or purpose of their own but gain those when proven useful within the new regime of truth. In other words the implements of the defended society do not exist until we learn to talk about them in particular ways, until they are rendered practical, until they are made subject. This transition from plague to panopticon marks power's transition from sovereignty to nascent versions of what Foucault will come to call biopolitics:

> Now an important phenomenon occurred in the seventeenth and eighteenth centuries: the appearance—one should say the invention—of a new mechanism of power which had very specific procedures, completely new instruments, and very different equipment. It was, I believe, absolutely incompatible with relations of sovereignty. This new mechanism of power applies primarily to bodies and what they do rather than to the land and what it produces. It was a mechanism of power that made it possible to extract time and labor, rather than commodities and wealth, from bodies. It was a type of power that was exercised through constant surveillance and not in discontinuous fashion through chronologically defined systems of taxation and obligation. It was a type of power that purposed a closely meshed grid of material coercions rather than the physical existence of a sovereign, and it therefore defined a new economy of power based on the principle that there had to be an increase both in the subjugated forces and the force and efficacy of that which subjugated them.[38]

"Bio" both because biopower courses through the entire social body (*bios*), capillary in its sedimentations and surveillance, and because the body gains a new significance within biopolitics. The individual body now matters—it now appears!—as the local site of the *bios* in general, society's emergency enacted as and on an anatomical organism. Biopolitics does not presume individuals to be acted upon—as if they exist there ready-made—as much as constitute the appearance of individuals by biopower's processes of individuation. One comes to be in the world because such a world has been made to matter; an "individual" is but part of a much larger concern called "the population" and only matters *as part of the population*. Within biopolitics, there are no individuals apart from the population, but as part of the population, the individual bears the total meaning of the population, and as such bears every imposition necessary to make the population come out right: safety, normality, productivity, efficiency, etc..[39] Within this *everything* now matters and so needs to be policed, from the architecture of town space to the maximum advantage of populations to public education and private behavior, all the way to the clothes people wear and the hygiene they practice.[40]

Foucault locates the origins of these burdens in the Christian pastoral and what he calls Christianity's revolutionary "economy of faults and merits" where a continuous and exacting confession of the flesh unfolds in a cycle of confrontation, contrition and confession, a "destruction of the self" within a vanishing horizon of endless recoiling humility.[41] While biopower matures the pastoral significantly, moving in different directions of extended productivity, still it retains the pastoral's continuous and exacting procedures of individuation (faults and merits in the pastoral; clothes, hygiene, and progeny for biopolitics). Because power no longer deals exclusively with the sovereign and his dealings, a new politics must be arranged to render visible all these multiple sites: "Biopolitics deals with the population, with the population as political problem, as a problem that is at once scientific and political, as a biological problem as power's problem."[42] Biopower's innovation lies in its ability to disperse a single logos that binds everything or everyone toward a conception of society as such, and so any number of arrangements can be made to work as long as they operate in reference to the "the society" or "the population." In this sense, "normalization" does not refer to a primordial conception (logos) of "normal" ("the norm") to be disseminated by a disciplinary apparatus called "normalization." Rather, "normal" comes to be realized within the disciplinary apparatus itself, the way the apparatus speaks and comes to speak about itself through its various serendipitously linked processes.[43]

Foucault considers biopolitics the great invention of bourgeois cultures, that which makes them possible, "one of the basic tools for the establishment of industrial capitalism and the corresponding type of society."[44] Biopower produced and was produced by a world that could not only permanently survive emergencies but could prove profitable within them. Capitalism displaced the occupancy of rulership from a king to individual subjects, making each individual king of his wealth, which now needed to be pursued and accumulated at all cost. Profit within this system became society's driving force (its plague) and each little king sought to establish and secure his kingdom (his panopticon); as his own apologist, no one needed to tell him to do so. A new sovereign subject appeared: the citizen of the bourgeois modern state. The threat of an unruly nature beyond the state's social contract—chaos and the state of nature—and its boogeyman of poverty proved highly effective as habits of speech and narratives of meaning. While theorists uttered illusions of a divided society—the haves and the have nots—biopower dominated exactly because the society was amazingly unified even if part of its unity was cemented by subscribing to such illusions. Combined with and enriching notions of normality and ensconced within fears of abnormality, these coherences galvanized a new society to be defended against enemies foreign and domestic: "A normalized society is the historical outcome of a technology of power centered on life."[45] The plague's lexicon finds a convenient home within the new scientism's biologism of race, to frightful but all too natural consequences: "the racist thematic is no longer a moment in the struggle between one social group and another; it will promote a global strategy of social conservatism ... we see the appearance of the State's racism: a racism that society will direct against itself, against its own elements and its own products. This is the internal racism of permanent purification, and it will become one of the basic dimensions of social normalization."[46] This war instills not the king's power over death but society's right to life: "Wars are no longer waged in the name of a sovereign who must be defended; they are waged on behalf of the existence of everyone; entire populations are mobilized for the purpose of wholesale slaughter in the name of life necessity: massacres have become vital."[47] Entirely new knowledges are founded through the development of technologies of life, labor, and language.[48]

Power

These revolutionary concerns for life elevate the role of the individual and coronate a newly appeared subject as the object of and herself the proprietor of concern: the person as her sex. Because the society's meaning (*raison d'être*) has shifted from the center to the whole, "the population" emerges as bearing meaning itself (*raison d'État*), warranting protection and becoming *the* issue for anyone who would so comprise it.[49] Procreation became everyone's business, the proliferation of the society's purpose through proliferation of the society: "sex is worth dying for."[50] What people did in the bedroom was now what they did for and before the whole state, a duty of the citizen's tacit responsibility to everyone. In the same way that fortification against invasion guarded plague society, its permanence required a new kind of militarization—make love not war, indeed. Why did hygiene, masturbation, bodily health, childhood virginity now matter when they hardly registered previously? Because "at the juncture of the 'body' and the 'population' sex became a crucial target of a power organized around the management of life rather than the menace of death."[51] Why does sex matter? Not because in its throes persons fulfill their wildest dreams (Foucault famously declared "sex is boring."). Sex mattered because it *broadcasts* our wildest dreams, into which sex was conscripted and then freighted with ultimate purpose. Nothing is any longer "just sex."

Foucault is adamant that he does not intend his conception of biopolitics to be a new theory of power, an all encompassing panoramic that explains every variety of power. Rather, he hopes it enables "a logical, coherent, and valid investigation of the set of these mechanisms of power and to identify what is specific about them." Power is not "a substance, fluid or something that derives from a particular source" and neither is it "along or on top of," "over and above" or "alongside" the relations it colonizes. There are not, Foucault thinks, relations that become coercive when invaded by power, because there are no relations without power and no power without relations. Instead, "Mechanisms of power are an intrinsic part of all these relations and, in a circular way, are both their effect and cause."[52] For Foucault, power is the most precise way of speaking of relations. To presume that this way of speaking—of relations as invariably tied to power—is "overly politicized" is to presume a realm of purity such that the presence of power within it could only be understood as impure, to believe that relationships can ensue without political consequence. For Foucault, this is not possible, and even the presumption and priority of apolitical space itself smuggles in political values—that space should and can be depoliticized. Such presumptions of purity in turn rely on undisclosed notions of pure indeterminacy—and their attending pictures of freedom, agency, and subjectivity, exactly the kinds of presumptions Foucault seeks to overturn on the way to portraying selfhood differently.

3. Power's Ruse

Foucault's sophisticated understanding of power offers a perspicacious lens through which we can examine contemporary existence, by first describing power's ubiquity and then showing how power "finds an anchor" in the most basic modes of relationality. According to Foucault, when dissatisfied with ordinary life we moderns long for abstractions, dreams of escape to worlds not held captive by the complexities of life situated with others, spinning yarns in order to cope with existence amidst the incessant presence of power within all relations and their productions and performances of biopower. Foucault writes, "power is tolerable only on condition that it mask a substantial part of itself. Its success is proportional to its ability to hide its own mechanisms."[53] Foucault here claims more than the clandestine nature of power's operations, though that is critical. According to Foucault power's significance lies in its totality, its capillary form that inundates all of life, making existence and its various emanations possible.[54] However power's ineluctability also hides a more sinister quality and its stealthy presentation—you can't see it because you see it everywhere—conceals its more potent manipulations. Power reveals itself just enough to further exert its putative mechanisms. By allowing the possibility of its unmasking, by allowing the subject the *pleasure* of knowing and through knowing consummating subjectivity, power further controls. Knowing satiates the will-to-truth as we voyeuristically gratify ourselves as "children of protracted solitude" finally in the know. This masturbatory affair with untold secrets romanticizes the unspoken, the oppressed, and the hidden, heralding the goodness of subversion: "We're getting away with it!" However, at this point, power most fully masters existence, for in the very promise of revolution/transcendence has power finally achieved complete control: now it colonizes dreams—the in-breaking of God, the intimation of an outside, "the coming freedom," the hope of the Eschaton—in order to simultaneously energize and pacify its adherents.[55] The voyeuristic gratification of knowledge gives hope for life after power but only within the given vestiges granted *by* power. And it is the ruse of freedom—"to speak out against the powers that be, to utter truths and promise bliss, to link together enlightenment, liberation, and manifold pleasures"[56]—that makes power "tolerable," the condition *sine qua non* that renders life among the powers palatable, while disguising power's true strategy, that it has capitulated only enough to further control "down to their slenderest ramifications."[57] By itself creating the myth of escape, the possibility of an after-power, power disguises its own workings; by the myth of freedom, the truth of power remains hidden in its "loquacious tactics."[58] Or more precisely, within the myth of freedom power conceals its most intolerable reality, that there is no outside, no escaping power. Understanding Foucault's conception of power on this score will be critical in the following chapter when we engage capitalism as a kind of Foucauldian power.

In the first volume of *The History of Sexuality*, Foucault demystifies an all too common view of desire and freedom, what I have been relating as the repressive hypothesis. In his other major works, Foucault had challenged modern myths like rationality, scientific objectivity, prison reform and others discourses that propagate, for the sovereign self, "a well-accepted argument."[59] Here, he reveals how commendations of sexual freedom arise by first setting repression in the past, an unmasking that exposes all such metanarratives as "a thing of this world" rather than "the reward of free sprits."[60] Rather than suffer these machinations, Foucault admonishes we

> locate the forms of power, the channels it takes, and the discourses it permeates in order to reach the most tenuous and individual modes of behavior, the paths that give it

access to the rare and scarcely perceivable forms of desire, how it penetrates and controls everyday pleasure ... in short, the "polymorphous techniques of power."[61]

Through an analytics of power one exposes the repressive hypothesis as an anodyne that allows us to esteem our liberation from oppression; seeing behind the myth, or under it, reveals that though sexual repression names something, whatever it names, *we* do the repressing. Mapping power illumines the self-policing (panoptical) features of "normalization" and a more frightening discovery: "you are always already trapped."[62] The allure of the repressive hypothesis was its ability to disguise these intolerable features, in their stead propping up myths of freedom and revolution—"*Aufklärung!*"—that cloaked the truth that through *self*-deception, we find ourselves most captive to the powers "always already present, constituting the very thing which one attempts to counter it with."[63] The repressive hypothesis posited power so diaphanous and flimsy that one could, if one so chose, see through and shake off power as easily as leaving behind self-incurred minority.

Instead, power courses everywhere as it "produces effects at the level of desire."[64] Here Foucault speaks of "power at its extremities, in its ultimate destinations," directing our "our bodies, our day-to-day existence."[65] Power deploys itself in these "material instances" and determines every moment of life an incessant drive toward "normalization," the status quo which in turn "create[s] a systemic blindness" to power's most potent forms, perpetuating myths of enlightenment.[66] Power does repress, but much more, ensuing as "a network or circuit of bio-power or somato-power, which acts as the formative matrix of sexuality itself as the historical and cultural phenomenon within which we seem at once to recognize and lose ourselves."[67] The panoptic nature of power disqualifies from the start the presumption of a neutral starting point to which one might return.[68] Power is no *thing*, nor is it *some*one; it exists only as its deployments in, through, and within every relationship through which selves get constituted.[69] Power is "everywhere; not because it embraces everything, but because it comes from everywhere."[70] Exactly because power is not someone or something acting upon us but exists within the interstices between and within persons, places, and things, there is no escaping power, no overthrowing or dismissing it. Rather than someone "out there" controlling power, power acts within us, on us, *as* us, in minute form, everywhere present, "the dissemination of micro-powers, a dispersed network of apparatuses without a single organizing system, centre or focus, a transverse coordination of disparate institutions and technologies."[71]

Seen through Foucault's genealogy, the modern age can be understood as the sentiment in which everyday life matters, where everything is at stake. The coronation of the ordinary however became "a place of maximum saturation."[72] Ordinary life became an "unrelenting system of confession" as everything now demanded disclosure and uniformity.[73] Every facet of life now became everyone's problem and the "putative mechanisms of power" justified war for the sake of all.[74] Power and life became synonymous in their "mobile relations." Just as there is no exteriority, nowhere beyond power, so there is no genuine interiority as selfhood is rendered a two-dimensional field for the smooth deployment of power, which comes to full flower only after colonizing our most intimate relations, those essential structures that bridge the particular and the universal: the family.[75]

> The family cell, in the form in which it came to be valued in the course of the eighteenth century, made it possible for the main elements of the development of sexuality (the feminine body, infantile precocity, the regulation of births, and to a lesser extent no doubt, the specification of the perverted) to develop its two primary dimensions: the husband-wife axis and the parents-children axis.[76]

Power comes home as family "provide[s] it with permanent support," developed webs of relations to exercise its surveillance and control in order to "anchor sexuality."[77] Family as "an obligatory locus of affects, feelings, love" has become in the modern era power's staging area from whence it travels through the entire social matrix. Amidst these relations, and their coordinated patterns in the cultural architecture, pleasure circulates with power, always its alter-ego, a cycle of knowledge and satisfaction, depth and confession, hiddenness and disclosure, a quiet war between and within individuals as the gaze floats just below the surface of quaintness.[78] Rather than interiority comprising modern selves, all gets pulled to the surface in "games of truth" and individuals *want* to lay bare their cherished secrets just as they *desire* their neighbors' confessions.[79]

Foucault advances Nietzsche's agonism toward a positive politics of immanence, "the multiplicity of force relations immanent in the sphere in which they operate and which constitutes their own organization."[80] On the one hand, Foucault occludes disavowal, that somehow we might gainsay the "perpetual relationship of force," that resistance to *power* actually means resistance *to* power. On the other hand, power's ubiquity means *anyone* can colonize power; in the same way that the state or capital usurps power "always already there" so others can redirect the flows of power. For Foucault, resistance does not speak of fleeing power; since there is no outside, the only resistance to be had takes place through appropriation: "resistance to power does not have to come from elsewhere to be real.... It exists all the more by being in the same place as power."[81] Only by first ensconcing ourselves within power's expansive grids, by becoming comfortable with its ubiquity, only by learning to stop worrying and love power, can we then mine power for our own uses. Abstractions like *Aufklärung* or the repressive hypothesis feign "a binary structure with 'dominators' on one side and 'dominated' on the other" rather than acquiring modes of resistance within power's many varied capillary expressions and material instances.[82]

Foucault writes, "What's effectively needed is a ramified, penetrative perception of the present, one that makes it possible to locate lines of weakness, strong points, positions where the instances of power have secured and implanted themselves by a system of organization.... In other words, a topographical and geological survey of the battlefield."[83] Surveying contemporary existence means first recognizing it as a battlefield, ripe for assertions and counter-assertions of power. Quietly here an absolute war unfolds as homogeneity orders behavior and spatial and temporal modes of socialization mobilize bodies under the battle cry of fitting in, "the great operations of discipline ... transform[ing] the confused, useless or dangerous multitudes into ordered multiplicities," as Foucault puts it in *Discipline and Punish*.[84] A "topological and geological survey of the battlefield" reveals normalization materializing at the level of desire and the very notion of repression—those making us do it—becomes a favored myth making contemporary life palatable. After all, the same preoccupations with homogeneity and order that conscript life in this world presuppose depth as the most sacred and invulnerable zone of personhood. At the level of desire and dream, we find ourselves most captured by the capillary powers of everyday life.[85] The very prevarication of recognition, the placing of one's hopes in the pretensions of an "outside"—another world that actually can meet our deepest desires deeply—demonstrates not genuine rebellion but the totality of this world. This belief in externality, and internality as the animating drive toward externality, marks the site at which power most potently grounds itself, for over against the repressive hypothesis, power is most power-like when it asserts not from some yet-to-be-identified intentionality but rather at the level where desire is affirmed as depth. Foucault's critique centers most squarely on notions of depth. On the one hand, he shows how knowledge in the modern period has been overly concerned with transparency, pulling everything to the surface and depleting interiority. On the other hand, Foucault does not in turn proffer an alternative interiority in order to create space somehow invulnerable to the gaze.[86]

4. "Courage to Begin Anew"

In a now paradigmatic assessment, the political philosopher Charles Taylor called Foucault's promise of resistance "ultimately incoherent," given Foucault's accounts of power and truth. In an exchange that appeared in the journal *Political Theory* around the time of Foucault's death, Taylor outlined what he understood to be three tenets of Foucault's philosophy and showed how if taken as premises, no meaningful account of political action could follow. The three tenets are: (1) against Enlightenment presumptions, we are no freer today than we were in the past; (2) we only conclude we are freer because we have been duped by power's latest ruse; (3) greater freedom will only come as we unmask the ruse.

In this chapter, I have already articulated the first two of Taylor's summary points, namely Foucault's genealogical and archaeological efforts to help us see that we are not as free as we would like to think we are and our captive notions of freedom are framed by hidden exclusions (unfreedoms). Taylor sees Foucault following these two by offering a way forward—an advance beyond deception and domination—by a dialectic of self-consciousness, that genealogy and archaeology gains us the advantage of showing us who we really are, given that we are not as we would like to think we are. This third step in the Foucauldian dialectic is the moment of liberation, by way of truth, by way of unmasking. Taylor summarizes, "This would be a notion of liberation through the truth, parallel to the Romanic-derived one, but different in that it would see the very notion of ourselves as having a true identity to express as part of the dispotif of control rather than what defines our liberation."[87] At this point Taylor believes he has caught Foucault in a contradiction: To the extent that he adheres to the Nietzschean line against truth—that there really is nothing behind the mask—how can Foucault speak meaningfully about gains in freedom, through unmasking or otherwise? If truth is simply power disguised as truth (tenet/premise 2), and getting behind this mask only reveals power once again, another mask, then we are stuck in the first position, and are not really *progressing* toward freedom at all. The best we can do is cycle back and forth between points 1 and 2 because within their terms, 3 is not a coherent possibility. Since Foucault does not believe in truth, neither can he say we are progressing toward greater freedom; it is incoherent for him to assert we are getting freer because "freer" (as a superlative) is a description that necessitates a zero point from which it can be measured.[88]

Taylor's assessment is important given my argument thus far. I have tried to show how within Foucault's terms, there is a coherent account of freedom even if there isn't a presumed account of truth. If Taylor is right then not only is he right about Foucault, then so am I wrong about Foucault, as is anyone who would rely on Foucault for a genuine alternative to the problems gripping modern existence. The only thing we could get from Foucault according to Taylor's reading is the sad irony of our foolishness—the depths of our captivity. In the following, I spend some time with Taylor in order to argue that he misses something critical about Foucault and, more central to my larger purposes, make that lacuna instructive for just how Foucault does offer a fully coherent account of freedom.

Taylor concludes his essay by turning to Foucault's later work, particularly his account of freedom as self-constitution which I have already began and will continue to lay out in this book. Even there, Taylor thinks, Foucault gets stuck on the same Nietzschean snag: "Indeed in offering us a new way of reappropriating our history and in rescuing us from the supposed illusion that the issues of the deep self are somehow inescapable, what is Foucault laying open for us, if not a truth that frees us for self-making?"[89] Taylor has other complaints about Foucault, notably that his documentary histories prove too lopsided to yield much benefit as insightful as they sometimes are. I'll focus on the complaint I outlined above since I agree with William Connolly that that specific target of Taylor's complaint proves to be, according to the complaint, "the ultimate incoherence in [Foucault's] project," the incoherence from which all other incoherencies in his work stem.[90]

In rejoinder to Taylor, Connolly turns Taylor's complaint on its head, showing how Taylor's complaint, if taken seriously, would undermine Taylor's own project. Connolly reviews how Taylor and Foucault both rely on epistemic claims that would be similarly delegitimized by modern foundational theories of knowledge. And yet, argues Connolly, Taylor deploys pressures that topple Foucault's illegitimate epistemology while shielding his own illegitimate account from such pressures. Their shared illegitimacy goes something like this: Foucault has a conception of truth and subjectivity that on foundational grounds (as rehearsed by Taylor in his complaint) cannot account for its *critique*; Taylor has a conception of truth and subjectivity that on foundational grounds cannot account for its *certainty*. Modern theories of knowledge cannot grant coherence to Foucault's critique given its Nietzschean adherence. As well, and this is what Connolly brings out, those same epistemologies cannot grant coherence to Taylor's beliefs either, given their pre-modern sources. So the negative pole of Connolly's critique is that Taylor allows himself leeway while stranding Foucault to charges that would render both of their claims illegitimate. The more interesting and constructive argument, and the one I think proves instructive to what Foucault *is* getting at, is that Foucault, unlike Taylor, has resources for legitimating his critique in a way that Taylor does not, precisely because unlike Taylor, Foucault does not take seriously those modern epistemic demands. Indeed, the very lopsidedness that Taylor's other complaints target does the work of showing why such demands ought not be taken seriously. "If the limits of the modern episteme do not constitute the limits to possible thought as such" as both Foucault and Taylor believe, then each *can* turn to that which is not respectively granted within modern foundationalism. But because Foucault majors on that which exceeds modern subjectivity while Taylor cannot help but see such excess as incoherent, Taylor is imaginatively precluded from talking about his own illegitimate claims. Not Foucault though, who "strives to stretch the established limits of the thinkable by concentrating on how otherness appears when it is presented as the product of a subjectivity that is itself produced."[91] Connolly's goals in this essay does not warrant detailing the otherness he thinks resourcing Foucault's (or Taylor's for that matter) project. But as these resources are critical for my interpretation I will delineate them here as instructive of Foucault's larger aims.

I started out by saying that Foucault's is a quasi-metaphysical philosophy. That classification is true if we freight metaphysics with traditional versions of transcendence and immanence. There is, however, another sort of transcendence in Foucault, and it is a crucial feature of his work, though one not visible to traditional philosophical registers. It is not the kind of transcendence onto-theologically posited as God or the ground of moral or epistemic judgments, and therefore not one legitimated within modern epistemes. Because he does not take those epistemes seriously—since his lopsided histories have, in his mind, discredited onto-theology—then he is able to figure an account of transcendence that makes possible freedom, truth, and subjectivity. Captive to the exclusions that makes it possible, the modern episteme focuses on what is included, even becoming an apologist for exclusion. By envisaging that which exceeds our immanent judgments (what Connolly calls "concentrating on how otherness appears when it is presented") Foucault's philosophy sees otherwise. As I will discuss at greater length in the following chapter we might think of this as a horizontal transcendence.

Foucault, as I portrayed him beginning this chapter, is searching for subjectivities beyond our exclusions. This search has to believe (for what other choice does it have?) that exclusions do not exhaust the stock of possibilities. Any one subjectivity is the byproduct of its native episteme, or set of exclusions. But that that episteme is neither necessary nor natural means that other subjectivities are possible. As Foucault says, "There is always a possibility, in a given game of truth, to discover something else and to more or less change such and such a rule and sometimes even the totality of the game of truth."[92] This is the whole point for Foucault, the attempt to speak of subjectivity beyond current exclusions, and even over against current exclusions. As Taylor and Connolly both agree with Foucault, "the limits of the modern episteme do not constitute the limits of possible thought as such." That which sits outside these limits then, which has not been expropriated or even anticipated, *transcends* those limits. The attempt to rethink the self is the attempt to think the self beyond the limits that make it possible, to rethink by unthinking the self. As Thomas Flynn writes of Foucault, "His 'ethics of thought' resembles a kind of self-transcendence. It is a self-distancing (*se déprendre de soi-même*) that is simultaneously a self-constitution: the self as other."[93] Hence Foucault's search for new subjectivities—genuine gains in truth and freedom—presumes these metaphysical conditions. This is what I take Foucault to mean by the ubiquity of power, the upshot of his discourse of power, "the necessity of excavating our own culture in order to open a free space for innovation and creativity."[94] Not only could Foucault account for his critique in a way that Taylor cannot, so Foucault has resources to receive Taylor in a way that Taylor cannot receive Foucault, since his receptivity to that/ those who transcend the reigning episteme (what Connolly called "concentrating on how otherness appears when it is presented") not only allows him to receive Taylor, but indeed seeks after such articulations of subjectivity. Taylor is right that Foucault's receptivity does not allow him to evaluate these various options, but neither does Foucault want to. The same evaluations that allow Taylor to render judgments (coherent, true, good, etc.) do nothing in Foucault's view but render judgments within exclusions (in the name of coherence, truth, goodness, etc.). Taylor recognizes that buying into foundationalism's games of truth (deciding who is in and who is out) will disqualify him, but he does not much care because he considers such games rudimentary for discerning what he calls elsewhere "the best account available."[95] Because Foucault is not so vested but is instead interested in as many accounts as possible, he has a keen interest in keeping the game open. As he rhetorically responds to a Taylor-like challenge, "Is progressive politics tied (in its theoretical reflexion) to the themes of meaning, origin, constituent subject, in short, to all the themes which guarantee in history the inexhaustible presence of a Logos, the sovereignty of a pure subject, the deep teleology of a primitive destination? Is progressive politics tied to such a form of analysis—rather than one which questions it?"[96] This allows him to let all manner of account in, including Christianity. And this is why the content of the last stage of Foucault's intellectual life cannot be divorced from the form of his reception. The fact that Foucault was able to find himself countenanced by games of truth he knew could be violent, exclusionary, and even hateful speaks volumes of the availability of his later thought.

For Foucault, exactly because history is comprised of accidental accretions—"blocks of historical knowledges that were present in the functional and systemic ensembles"[97]—rather than solid states of nature and necessity, then any regime of truth can be overturned. That doesn't make them, as Taylor rightly observed, *more* truthful; but they are true, as much as something can be true, as embedded in modes of enforcement that regulate a society around them as true, history books as "textbooks on public right."[98] Resistance then begins by questioning those truths and undercutting the regulated society, disbursing the bios toward new assemblages around new knowledges. Along the way Foucault archaeologically surveys "the law of *existence* of statements, that which rendered them possible—them and none other in their place: the conditions of their singular emergence"[99] and genealogically investigates the options of alternative knowledges and assemblages that might be gathered as counterhistory:

> Not only does this counterhistory break up the unity of the sovereign law that imposes obligations; it also breaks

the continuity of glory, into the bargain. It reveals that the light—the famous dazzling effect of power—is not something that petrifies, solidifies, and immobilizes the entire social body, and thus keeps it in order; it is in fact a divisive light that illumines one side of the social body but leaves the other side in shadow or casts it into the darkness.[100]

Genealogy reaches back to this casted shadow and brings forth new stories, which in turn reveals the architecture of the current regime of truth as simply one among many possibilities—that society was made, that it can be unmade, that we can begin anew.

Earlier I mentioned what Foucault called "the economy of faults and merits," speaking of "the absolutely new form of power" that proved a seminal form of biopower's exhausting, exacting, and permanent individualization. Describing this historical innovation, Foucault writes, "What the history of the pastorate involves, therefore, is the entire history of procedures of human individuation in the West. Let's say also that that it involves the history of the subject."[101] Foucault traces a newly emergent self with these processes of individuation—the self "appears" in the confession of her faults and merits—within this new economy of power which he labels, "governmentality." Because Foucault sought to situate biopolitics beyond the confines of the sovereign and instead displace power at every site of relationality, so governmentality meant not simply being governed but also governing. It is precisely this duality of govermentality, "the government of oneself and other" that reveals power's double-agency, and here resistance can be envisaged as fully coherent within Foucault's larger philosophical project. After all, we started this chapter by observing that Foucault thought himself not finally a theorist of power but freedom. Biopower's multidirectionality means that one can speak of power as genuinely agential, doubly so, both assertion and resistance (counter-assertion). Nowhere is this clearer than in Foucault's etymological analysis of the verb on which he founds his account of governmentality:

> Conduct is the activity of conducting (*conduire*), of conduction (*la conduction*) if you like, but it is equally the way in which one conducts oneself (*se conduit*), lets oneself be

conducted (*se laisse conduire*), is conducted (*est conduit*), and finally, in which one behaves (*se comporter*) as an effect of a form of conduct (*une conduite*) as the action of conducting or of conduction (*conduction*).[102]

The sheer uses of the verb lend insight into the multifarious forms agency can adopt within the Foucauldian power lexicon. Most notable is the reflexivity of governing (*se conduit*) and the subjectivity implied within self-governance's passive agency (*se laisse conduire*) and most telling is Foucault's potent "counter-conduct."[103] We are now far-removed from the juridical account of power, in its Classical or Marxist forms, that posits power within zero-sum analyses of action. Counter-conduct instead illumines power as ubiquitous, and here Foucault points to the anti-pastoral modalities of scripture, community formation, mysticism, and eschatology that bespeak a plentitude that exceeds what can rendered visible and captive by biopower, or more precisely, biopower as abiding this plentitude.[104] Foucault offers us a fluid, exhilarating, and even hopeful account of political existence at an unimaginably personal level: power as the ethics (*ethos*) of self-conduct. Power speaks to how I conduct myself as self-governance, how others conduct me through dominance, how I do and do not allow that conduction, and how at each moment I have available to me counter-conduct. Each circuit of conduction crisscrosses multiple lines of possibility in rapid succession of action, compulsion, and resistance. Hence, instead of questioning, "Can there be resistance to the omnipresent pastoral?" we ask "By what resistance did the pastorals themselves emerge?" and "What resistances did the pastoral over its long history entail and even instigate?" Especially by emplacing them on the vanishing horizon of a recoiling humility (recall Christianity's anti-pastoral asceticism[105]), the pastorals themselves become new modes of self-conduct: "By whom do we consent to be directed or conducted? How do we want to be conducted? Towards what do we want to be led?" as embodied in Wyclif's dictum for and against the pastorate: *Nullus dominus civilis, nullus episcopus dum est in peccato mortali*.[106] When these "insurrections of conduct" cohere in the production of new selves and their gathered publics, one arrives at what is perhaps

Foucault's most audacious articulation of resistance, the creation of an alternative political society:

> there is a political party, which has ceased being clandestine for a long time however, but which continues to have an aura of an old project that it has evidently abandoned but to which its destiny and name remain linked, and which is the project of giving birth to a new social order and creating a new man. That being the case, it cannot fail to function to a certain extent as a counter-society, another society, even if in fact it only reproduces the society that exists, and consequently it appears and functions internally as a sort of different pastorate, a different governmentality with its chiefs, its rules, and its principles of obedience, and to the extent it possess, as you know, a considerable capacity both to appear as a different society, a different form of conduct, and to channel revolts of conduct, take them over, and control them.[107]

In the next chapter, I turn to how Michael Hardt and Antonio Negri envision this "considerable capacity" for revolts of conduct in the face of the crushing pressures of late capitalism. Taylor is correct that from certain perspectives, including his own, it will not be clear that such revolts are advances. For Foucault, just the moreness of these differences is enough, if only to remind us that alternatives exist. For Foucault, that would be an advance.

Chapter 2
Capitalism, Totality, and Resistance

Since there is no truths to values and since heaven is in shreds, let each man fight for his gods, and a new Luther, sin resolutely.
—Max Weber

If certain theorists are to be believed, a new age of empire is upon us. Compared to the historical empires that came before, this new empire is both more diffuse in its articulation—transcending and even subsuming nation-states—and because of that, more pervasive in its authority. We now belong not to empires, but reportedly, Empire. The theorists of Empire are of course referring to global capitalism, or what we might simply call late capitalism because by its nature capitalism has always tended toward globalization. The empire of capital is totalizing in its effects, and as significantly, in its theorization. Not only does it seek to dominate all, it seeks to determine how we think about its dominance. For example, ask any reputable economist for coherent alternatives to global capitalism and you will be met with a quizzical look. The pressing issues in relation to globalization within contemporary economics are entirely directed toward trends *within* globalization; imagining an alternative now seems passé if not irresponsible.[1] Hence, Empire in terms of globalization seeks to encompass the political, economic, social, *and* methodological landscape. Totality is a key feature of capitalism; it wants nothing else. Part of the goal in this chapter will be to take seriously this totality—and in this Foucault will prove helpful—while also canvassing what alternatives still remain—and in this Foucault will prove indispensible. Foucault's conception of power helps us understand this new empire and its alternatives.

Capitalism, Totality, and Resistance

This chapter visits the most articulate and audacious expression of globalization by considering the work of Michael Hardt and Antonio Negri. Understanding globalization through Hardt and Negri will assist us in understanding both capitalism and Foucault because Hardt and Negri's capitalism as Empire demonstrates with detailed relief Foucault's notion of power. As they observe beginning their ambitious project, "In many respects, the work of Michel Foucault has prepared the terrain for such an investigation of the material functioning of imperial rule."[2] My contention will be that Hardt and Negri tow the Foucauldian line toward multiple convergences that illumine with great clarity the world in which we find ourselves, and the modes of resistance and even witness available to us. Hardt and Negri's innovation through Foucault is not the recognition of Empire's pluriform occupation vis-à-vis biopower; rather, it is the rather startling claim that Empire in just this sense offers, along with despair, reasons for hope; the novelty of such a claim—that the new age of empire is cause for hope—can only be appreciated within a Foucauldian cosmology. The ways Empire names the complex convergence of hope and despair illustrates how the purported contradictions within Foucault's thought issue in productive tensions: "where there is power, there is resistance." While globalization leaves no remainder in terms of conceptual alternatives, it does shift prior theoretical lenses toward new vistas, and hence, new ways of being in the world (including renewed ways of being in the world). Like Foucault, Hardt and Negri insist that "Manichaen" promulgations of power situate resistance in all-or-nothing analyses which demand of resistance total revolution, the complete eviction of power. Foucault caricatured this picture of resistance as cutting off the king's head. In contrast, a non-Manichaen analysis pays greater attention to power's double agency, minding both its disciplinary governance and its capacities for freedom. In this line, Foucault proves quite helpful to the Christian church by highlighting political action sighted along the index of witness within the context of this present darkness. Foucault through Hardt and Negri helps the church rightly despair capitalism while also substantiating her own reasons for hope.

1. "Immanence in Its Simplest Form"

Utilizing Hardt and Negri as an explanatory grid through which to understand Foucault raises an important issue regarding the compatibility of Foucault and Christian theology, namely whether Foucault remains wedded to a Nietzschean ontology that views transcendence as only will to power imposing on immanence Schmidtian injunctions of theological justification. When Foucault speaks of power's ubiquity and utilizes genealogy to unmask the ruse of the universal, as discussed in the previous chapter, it would seem that he follows Nietzsche at least on this score, and so propones what John Milbank disparages as "an ontology of violence"[3]—agonistic forces of power disguised as benevolent play of difference. In this vein Foucault seems to share little in common with Christian theology, which conceptualizes at minimum transcendence as the difference between God and creatures. I have no intention of trying to contort Foucault or Christianity so that this disjunction can be passed over. However, I also think that leaving the matter at that, that because Foucault lacks a Christian transcendence he can be no friend of Christianity, does little for our understanding of either Foucault or Christianity. The ontological differences between Foucault and theology should chasten Christian appropriations of Foucault. Still, if the church can put Foucault's politics to use while remaining cautious of its atheistic immanence she will discover in Foucault a friend in her struggles against *certain* common enemies, and may even come to appreciate how his reworked transcendence makes possible that political friendship, what I called earlier the availability of his thought.

For Foucault as for Heidegger (as I will show in the fourth chapter) transcendence ensues on the order of immanence. Unlike Heidegger, Foucault does not wed himself to the work of ontology, and so his figuration of transcendence in immanence is a bit friendlier to Christianity, just as his philosophy is political in a way Christianity is directly so and Heidegger is only indirectly so. Responding to the charge that their Foucauldian politics precludes transcendence, Hardt and Negri insist: "We are merely insisting that society be able to organize itself with no superior power ruling over it. This would be a politics of immanence in its simplest form."[4] They desire a version of political life that refuses to trade on Schmidtian imperatives of divinely sanctioned political authority, what Foucault calls "the guarantee provided by a primitive foundation or a transcendental teleology."[5] Hardt and Negri seek after a common life where people are answerable only to one another, what Richard Rorty considers the minimum condition of democracy.[6] Proposing democracy, they rework traditional categories of transcendence and immanence through Foucault (and at times Spinoza and Gilles Deleuze). They begin the third installment of their *Empire* trilogy with characteristic aplomb:

> War, suffering, misery, and exploitation increasingly characterize our globalizing world. There are so many reasons to seek refuge in a realm "outside," some place separate from the discipline and control of today's emerging Empire or even some transcendent or transcendental principles and values that can guide our lives and ground our political action. One primary effect of globalization, however, is the creation of a common world, a world that, for better or worse, we all share, a world that has no "outside." Along with nihilists, we have to recognize that, regardless of how brilliantly and trenchantly we critique it, we are destined to live in *this* world, not only subject to its powers of denomination but also contaminated by its corruption. Abandon all dreams of political purity and "higher values" that would allow us to remain outside![7]

Leaving behind vaunted notions of an outside, Hardt and Negri think, frees us for "a politics of immanence in its simplest form." By "simplest form" they mean immanence without a presumption of transcendence that grounds political action. They worry that ideas of an outside too easily excuse us from the careful work of politics because such ideas presuppose that something else, other than our work of politics, will take care of us.[8] Given the conditions they describe—"war, suffering, misery, and exploitation"—they believe we have no room for those kinds of excuses, especially since they have only contributed to the conditions' "increasing" character. Leaving those ideas behind, they call us forward to the business at hand.

Foucault and Theology

Hardt and Negri subscribe to what I referred to earlier as Foucault's horizontal transcendence, where an ontology can be suspected but is not explicitly declared. Making use of Foucault first requires we make careful distinctions, and then bracket certain ontological speculations about what he doesn't say. For example, Foucault's explicitly non-centrist non-sovereign view of power signals a critical departure from an easy schematics of transcendence and immanence; Foucault here questions not only the Platonic transcendent Good but notions of political theorizing that presume it, including those that begin with ontology. In reading Foucault, one should not begin with ontology—remember, he says "Let's suppose that universals don't exist."[9]—but trace from his politics the ontology operating in his politics. Hardt and Negri's political theorizing aids us because they move the conversation forward in this way, delimiting what Foucault did not say in terms of what he did in order to understand a politics that not only escapes the pull of traditional metaphysics but in some important ways overcomes it. Hardt and Negri in their use of Foucault acknowledge a certain transcendence but question, "what is gained by such a statement?"[10] The same can be said for Foucault for whom transcendence obtains on the order of immanence, but preoccupation with these matters *as* polemical concerns (i.e., transcendence *versus* immanence) "could mask or confuse the difference between resistance and power and thus make it seem that there is no way to go beyond the limits of power, be they transcendent or transcendental."[11] In contrast to polemics, they propose revising transcendence as we know it, "a strange kind of teleology because no telos stands at the end and pulls the process forward. There is no end point but merely a vector that extends from the present in the direction of the desire of the multitude ... When the political desires and constituent powers extend in time to construct new institutions and forms of life, they follow a telos that the imagination has designed."[12] Hardt and Negri, following Foucault, buck inscribing transcendence in terms of sovereignty and certainty, instead plotting it in relation to immanence. They speak of subjectivity by invoking Foucault's conception of dispotif and hence existence and resistance in terms of emergent subjectivities, the proliferation of which conditions the world "of historical and ontological overflowing" toward the arrival of "the becoming-Prince of the multitude."[13] Hence they offer us an immanent apocalypse—what they call "a kind of secular eschatology" in the likes of Franz Rosenweig and Walter Benjamin[14]—that issues for them in a politics that expresses a construed ontology of love, "the power of creation that resides and is born again and again in the encounters between and among us."[15] Turning to their politics and how Foucault founds it will flesh out my construal of Foucault's account of totalizing power and its dictum, "where there is power, there is resistance."

2. The Demise of the Nation-State

The public intellectual Naomi Klein recently described utopianism as the ability to "think our way out of the present," aerating what political theorist Sheldon Wolin understands as the present constellation of power.[16] If we take utopianism in these terms, then one will not find in recent years a utopian vision more audaciously compelling than that offered by Michael Hardt and Antonio Negri in their *Empire* trilogy. Clearly this work utopicly tries to think its way out of the present. Whether it succeeds in doing so remains to be seen, but one cannot easily resist its infectious vision.

In the trilogy's first volume, *Empire*, Hardt and Negri depict the emergence of a new political order,

> In the passage of sovereignty toward the plane of immanence, the collapse of boundaries has taken place both within each national context and on a global scale. The withering of civil society and the general crises of the disciplinary institutions coincide with the decline of nation-states as boundaries that mark and organize the divisions of global rule. The establishment of a global society of control that smoothes over the striae of national boundaries goes hand in hand with the realization of the world market and the real subsumption of global society under capital.[17]

For the most part, nation-states, including America, have missed this passage. This is so because nation-states tend to conceptualize the world within the horizon of the nation-state as an idea.[18] The nature of the state's power (centralized, juridical, intentional) blinds it to the appearance of subjectivities that do not so easily fit within its form of authority.[19] Equating the nation-state with rationality, as classic political theory tended to do, fuels imperialistic expansion within its own domain, across new territories and over rival political, social, and economic orders but also delimits the nation's imaginative encounters. An immature capitalism relied on European imperialism and its "partition of the world among the dominant nation-states, the establishment of colonial administrators, the imposition of trade exclusives and tariffs, the creation of monopolies and cartels, differentiated zones of raw material extraction and industrial production, and so forth."[20] Yet to the extent that capital rode imperial expansion in order to make use of its regnant power apparatus, capital tied itself to a nation-state world, that is a world cordoned by borders that artificially delimited capital's expansion: "Although imperialism provided avenues and mechanisms for capital to pervade new territories and spread the capitalist mode of production, it also created and reinforced rigid boundaries among the various global spaces, strict notions of inside and outside that effectively blocked the free flow of capital, labor, and goods—thus necessarily precluding the full realization of the world market."[21] The nation-state's border extending enterprises suited capital's expansionist agenda but the nation-state's constitution by delimitation (borders) also proved its undoing: "Imperialism is a machine of global striation, channeling, coding, and territorializing the flows of capital, blocking certain flows and facilitating others. The world market, in contrast, requires smooth space of uncoded and deterrialized flows."[22] As economist David Harvey writes, "Capital is not a thing but a process in which money is perpetually sent in search of more money . . . There is, therefore, within the historical geography of capitalism a perpetual struggle to convert seemingly absolute limits into barriers that can be transcended or circumvented."[23] When capital eventually outgrew the nation, it had no interest in abiding the nation's trumped transcendence as embodied in its rationalistic bureaucracy:

> Capital . . . operates on the plane of *immanence*, through relays and networks of relationships of domination, without

reliance on a transcendent center of power. It tends historically to destroy traditional social boundaries, expanding across territories and enveloping always new populations within its processes ... Traditions, cultures and social organizations are destroyed in capital's tireless march through the world to create the networks and pathways of a single cultural and economic system of production and circulation.[24]

Labor entered into new modes of abstraction; whereas in the industrial economy, as theorized by Marx, commodification alienated the worker, in the post-industrial economy, her labor was never "hers" to begin with; rather, it only emerged within the discourse itself. Transforming itself, capital found a new home in the multinational corporation which rose in influence and power because it could go where the nation could not. "The declining sovereignty of nation-states and their increasing inability to regulate economic and cultural exchanges is in fact one of the primary symptoms of the coming Empire."[25]

3. Empire

Hardt and Negri are quick to acknowledge the new capital's violence, including the overrunning of the state as political form and idea; after all, "The end of the dialectic of modernity has not resulted in the end of the dialectic of exploitation."[26] However, for them the transition from these forms and ideas heralds tremendous opportunity. As they say, "Our ultimate objective in this analysis ... is to recognize the terrain on which contestation and alternatives might emerge."[27] Just as capital eventually broke free of state-based imperialism (and its own amazing propensities for violence) and just as power took form in that particular instance of dominance, so too the new capital engenders other instances of innovative freedom. Recall Foucault's words from the previous chapter: "What's effectively needed is a ramified, penetrative perception of the present, one that makes it possible to locate lines of weakness, strong points, positions where the instances of power have secured and implanted themselves by a system of organization ... In other words, a topographical and geological survey of the battlefield."²⁸ Following Foucault's lead, Hardt and Negri survey a "pyramid of global constitution" and describe this present battlefield as "Empire": "Empire constitutes the ontological fabric in which all the relations of power are woven together—political and economic relations as well as social and personal relations."²⁹

Atop the triangular configuration sits the United States as something both more and less than a nation-state, more in that partnership with capital bequeaths monarchical status, less in that Empire's monarch serves at the pleasure of capital. And why has capital chosen America? The accidents of its historic proximity to capital's past and present make it a natural fit. That this arrangement is both made possible by and makes possible America's "hegemony over the global use of force" indicates the protean mobility of capital and the radical impermanence of this arrangement.³⁰ The rule of Empire, in good Foucauldian fashion, prescinds as a set of relations that depends on but is not identical with any one of its organs. Empire as an instance of power is, in the words of Hardt and Negri, "a decentered and deterritorialized apparatus of rule that progressively incorporates the entire global realm within its open expanding frontiers. Empire manages hybrid identities, flexible hierarchies, and plural exchanges through modulated networks of command."³¹ The mastery of the new capital obtains in its ruthless lack of partisanship: only to the extent that America suits its interests (increasingly America will not, while nations like China will), will Empire grant America its privileged role.³²

Below the monarchy sits a mediating tier populated by political and economic elites: multinational corporations, supernational institutions, and their client states, together comprising "filters of the flow of global circulation and regulators of the articulation of global command; in other words, they capture and distribute the flows of wealth to and from global power, and they discipline their own populations as much as this is still possible."³³ None of these nation-states can match America's political clout but each finds ways to siphon off the economic flows they host and supply. This second plane becomes the great equalizer as capital deals with anyone so willing. Empire's totalizing inducements means few can long abstain from participating. Non-participation only intensifies demand, especially because "outside" designates yet-to-be-colonized territory: "from the standpoint of capital, it is all the outside: potential terrain for its expanded accumulation and its future conquest."[34] Empire travels by nature, not because it lacks for something, but because by its nature it is nothing else. "In other words, Empire presents its rule not as a transitory moment in the movement of history, but as regime with no temporal boundaries and in this sense outside of history or at the end of history."[35]

At bottom, with an inverse proportion of area to authority, lives "the multitude." Resistance is most able to occur here.[36] But so is discipline. Hardt and Negri utilize the term "multitude" in order to highlight the diffuse, variegated, and incalculable lives of peoples simultaneously subject and free. Given how representation determines imaginative encounters, Hardt and Negri theorize this third tier in terms of its possibilities. They readily admit, "It is certainly an open question whether the development of this biopolitical fabric will allow us to build sites of liberation or rather submit us to new forms of subjugation and exploitation."[37] When global capital gains control of the multitude, it profits immensely, though not by inhibiting but tapping into the multitude's infinite productivity. Remember that Foucault posits power as productive of subjectivity insofar as it individualizes.[38] As Hardt and Negri put it, "There is indeed something mysterious about the act of creation, but it is a miracle that wells up from within the multitude every day."[39] Capital preys on this creativity, extracting from the multitude energies released from its infinite miracles. Empire will utilize every tactic available, from blunt instruments like the monarchy's "use of force" to more subtle stratagems like the repressive hypothesis. The greatest stores of renewable resources run just below Empire's perch and whenever capital divines multitude's next steps, it can anticipate how to make use of the multitude, including its resistance, for its own benefits.

Hardt and Negri portray capital as parasitic on biopower's infinitude—drawing its own life from the lifeblood of the multitude's vibrancy—so as to demonstrate the anteriority of freedom. Hardt and Negri write, "Here we can appreciate the full importance of Foucault's claim that power is exercised only over free subjects. Their freedom is prior to the exercise of power, and their resistance is simply the effort to further, expand, and strengthen that freedom. And in this context the dream of an outside, an external standpoint or support for resistance, is both futile and disempowering."[40] Tied to the multitude in these ways, capital must exact every discipline necessary to maintain control of the multitude's capillary flows and formations. Empire must stay one step ahead by producing technologies of control through discourses and performances that cultivate and harvest the multitude's field of immanence. At bottom, the multitude represents the possible and by parasitically sapping potentiality, Empire at once energizes and enervates the multitude while growing stronger off the torsion.

Empire's dominance is only matched by the multitude's ability to continuously recreate itself; the products of its labor include not only immaterial goods (such as knowledges, styles of communication, and relationships) but by engendering social relations and forms of life, the multitude *creates* the multitude.[41] "The passage from the virtual through the possible to the real is the fundamental action of creation. Living labor is what constructs the passage way from the virtual to the real; it is the vehicle of possibility."[42] In order to stay ahead, capital must harness the masses long enough to sap their energies, distract their politics, invade their imaginaries, drain their energies, and hijack their strengths. Capital has no biopolitical productivity of its own; it is only parasitic. The multitude alone produces and reproduces and becomes the source not only of Empire's survival but the multitude's own becoming.

The relations between the three tiers are both totalitarian, as capital seeks to subsume thought and action, while at the same time radically democratic. Since power is diffuse, taking many different shapes in different places and because capital can only exert and sap capillary power but never completely control it, domination and resistance occur simultaneously. Hardt and Negri write, "Since it has no center and almost any portion can operate as an autonomous whole, the network can continue to function even when part of it has been destroyed. The same design element that ensures survival, the decentralization, is also what makes control of the network so difficult."[43] Within the "mixed" constitution of this new political representation of "the people" collude the usual manipulations vis-à-vis conglomerations, nation-states, or global corporations.[44] These elites both seek to represent the masses by reducing them to staid conceptions of community (recall Foucault's "the population") flattened in the simplistic terms of supply and demand (recall Foucault's "maximum advantage") and disparages representation when those conceptions prove unruly (recall Hardt and Negri "the multitude").[45] Accordingly, representation (what Foucault calls "self-writing" as explicated in the next chapters) belongs to the multitude itself: "The strategic production of knowledge . . . implies immediately an alternative production of subjectivity."[46] Given the totalitarian programs of the monarchy and the elites, the many can only "speak" and be "seen" when gathered, which can be amazingly difficult given capital's abilities to draw solitary individuals qua consumers into the open as nodal points of free market productivity.

Assembled, the publics that comprise the multitude become much less manageable.[47] Borrowing Hardt and Negri's phrase, the "moment of creation" names this mobilization, where gathered publics gain visibility hitherto impossible as individuals: "We need a force capable of not only organizing the destructive capacities of the multitude, but also constituting through the desires of the multitude an alternative."[48] Here at bottom reside the possibilities for multifarious gatherings. The profusion of capital through its conglomerate, corporate, and nation-state structures, to be sure, shifts as well, but given those structures, conservatively lest it slips off its power base. At bottom, in contrast, the multitude bustles, differentiated and diffuse in every possible way; here movement defines existence and continual gathering and dispersing, infusing and defusing, agitating and convulsing toward "moments of creation," rendering movements above glacial in comparison. "Every singularity is a social becoming. What the multitude presents, then, is not a *sociedad abigarrada* engaged in common struggle but also a society constantly in the process of metamorphosis."[49] This can be difficult to appreciate when the rapid development of new technologies of production suggest responsible politics can only be populated by the conglomerates, and so while the multitude holds the greatest potential, the ubiquitous presence of global elites can nullify that potential. The gathered publics become visible when they choose purposes, identities, and practices that overwhelm the gaze of capital:

> These virtual, constituent powers conflict endlessly with the constituted power of Empire. They are completely positive since their "being against" is a "being-for," in other words, a resistance that becomes love and community. We are situated precisely at the hinge of infinite finitude that links together the virtual and the possible, engaged in the passage from desire to a coming future.[50]

Significantly, Hardt and Negri term their politics "political realism."[51] The multitude in transgressing and overflowing delimitation expresses the reality of things: "only space that is animated by subjective circulation and only a space that is defined by the irrepressible movements (legal or clandestine) of individuals and groups can be real."[52] Hardt and Negri champion migration and the ineluctable movement of life, which tests and overflows boundaries, especially those policed by Empire's violent security apparatus. As much as Empire seeks to corral the multitude's genesis and hijack its surplus value, as much as Empire succeeds for moments at a time, and as much as those moments entail great violence and suffering, still, in the same way that capital escaped the reigns of the colonial and nation-state form, multitude breaks free of Empire toward "a new cartography," a new way of living:

> The movements of the multitude designate new spaces, and its journeys establish new residencies. Autonomous movement is what defines the place proper to the multitude. Increasingly less will passports or legal documents be able to regulate our movements across borders. A new geography is established by the multitude as the productive flows of bodies define new rivers and ports. The cities of the earth will become at once great deposits of cooperating humanity and locomotives for circulation, temporary residencies and networks of the mass distribution of living humanity.[53]

By mapping contemporary existence onto Hardt and Negri's cartography of "love and community," one finds available new ways of engaging power's ubiquitous presence, the goal of the Foucauldian project. This re-imaging of the political makes visible various publics previously disappeared by colonized theoretical indicies. Through Foucault, Hardt and Negri make immediately perceptible new bodies and gatherings. No wonder that at the same time they delineate and demonstrate Empire's vast rule they also show within and beyond Empire possibilities for resistance and alternative modes of flourishing in a world ruled by Empire. Thus, they write, "the key to these transformations resides in the democratic moment, and the temporal dimensions of the democratic moment has to refer ultimately to the multitude."[54] Empire's primacy resides in its ability to tell only one story. Genealogy for Foucault meant rethinking the present by retelling the past. In order to undermine that present, Foucault tried to detect the fissures comprising its totalizing histories. Similarly, in order to rethink the terms of Empire, one first discovers the fissures of its theorizing. Transformative theorizing arises from new exposures and experiences. The massive shifts from imperialism to nation-states to Empire each occasioned opportunities for renewal. Hardt and Negri write, "the rupture within capital and the emerging autonomy of biopolitical labor present a political opening. We can bet on the rupture of the relation of capital and build politically on the emerging autonomy of biopolitical power. The open social relation presented by capital provides an opportunity, but political organization is required to push it across the threshold."[55] For example, publics gather when isolated subjectivities make use of globalization's glutted communication lines and share stories of suffering, corroborate local surveys of Empire, and go about the hard work of political organization *within* Empire's many blindspots. Through this, the multitude makes passage into peoplehood, "from *being* the multitude to *making* the multitude."[56]

4. The Church's New Visibility

Hardt and Negri's outline of emerging global political orders renders new possibilities for what is "seen" as effectively political. Over against political liberalism's policied borders, the new capital shifts the register of the political exactly because it refuses to proffer a realm of purity as the constitutively political. But what does this accomplish for Christianity? After all, it may seem as if this new visibility allows the church to return to Christendom, where "visibility" signals a return to a constantinian presumption and visibility denotes rulership. Certainly as the church continues to lose authority in the West, some affective positioning on a global scale might return the church to a luster of old. Considering the varied crises that threaten all notions of the good—what Alasdair MacIntyre has infamously referred to as "the new dark ages"[57]—repristinating an authoritative magisterium would be received by some as a gain. That is, unless one remembers the many excesses Christendom imposed through its own modes of totality, impositions that prepared the ground for the nation-state's ascension to political rule. Those clamoring for the next Christendom would find Empire wanting only to the extent that it awaits the blessing of the bishops.

Hardt and Negri's "triangle of global constitution" and its Foucauldian ubiquity of power can help fend off these kinds of temptations insofar as its cartography envisages the multitude replete with potencies so as to expose those temptations as inabilities to rethink the political beyond political liberalism, which is why religious fundamentalism is less the ostensible revitalization of purity as much as aspiration to relevance within liberal sequesters of political discourse. Though the multitude is neither Empire nor its vessels of domination, neither is it ossified in forms that must *retain* dominance. As Hardt and Negri assert, "only subjectivities at the base of the productive and political processes have the capacity to construct a consciousness of renewal and transformation."[58]

Power at bottom gives the church access to an infinite variety of flows that too may be siphoned for the church's purposes. Concluding *Empire*, Hardt and Negri offer a surprising exemplification for the potential of multitude and its subjective expressions: "There is an ancient legend that might serve to illuminate the future of communist militancy: that of Saint Francis of Assisi . . . Francis in opposition to nascent capitalism refused every instrumental discipline, and in opposition to the mortification of the flesh (in poverty and in the constituted order) he posed a joyous life."[59] Hardt and Negri's appropriation of Francis does little work to open up the rich theological tradition continued through and embodied in Francis, his naked admonition to the church to more fully clothe itself as church, and the theological rigor through which Francis understood and positioned his militancy against a complacent Christendom. Still, Hardt and Negri convey the political possibilities of Christian faithfulness as a reverberating alternative to imperialism of any stripe. The life of Francis poignantly articulates Foucault's ubiquity of power and Hardt and Negri's summoning of the multitude. Foucault reminds us that the political is often witnessed in the least political of places. As the church has long witnessed, power comes as both opportunity and temptation. These are not, finally, new realities.

Power's availability to the church as multitude in turn should enliven the church's availability to the multitude. This does not mean that the church need submit to Milbank's "ontology of violence" where the presumption of *agon* supplants theological affirmations of trinitarian peace. It should mean that the church can resist the language of resistance as I prefaced in the Introduction, especially in the way that resistance discourse tends toward violence. Because the church's primary language is one of witness and not resistance, it is less prone, or at least should be, to war (just or otherwise) because witness, unlike resistance, is not charged with securing its own victory. Witness makes present the Lamb of God whose eternal victory rendered unnecessary securing right.[60]

Part 2
Self-Writing

I am no doubt not the only one who writes in order to have no face. Do not ask me who I am and do not tell me to remain the same.

—*Michel Foucault*

But, then, what is philosophy if not the critical work that thought brings to bear on itself: in what does it consist, if not in the endeavor to know how and what extent it might be possible to think differently.

—*Michel Foucault*

Chapter 3
Biography and Biopolitics

Gradually it has become clear to me what every great philosophy so far has been: namely, the personal confession of its author and a kind of involuntary and unconscious memoir; also that the moral or immoral intentions in every philosophy constituted the real germ of life from which the whole plant had grown.
—Friedrich Nietzsche

Michel Foucault once asked whether Nietzsche's day planner and laundry lists should be published along with the rest of Nietzsche's work, and if not, why not?[1] His musings on Nietzsche's day planner, and the larger question of what constitutes a life, reminds us that those who find Foucault elusive can be certain he would have liked it that way. Perhaps the only thing we can say definitively about Foucault is that he defied final conclusions about everything, including Michel Foucault. Which makes writing his biography tricky business. After all, Foucault was not only a philosopher (those who spend their time asking questions like "What is a pipe?") but a philosopher disposed to very peculiar sorts of philosophical questions (ones like "What is an author?"). Along with his sometimes friend/sometimes rival Jacques Derrida, no one has problematized more the notion of biography. Adding to the trickiness, Foucault's biography is rather unique among theorists and academics in that his life proved almost as interesting as his written work; indeed, among influential twentieth-century academics, one would be hard pressed to find a life more interesting than Michel Foucault. And here we find an immediate likeness to Christian theology, which refuses easy distinctions between truth and embodiment. As radical as was Foucault's political theory, he lived those politics. This makes him not simply one of the great thinkers of the century, but one of its great characters.

Indeed, I would venture to say that more so than his written work, Michel Foucault's life epitomized the great passions and pathologies of an oft passionate and pathological century; he was the twentieth century's saint. Foucault to be sure would have shunned these characterizations. But he was also wise enough to know that characterizations are all we have. And so he might forgive us if at least we acknowledged as much up front. In this chapter I will not attempt to write Foucault's biography. Instead, I look at the complexity of such an endeavor by reviewing one such biography, the controversy it raised, and what that controversy tells us about Foucault's work, if not his life.

Readers familiar with English translations of Foucault's work will recognize the author bio prefacing the now iconic Vintage Books editions of Foucault's work:

Michel Foucault was born in Poitiers, France, in 1926.
He lectured in universities throughout the world; served as the director at the Institute Français in Hamburg, Germany, and at the Institute of Clermont-Ferrand, France; and wrote frequently for French newspapers and reviews.
At the time of his death in 1984, he held a chair at France's most prestigious institution, the Collège of France.

The brief note on Foucault's biography is more than Heidegger legendarily offered for Aristotle—"Aristotle was born, worked, and died"—but not much more. It does not tell us for example that Foucault considered himself "a total Atheist" though he came from a Catholic family and spent the last years of his life pouring over patristic literature in the Dominican Bibliothèque du Saulchoir, or that much of his work was informed by direct engagement with the topics of his researches (mental hospitals, government protests, prisons, etc.).[2] We don't learn that Foucault not only suffered and died from AIDS but also that he suspected, somewhat rightly, that the mythic rumors of its occurrence were not to be trusted. In other words the brief biography does not present us with Foucault's day planner or laundry list. These features of Foucault's life mattered, and while we should resist mapping them directly onto the various contours of his intellectual work,

Biography and Biopolitics

we also cannot avoid them as Heidegger does regarding Aristotle. If biography matters, how does it matter?

1. What Is Biography?

Given Foucault's claims about biographies (discussed below) and his own rather fascinating biography, we should not be surprised that one attempt to tell his story raised a controversy. In 1993 James Miller published *The Passion of Michel Foucault*.[3] One observer described the reception of Miller's Foucault: "The usual placid surface of a scholarly presentation turned into roiling waters as people stood and almost screamed their disapproval. They accused Miller of every imaginable intellectual offense and clearly felt that they had to defend the memory of Foucault against a threatening assault by an unsympathetic outsider."[4] Like other Foucault biographies before and since, Miller's offered a detailed account of Foucault's life and letters and utilized philosophical training to make valuable connections between the two. Like any successful intellectual biography, Miller's book helped us understand Foucault's thought by helping us understand Foucault's life. Indeed, as this chapter is arguing about theology, Miller's biography powerfully demonstrates that one's biography and one's thought mutually inhere—getting at how is a much more complicated issue and will be the ultimate goal of this chapter.

Miller's efforts ran afoul with critics where he seemed to reduce the whole of Foucault's work to certain moments of Foucault's life. David Halperin has been the most ardent and astute critic of Miller's work and puts it this way: "It purports to 'explain' Foucault's thought by tracing its origin to the 'truth' of his psychographical knowledge with the power of normalizing judgment in a single gesture whose effect is to strengthen the very disciplinary controls that Foucault's whole life was dedicated to resisting."[5] Namely, Miller was interested in Foucault's sex. Miller characterized Foucault's intellectual career as evermore-daring attempts to access "limit-experiences" transgressed through evermore-daring sexual ventures into the realm of death, making Foucault's eventual death from AIDS a natural progression within the logic of not only his life but his intellectual development. In a speech two years before *The Passion of Michel Foucault*'s publication, Miller summarized its thesis, and his version of Foucault, hence,

> the inner logic of his philosophical odyssey, and also of his public political statements and actions, is unintelligible apart from his lifelong, and highly problematic, preoccupation with limiting the limits of reason, and finding ways—in dreaming, at moments of madness, through drug use, in erotic rapture, in great transports of rage, and also through intense suffering—of exploring the most shattering kinds of experience, breaching the boundaries normally drawn between the unconscious and conscious, order and disorder, pleasure and pain, life and death; and in this way, starkly revealing how distinctions central to the play of true and false are pliable, uncertain, contingent.[6]

Miller further enraged readers by suggesting that Foucault knowingly risked AIDS in the early 1980s. This latter point, as contentious as it may be, was simply internal to Miller's larger argument regarding Foucault's increasing sensitivity to the disciplinarity societies muster in order to normalize human subjectivity (i.e., Foucault's actions during this time was about pushing imposed limits, not knowingly spreading a deadly disease, which given the time frame would be an anachronistic inference). Foucault's sex was fair game because for Miller's Foucault, sex was never just sex, but an indelibly political enterprise.

Miller, in an academic article that appeared shortly before *The Passion of Michel Foucault*, brings up the graphic detail Foucault utilizes in recounting the regicide Damiens' execution at the unforgettable beginning of *Discipline and Punish*. Miller writes of Foucault's report: "Reading, we recoil: The scene provokes nausea, disgust, revulsion—but also a perverse fascination with the details."[7] Might the same be said of the revelations of Foucault's sexual habits conveyed in *The Passion of Michel Foucault*? Might we ask similarly of Miller: "What are we to make of *his* apparent fascination with death by torture?"[8] As intellectual biographer, Miller utilizes a strategy that is not unfamiliar even if the content of its provocation is odd. Other biographers have as well attempted to explain a thinker's biography by the substance of that thinker's intellectual career. For example, in his fine biography, Rüdiger Safranski goes to great lengths to situate Martin Heidegger's temporary sojourn with the Nazi's as a mistaken attempt to pursue the purity of being (*das Seiende seiender*) as conjectured in Heidegger's work following *Being and Time*.[9] Without explaining away, Safranski's explanation contextualizes these dark moments within Heidegger's thought (and vice versa). However, Miller on Foucault employs a strategy that is strikingly different than that used by Safranski on Heidegger. Whereas Safranski's biography achieved the intended effect of drawing the reader further into the sophisticated nature of Heidegger's thought on the apolitical constitution of being, Miller seemed most intent in talking about Foucault's sexuality with discussion of his intellectual work luring the reader there. In other words, Safranski's biography makes Heidegger's life *as* interesting as his thought; Miller's makes Foucault's life *more* interesting than his thought. Miller reduces Foucault to his sex. For Foucault the person, even more so than Foucault the intellectual legacy, this is a heavy burden to bear given his sexuality, almost foisting upon gay sex the suggestion of "limit-experience" as such. Making Foucault's life more interesting than his thought is no small feat, given how amazingly interesting his thought was, and so Miller succeeded on that score even if he played fast and loose with Michel Foucault in the process.

Foucault believed that the modern expansion of knowledge coincided with an expansion in surveillance and control, the will to truth as the will to power. Hence, Foucault thought he had good cause for disregarding what must have felt like colonized rumors of an emerging new disease in the early 1980s. The historical coincidence between knowledge and control seemed to be playing out once again as panic spread within the gay population, which by coincidence had just then been experiencing a significant political renaissance. Miller's biography seems to recognize this about Foucault and Foucault's thinking during this period. Yet this only further illumines the way Miller's biography misfires by pushing the envelope about what needs to be known about a thinker's life. In his later work, Foucault spoke of a dialectical progression involving repression, knowledge, and pleasure. *The Passion of Michel Foucault* not only instills this dialectic (its pleasures of getting behind the text) but does so without irony considering its subject matter. Whether this is for Miller a glaring oversight or a peculiar masochism ingeniously parodying Foucault's life and work is unclear. Undoubtedly, Miller has capacities for genius, and *The Passion of Michel Foucault*'s comprehension of Foucault's thought, relative to the controversy of its thesis, has gone largely unquestioned.

Miller justifies his preoccupation with Foucault's sex by invoking Foucault's desire to see one's life as a work of art, to see living as writing. Attempting to adhere to Foucault's wishes Miller turns to Foucault's life as one would his books. In a later article, Miller restates Foucault's now well-known desire to fashion life as art and contends that to understand Foucault's *work* one must attend to Foucault's life as aesthetic vocation.[10] Miller's Foucault produced his masterpiece in twin forms: *Surveiller et punir* and the limit-experiences undertaken in his final years: "For Foucault in the last years of his life, what finally mattered was not so much saving the world—a project doomed to miscarry—as it was achieving a certain piercing truthfulness, conveyed with exemplary beauty and wit, and combined with a sense of unashamed pleasure in the living of one's life."[11]

In his own words, Foucault associated what Miller would come to call "unashamed pleasures" with the creativity of artistic life. In one interview, Foucault spoke of "the innovations" implied in "the real creation of new possibilities of pleasure," saying, "Sexuality is something that we ourselves create . . . sex is not a fatality; it's a possibility for creative life."[12] If there is death in the creative act, it is not the death of shame imposed by disciplinary societies who delimit the pleasure of self-creation. Rather, death denotes the becoming of sexuality itself, the author's demise in the author's creativity, death as life constituting. While Miller's forays into Foucault's sexual habits come uninvited and feel distasteful, Foucault's own thought seemed to require analysis of the author *and* his life. In this regard Miller fails Foucault only in heading the wrong direction. In his famous essay "What Is an Author?" Foucault makes an inexorable link between authors and their works, but in the direction of their *works*, the death of the author in the birthing of his creation. The details of the author not only dissolve into his creation, but even more so are produced there. It is not like there is, for Foucault, "this figure who is outside and precedes" a text; in a very real sense for Foucault, the author is born *as* his text.[13] Or better yet, the author dies in the process of creation. "Writing is now linked to sacrifice and to the sacrifice of life itself; it is a voluntary obliteration of the self that does not require representation in books because it takes place in the everyday existence of the writer" and then critically as related to Miller's ambitions: "If we wish to know the writer in our day, it will be through the singularity of his absence and in his link to death, which has transformed him into a victim of his own writing."[14] Foucauldian biography does not seek "this figure who is outside and precedes" the text but would find him in his books, the author living in texts. For Foucault the *author* lives in his texts—so he speaks of "writing so as not to die" in the essay "Language to Infinity"[15]—as themselves mirrors to death. The writing swallows the writer in a life-death process "primarily concerned with creating an opening where the writing subject endlessly disappears."[16] Akin to Nietzsche's claim that belief in God remains to the extent that grammar remains, so Foucault thinks that positing authors behind texts re-inscribes a transcendent realm of origin (and a concomitant necessary and sufficient causal relation between author and text). Rather, writing denotes the immanence of becoming and an inverse dissolving (the ontology of which will be discussed in the following chapter through Foucault's Heideggerian debts). One could excuse Miller as conducting researches into Foucault's sexual habits as an innovative textuality, that is, Foucault's sex as Foucault's (greatest) creation. But this maneuver could only be attempted with a keen awareness of the dominative tendencies of knowledge, and the will to power lurking within claims of knowing. It remains unclear to me whether Miller pulls this off, and hence I am unsure what to make of his obsession with Foucault's sex.

2. *Salmagundi 97*

In 1997, the literary magazine *Salmagundi* published a series of responses to Miller's book, including comments by Miller in which he states, "My book is not a biography . . . It is, rather, a narrative account of one man's lifelong struggle to honor Nietzsche's gnomic injunction, 'to become what one is.'"[17] The noteworthy respondents, which included Richard Rorty and Alasdair MacIntyre, quickly turned to the question of biography while commenting on Miller's book. Lynn Hunt offered the most generative reading of the Miller controversy, suggesting that the form of controversy constitutes itself the content of Miller's argument:

> If Miller has manipulated us, it is in the most unusual way. He has generated a reaction—a visceral feeling, whether it be fury, rejection, amazement, disgust or just uncertainty—that in some sense proves his central contention: that experience matters. It sounds simple, but actually involves very big stakes. At issue is not just the correct interpretation of Foucault's work but by implication the interpretive strategies of postmodern criticism. Miller uses the most traditional tools of history and literary criticism (biography and thematic analysis) to paint a new picture of one of the leading masters of postmodernism. In the process, he raises disturbing questions about the relevance of an author's life and, more profoundly still, about the possibility of the self in the modern world.[18]

Hunt observes that contrary to Foucault's doubts about the continuity of the self, Miller presents Foucault as a unified self (and his sex as its unifying center), with depths that Foucault spent a lifetime denying: "Foucault may have wanted to efface himself or decenter all of mankind, but Miller just won't let it happen."[19] Absolving himself of our indictments, Miller does not think he has failed because he was not attempting to be faithful to Foucault's thought, only his life. He was not through *The Passions of Michel Foucault* maneuvering to be a follower of Foucault but only a biographer of Foucault, and hence is *like* Foucault only in the sense that admixing the critical with the historical means obstinately disallowing Foucault from naming himself. Defending himself, Miller writes, "Such a mode of analysis (which is indeed indebted, in different ways, to styles of interpretation pioneered by Nietzsche and by Freud) inevitably involves treating texts, not with reverence, but rather with systematic suspicion, thus subjecting them to a kind of interpretive 'violence.'"[20] Thus, when David Halperin, with his own self-styled "hagiography" of "Saint Foucault," complains in *Salmagundi 97* that Miller fails to remain true to Foucault—"My quarrel with Miller's book, in short, is not that its author is uncomprehending of Foucault's project. It is that he is politically opposed to it"—he reveals he has not yet come to terms with what Miller was trying to do.[21]

If Miller failed to acknowledge the irony of his biography, so too have his detractors missed the more convoluted irony of their vitriol, their ire that Miller got Foucault "wrong." There is no one Michel Foucault. That self, on Foucauldian grounds, is up for grabs, making Miller finally more Foucauldian than his detractors admit. It was Foucault, we must remember, who praised Nietzsche's genealogist: "if he listens to history, he finds that there is 'something altogether different' behind things: not a timeless and essential secret, but the secret that they have no essence or that their essence was fabricated in a piecemeal fashion from alien forms."[22] One might extend Foucault to say that we need biography as we "need history," in order to "dispel the chimeras of the origin, somewhat in the manner of the pious philosopher who needs a doctor to exorcise the shadow of his soul" and so use biographies, including those as wily as Miller's, for "its jolts, its surprises, its unsteady victories and unpalatable defeats."[23] It may be true that there is too much Miller in Miller's biography, but given Foucault's belief that such things cannot (should not) be avoided, so what? Was it not Foucault who lampooned "the demagogue" who "denies the body to secure the sovereignty of a timeless idea . . . he is divided against himself: forced to silence his preferences and overcome his distaste, to blur his own perspective and replace it with the fiction of universal geometry, to mimic death in order to enter the kingdom of the dead, to adopt a faceless anonymity"?[24] Miller's detractors may not like his Foucault biography for its jolts and surprises (or its kinds of jolts and surprises) but it remains unclear how Foucault could support that dislike. This is not to deny that within some epistemes some biographies are better than others, and that we might prefer on grounds of veracity some biographers over others (e.g., Halperin prefers

David Macey's *The Lives of Michel Foucault* over Miller's *The Passion of Michel Foucault* on the gauge of "complete and accurate information"[25]), but Foucault would caution us against overmuch respect for such epistemes and their preferences (e.g., what could Halperin's "complete and accurate" mean that it doesn't imply?). When Halperin complains that Miller's biography is "revisionist history" one might wonder, why would *that* be a problem; on genealogical grounds (remember, Halperin, unlike Miller, purports allegiance to Foucault's arguments) what history isn't "revisionist"?[26] Instead of dismissing Miller in the name of truthfulness, those who dislike Miller's biography might better serve their Foucauldian commitments by a different tactic: write a different biography; put the pieces together in another way. We are after all talking about the legacy of Nietzsche, the nihilism of truthfulness and the wilds of life: "It is no longer a question of judging the past in the name of a truth that only we can possess in the present; but risking the destruction of the subject who seeks knowledge in the endless deployment of the will to knowledge."[27] Or as Paul Veyne writes of Foucault's historiography: "Despite what the justificatory or self-protecting philosophers assert, the spectacle of the past brings to light no reason in history other than the struggles of men for something that is undoubtedly neither true nor false but that imposes itself as truth to be told. If this is so, a philosophy has only one possible use, which is making war: not the war of the day before yesterday, but today's war."[28] Miller's detractors might rather follow Veyne's injunction: "'Yes' to war, 'no' to patriotic brainwashing."[29]

3. The Modern Self's Biography

Foucault begins *The Order of Things* with a task that will occupy him over the next 300 pages, and in some ways, the remainder of his career: analyzing human modes of knowing, which he refers to in this text as epistemes.[30] For Foucault, the chief epistemic concern during the Classical period was representation, relating the truth of things by way of resemblances. Foucault concerns himself with the shifting ground of knowing, such that knowing does not refer *immediately* to the world (as the *un-shifting* ground of knowing) but rather pictures of the world. He speaks of his task as "an inquiry whose aim is to rediscover on what basis knowledge and theory became possible; within what space of order knowledge was constituted; on the basis of what historical *a priori*, and in the element of what possibility, ideas could appear, sciences be established, experience be reflected in philosophies, rationalities be formed, only, perhaps, to dissolve and vanish soon afterwards."[31] In order to accomplish this task, Foucault juxtaposes these modalities in all their complex certainty; the confidence of each episteme displays itself through ornate composites proffered as senses of the world. Sometimes the epistemes follow on one another such that coherent periodizations follow. More often they do not, so, Foucault need only lay them side by side, showing without comment periodization itself a sense of the world. Foucault's history of the appearances and institutionalizations of these epistemes and their eventual dissolutions and disappearances is his biography of the modern self, how it came to appear, how it must be continuously established, and its dissolution and disappearance, what he describes as its face washed from the seashore.

Beginning, Foucault focuses on the Classical painting by Velázquez, *Las Meninas*. Right away the painting strikes one as odd because it seems to make its subject matter painting itself, a second-order painting of painting: "there exists by Velázquez, the representation as it were, of Classical representation."[32] *Las Meninas* captures Velázquez painting himself painting the Spanish monarch King Philip IV and his family. However, for us as viewers of *Las Meninas* the monarchy, standard subject matter for Classical painting, is hardly the subject, their identity barely revealed by a minor mirrored reflection. Instead, Velázquez himself becomes the subject, or more precisely, the interaction between him and his subject, the royal family. Stranger still is *Las Meninas*'s portrayal of the backside of the painting, most improbably the wooden framing of the canvas, the part of paintings never meant to be seen. Years before he will turn his full attention to it, Foucault seems already poised on the relationship between power and knowledge. Successful portraitures of royalty represent power without remainder, as if power were bestowed beyond this world, and the fate of the world but the destiny of God, truth, and history. A portrait means to draw viewers into its world, provoking participation in the world as given by the portrait: King Philip as unquestioned ruler. Exposing a portrait's wooden frame reveals its constructed nature, the present order of things as simply a thing of this world, a *product* of representation: "a profound historicity penetrates into the heart of things, isolates and defines them in their own coherence, imposes upon them the forms of order implied by the continuity of time."[33] *Las Meninas* expresses a reality that surpasses its imagination, something too embarrassing, politically inexpedient, and epistemologically impossible: "We are observing ourselves being observed."[34] As Jürgen Habermas summarizes, for Foucault, "the real point lies in the fact that the Classical picture frame is too limited to permit the representation of the act of representing as such—it is this that Velázquez makes clear by showing the gaps within the Classical picture frame left by the lack of reflection on the process of representing itself."[35]

Something similar is going on in the pages of *Salmagundi 97*, representation without proper dissonance, or as I have been speaking of, irony. The discourses of representation reverberating through Miller on Foucault and Halperin on Miller on Foucault are doubtless different than that of the Classical Age of Velázquez' *Las Meninas*, but we see in them something comically similar: embarrassing, inexpedient, and impossible. Miller sits before himself the vaunted legacy of Michel Foucault. Here the viewer sees the biographer capturing the genealogist capturing the world. Yet, Miller like Velázquez is driven by a transcendental need to reveal and expose Foucault's framing: the quest for limit-experience, Foucault framed by his sex. *Salmagandi 97* exposes representation, embarrassing, undermining, and spoiling portraits that hold worlds together, recoiling reflexivity of representation thrice removed, toward recoiling orders of reflection.

Near the end of *The Order of Things*, Foucault advances Nietzsche's famous aphorism about God's death toward the death of man: "Nietzsche rediscovered the point at which man and God belong to one another, at which the death of the second is synonymous with the disappearance of the first, and at which the promise of the superman signifies first and foremost the imminence of the death of man."[36] For Foucault the life of man within Western thought was invariably tied to the life of God, what he called "The correspondence between an omniscient God and subjects capable of knowledge," and so the death of one evinces the death of the other.[37] Western conceptions of subjectivity, and their attending representations, relied on the presumption of a ground of such subjectivity, namely God as the anchor of knowing and being. The idea of representation (e.g., biography) came with the presumption of an objective unity Foucault identifies with Kant, what he elsewhere called "the formal ontology of truth."[38] Biography as representation presumes transcendence and the episteme of representation relies on a very specific, and novel, account of the self, that is, the self as knower. Foucault describes the episteme of representation as that "in which things address themselves (always partially) to a subjectivity, a singular effort of cognition, to the 'psychological' individual who from the depth of his own history, or on the basis of the tradition handed to him, is trying to know."[39] In the process of knowing and representing the subject comes to be through that which he makes by representation. In this sense Foucault speaks of an author being born in his works. However, in the same way that the self appears in its work, so the self also dissolves *in* the biography of a particular episteme, showing that the self was not always there, has a history, and is now dying. As Velázquez betrayed the royal family by exposing its composition, so Foucault thinks that transcendental critique finally betrays itself, showing its composition and hence undermining its own authority (Foucault's post-structuralism). What surveying the history of western thought reveals for Foucault is the fragility of that ground, and its inevitable collapse. The history Foucault tells here, and elsewhere, presages the apocalyptic, emplotting the moral, social, economic, and political orders made possible by man/God giving way to new modes of being in the world traced through speech about language, economics, and natural science. The loss of these grammars avails new ways of speaking, and hence new grounds for new emergences: "It is no longer possible to think in our day other than in the void left by man's disappearance. For this void does not create deficiency; it does not constitute a lacuna that must be filled. It is nothing more, and nothing less, than the unfolding of a space in which it is once more possible to think."⁴⁰ And so Foucault ends the book with his prophetic announcement of man's death:

> If those arrangements were to disappear as they appeared, if some event of which we can at the moment do no more than sense the possibility—without knowing either what its form will be or what it promises—were to cause them to crumble, as the ground of Classical thought did, at the end of the eighteenth century, then one can certainty wager that man would be erased, like a face drawn in the sand at the edge of the sea.⁴¹

Man's portrait of himself as a self, a subject preternaturally endowed with reason (reason which in turns allows him to separate himself from those overrun by animality, and hence a self that is not animal), was always only that for Foucault. By stepping into the episteme of the Classical Age, Foucault shows, as Velázquez does, the construction of its accounts of truth, and hence, its accounts of self. Like the Royal family, we moderns project selves bidden to power, constructed by the same mundane elements (wood, canvas, paint, imagination, power) that so constitutes all portraits. The self, finally, is a portrait. Something created. Something of this world. Like a face drawn in the sand before the always encroaching sea, it will soon wash away, replaced by something else.

For Foucault, like Nietzsche, this is cause for celebration and only those who cherish particular portraits and certain faces lament what is lost: their convenient relationships to power, their grammars of truth and God, their esteemed moralities, and their economic, political, and social orders. For Foucault, these are always at stake in a face, a life, in portraits and their representations. And so he chronicles the biography of man in his age, his birth, work, and death. To those who mourn, Foucault writes, "It is comforting, however, and a source of profound relief to think that man is only a recent invention, a figure not yet two centuries old, a new wrinkle in our knowledge, and that he will disappear again as soon as that knowledge has discovered a new form."⁴² He hopes this particular biography will reveal for us something about ourselves, our need for representation, for grammar, for tidy accounts of self and God. Of *Las Meninas*, he writes, "it isn't a picture: it is a mirror."[43] Representations of the self relied on represented gods and so the death of God means, as Nietzsche announced earlier, the wiping way of horizons and the earth unchained from its sun. No God means no ground on which to stake the certainty of the self. Hence Foucault infamously wrote, "you may have killed God beneath the weight of all that you have said; but don't imagine that, with all that you are saying, you will make a man that will live longer than he."[44]

Accordingly James Bernauer describes Foucault's project as a version of negative theology. According to Bernauer, the Cartesian cogito replaces God "as source of the world's reality and intelligibility" and Kant, Hegel, and Nietzsche complete the philosophical project while the scientific revolution fashions the practical technologies that implement its divinization. Bernauer goes on, "Parallel to the death of God was a divinization of man. Claiming a firm knowledge of this figure humanism made humanity's happiness its ultimate goal and human perfection its permanent project." For Bernauer, Foucault's negative theology undercuts human divinity in order to recast transcendence, even as the content of that transcendence, for Foucault, remains unnamed.

> The religion of the God Humanity, with its priesthood of scientific experts as advanced in Comte's positivist philosophy, is not only an integral element of that philosophy but of the logic of the modern age itself. Faced with a sacred history constituted by man's revelation to himself of his ever advancing perfection, Foucault has attempted to demythologize the historical reality in which the modern identity of man and the sources of his humanistic knowledges are lodged.[45]

Undoubtedly Bernauer, the most elegant interpreter of Foucault's theological significance, is right to emphasize Foucault's deconstructive task. Yet Foucault also wants to fill in his account of transcendence with more content than Bernauer acknowledges.[46] There is a constructive mirror to the critique of humanism Bernauer so aptly describes as negative theology. For Foucault, the subverting of man's divinization is not meant to avail space for the transcendence of Pseudo-Dionysius' and Karl Barth's trinitarian mystery whose transcendence is brought near by immanence (God *shows* creation the difference between God and it; creation does not discover this on its own, a proposition that relies on the presumption of humanity's elevation by will and mind toward a human *recognition* of the Trinity *as* mystery), but rather to clear the ground for transcendence's immanent new becomings (discussed in the previous chapter as Foucault's quasi-metaphysicalism). As will be shown in the following chapter, Foucault still wants after freedom, but by way of the death of humanism. As the death of God meant for Nietzsche new gods, so for Foucault the death of the modern self means new selves, the proliferation of ways of being in the world, and their representations.

4. Biography and Absence

The question of biography grows more complicated when held under the light of Foucault's later formulation, "self-writing," the self as text and creation. What particularly worried Foucault was contemporary society's unwillingness to reserve sacred space. For Foucault, modern-day surveillance forced incursions into every zone of existence, the intrusion of the gaze on every body under the ruse of benevolence and knowledge. On this score David Halperin's critique of *The Passions of Michel Foucault* hits its mark. Namely, he shows biography to be especially detrimental to those already burdened with society's taboos. He takes Foucault's discussion of the "author function," intensifies it in terms of biography, and then freights it with the question of heterosexual biographies of homosexual men.

> the perennial threat of discreditation through biographical description becomes painfully acute, and the need to resist it becomes pressingly urgent, when the biographical subject is gay. The struggle for interpretive authority and for control of representation, intrinsic as it may be to the biographical situation in general, acquires an absolutely irreducible political specificity when it is waged over a gay life.[47]

Biography and Biopolitics

Not only does biography force into the open those who might find hiddenness safer and not only can it violate the integrity of a life, but, moreover, biographies of so-called social deviants do so for the sake upholding social norms. In other words, such biographies have a social function.

Furthering the Deleuzian imagery, we can envisage Foucault as creating sacred territory, new lands for the arrogation of new selves. For Foucault, technological cultures make no allowance for absence, for hiddenness, for that which escapes control and manipulation, that which refuses commodification. Accordingly, writing for Foucault is verdant, the growth of a text watered by the death of its author, the self's flowering fertilized by its demise. In this way we might rather talk about "Foucault" than Foucault, who comes to be in his texts. (From Foucault's perspective, what is being produced in Foucault biographies is not Michel Foucault as much as the biographer, biography as autobiography. Of course *The Lives of Michel Foucault* is Miller's story; who else's could it be?) As Foucault stated,

> I don't feel that is necessary to know exactly who I am. The main interest in life and work is to become something else that you were not in the beginning. If you knew when you began a book what you would say at the end, do you think you would have the courage to write it? What is true for writing and for a love relationship is true also for life. The game is worthwhile insofar as we don't know what will be the end.[48]

Within this vein, one can see the banality of biography as its static temporality: "*This* is who this person *is*." Biography presumes the indeterminacy of the historical past (the biographer as excavating that past) and relies on a rigid temporal framework, while Foucault is much more interested in questions of becoming, the discovery of the past revealed by futural becoming. Combined with his prior analysis of disciplinarity, one can begin to see banal biography as police work, investigating one's secrets, interrogation under the guise of popular or scholarly pursuit, pulling everything to the surface and laying bare under the all seeing gaze. Under this light, the self can only become what is allowed, conscripted under the terms of another's narratival imposition. More nefarious still is the biographer's normalization of the subject, prognosticating idiosyncrasies under diagnoses that explain away difference, inscribing the subject under terms readily available to all, simultaneously more bizarre, peculiar, and alien while less threatening, less wild, less other, using people's lives to balance the scales of social normality. Here individuality is stripped away, difference simply a curiosity, a life packaged and sold for the price of admission. And so a biography that seeks to remain true to Foucault's thought—as Miller's does not—would need to sustain absence, rather than vanquishing it in the name of presence. It would skillfully if gingerly hold absence and presence together: presence as the abeyance of absence, and absence as a precursor of an inexpugnable absence/presence, and hence the presence of a genuine absence. In presenting a life, it could at best provide a snapshot on the way to becoming, freeze a moment without implying completion. It would invoke the desire for more without denying each moment its fullness. What would it mean to write biography that grants publicness while denying the gaze? The brilliance of Velázquez' portrait is the way it destabilizes the episteme of the portrait, how it represents representation and hence undermines its own authority and (re)frames subjectivity. As Foucault writes,

> No gaze is stable, or rather, in the neutral furrow of the gaze piercing at a right angle through the canvas, subject and object, the spectator and the model, reverse their roles to infinity. And here the great canvas with its back to us on the extreme left of the picture exercises its second function: stubbornly invisible, it prevents the relation of these gazes from ever being discoverable or definitely established. The opaque fixity that it establishes on one side renders forever unstable the play of metamorphoses established in the centre between spectator and model. Because we can see only the reverse side, we do not know who we are, or what we are doing. Seen or seeing?[49]

The intersecting lines of visibility undermine overmuch respect we might otherwise grant to our vision, complicating certain positional politics of subject and object. The gaze turns in on itself, undermining its power by laying itself bare. Agreements of presence—that the subject of the painting should be present—are blurred when the royal family is rendered barely present, put to the side by new subjects, made the object of another's gaze. Presence is rendered absent, and absence (that King Philip is *not* there) becomes the painting's new subject; staged front and center, a new presence takes command (the painter himself). Hence Foucault reverses roles for the sake of new productions, representations, and biographies and infinite new selves emerging from such productions; "the painter's gaze, addressed to the void confronting him outside the picture, accepts as many models as there are spectators."[50] The proliferation of new models, spectators, allows for a commanding absence to penetrate presence just as presence invades the world of absence. "Among all these elements intended to provide representations, while impeding them, hiding them, concealing them because of their position or their distance from us, this is the only one that fulfils its function in all honesty and enables us to see what it is supposed to show."[51] What *Las Meninas* is *supposed* to show is absence, the profound and resolute invisibility of presence, its incapturability. It does so by trading on the one presence that cannot be questioned: the invisibility and hence supremacy of the sovereign self, the aesthetic viewer as sovereign knower. "It may be that, in this picture, as in all the representations of which it is, as it were, the manifest essence, the profound invisibility of what one sees is inseparable from the invisibility of the persons seeing—despite all mirrors, reflections, imitations, and portraits."[52] *Las Meninas* pushes the traditional subject to the side and forces into the open the imposed invisibility of its spectator, switching roles, trading visibilities. Foucault's genealogies yield this double effect: shattering one image while producing another. Foucault not only writes the biography of modern man, but rewrites it, offering a new history by offering a new telling, of its demise as its birth, its visibility by its invisibility. He does so at the interface between presence and absence. In the same way that the gaze rendered visible every self, so Foucault's researches on modern representation made visible the gaze, stripping its powers by laying it bare. By making visible the gaze, he foments new zones of invisibility through approbations for absence.

Biography belongs, finally, to the subject herself and so fails when claiming completion because the subject cannot finish her own story. Michael Peters fashions biography in terms of the self-writing he sees summoned by Foucault and Ludwig Wittgenstein: "Like philosophy itself, there is no final resting place for the autobiographical subject, no final self-overcoming: the subject in relation to itself must continually work on its self on the understanding that such work is worthwhile but is never completed and that, inescapably, as such subjects 'we' return to our selves everyday."[53] Biography as autobiography, as self-writing, connotes the self's coming to be in the world, self-disclosure as world-disclosure, disclosure that both shows the self and the world.

5. Biography as Theology

In his incisive critique, Halperin contrasts Miller's biography with David Macey's *The Lives of Michel Foucault* and Didier Eribon's *Michel Foucault*. Compared to Miller's, the Macey biography's "matter-of-fact posture" lacks "a particular story to tell about Foucault's life or by means of it."[54] Eribon's, in comparison to Miller, "mistake is to reduce Foucault's personal life to the merely private, neglecting the connections between Foucault's thought and his experience of sexual, social, and political subjection."[55] So according to Halperin, Macey fails to trace the political implications of Foucault's thought and life while Eribon forgets to say how Foucault's life related to his thought. Obviously Halperin does not consider Miller a positive alternative to Macey's and Eribon's negative cases. Rather, what Miller does for Halperin is show what Macey and Eribon should have done, even if in doing so Miller goes too far. "If what was missing in Eribon and Macey was a willingness to interpret systematically the meaning of Foucault's life, with James Miller we have the return of interpretation with a vengeance."[56] Yet Halperin does not tell us *how* he decided Miller had gone too far. If Miller got the trajectory right but went too far, how are we supposed to know what "too far" means? Halperin writes that Miller's limit-experience thesis is only made possible by "some extraordinary critical acrobatics," but like "complete and accurate" it remains unclear what such claims could mean.[57] After all, one must remember that Foucault's own histories were scorned on these very grounds. In fact, on one occasion Halperin himself described *The History of Sexuality* as "full of hollow assertions, disdainful of historical documentation, and careless in its generalizations."[58] Halperin explains, "Despite his critique of truth as a regulatory concept in the human sciences, Foucault did not feel at all inhibited about appealing to truth when attempting to expose the realities of torture, police brutality, and governmental injustice."[59] Yet Halperin does not clue us into why Miller's inconsistencies specifically should be so worrisome and why certain "realities" warrant exceptional epistemic allowances. He states only that Foucault "played fast and loose" with some of his core concepts, but offers no interpretive key for when those permissions should be granted.

At this point the reader of Halperin's *Saint Foucault* begins to suspect an evaluative claim that Halperin does not acknowledge. In his critique of Miller, Halperin states that he does not expect Miller, or any biographer, to agree with Foucault. He wants only for him to be a biographer, which given his critiques of Macey and Eribon, means something like relating elements of a subject's life to the political articulation of that subject's thought. In other words, a properly disposed biography should serve as an ad hominine argument for the subject's thought. Beyond that, "Miller is under no obligation as Foucault's biographer to agree with anything Foucault's said or wrote."[60] At least on these two obligations of the biographer, Miller has lived up to his end of the bargain; he does what Halperin thinks a biographer should do, and the very things Macey and Eribon fail to do. So what exactly is Halperin's complaint? My sense is that even though Halperin says that an intellectual biographer does not need to adopt the convictions of his subject, his primary problem with Miller is exactly Miller's refusal to adopt a Foucauldian perspective and most specifically a Foucauldian perspective on Michel Foucault. He states as much near the beginning of the critique: "My quarrel with Miller, then is not that he is uncomprehending of Foucault's project. It is that he is politically opposed to it."[61] Though he states his desire to avoid "the politics of biography" what else *could* Halperin be doing by all his truth-baiting?

I have no quarrel with Halperin on this score as I think biography is always politicized. I happen to believe that Halperin is right to question a biography because of its politics. On Foucauldian grounds it is largely unclear to me how politics can ever be avoided in biographying another's life. Halperin is surely right that part of the point of biography is to tell a story that has political implications and also right that an effective intellectual biography should relate the subject's thought to her life. I have my complaints, previously noted, that Miller effectively makes Foucault's thought less interesting than his life, but I am in agreement with Halperin on Eribon, that such mapping is largely the point of biography. I quarrel with Halperin only in that he is not transparent about his own concerns, and his confidence that biography should be depoliticized creates that opacity.

Halperin's disingenuousness here is unfortunate to the extent that his worries are unnecessary. Biographies should be politicized in order to make evident that lives matter for the truthfulness of intellectual claims. Returning to Lynn Hunt's comment for a moment: what Miller's Foucault shows us is that experience matters. That is why, as Halperin pushes Macey, biographies at their best demonstrate the political consequence of intellectual thoughts and commitments. This can only be shown. As well, as Halperin rightly pushes Eribon, one's thought and one's actions mutually inform one another; biographies are meant to reveal this mutuality. This also must be shown, and can only be shown by personal display, that is, biography as the political self-showing of a life. Foucault is a saint not in the sense that the content of his life was "saintly" (in some important ways it was, and others it was not[62]) but just to the extent that there endures some remarkable continuities between the extraordinary nature of his thought and the extraordinary reality of his life. The consistency of Foucault's life to his thought—the way his life embodied his thought and the way his thought embodied his life—and Miller's ability to narrate just that, are emblematic of how Christians think about witness. Unlike Halperin, theology has no need to shy away from such claims and thence disparage politicized biographies. For Christian theology, the lives of the saints make *political* theological claims. The fact that Halperin feels the need to so vociferously defend Foucault from the likes of Miller indicates he does not get this, or if he does lacks the courage to allow the display of Foucault's politics to speak for itself, even against those who would misconstrue, exaggerate, or orientalize. I think Halperin at his most perceptive is quite right, that Miller puts an unfortunate but sadly characteristic burden upon Foucault's sex, making it more interesting than Foucault's undeniably brilliant work and life. But that is the thing about brilliance; it can abide such burdens, and Foucault *has* survived and outlasted *The Passion of Michel Foucault*. To be sure, Halperin's larger concern is whether gay and lesbian men and women can survive the gay-baiting he thinks exemplified by *The Passion of Michel Foucault*. He is right to worry since while we can currently acknowledge a universal appreciation for Foucault's thought, we are still far from achieving the same for his life, or at least those features of it reduced to sexuality. But it is exactly here that activists and intellectuals like Halperin have something to learn from the church, which has never feared (or should never fear) misunderstanding, even death-dealing misunderstanding.[63] And maybe in this way, biography for Christian theology means something different for the church than it does for others. For Christianity biography taps into the courage of letting one's life make clear (or unclear) one's work, the courage of letting one's life do all the talking, what I have called witness. It does so not in the sense that one's thought is the upshot of one's life but rather the reverse, that one's thought helps clarify what one's life was primarily about.[64] This is why truth is inexhaustibly political for Christian theology and why it maximally claims (similar to Hunt's "experience matters" claim): bodies matter. In doctrinal language, biographies bespeak incarnation.

This is what I understand James McClendon to have been arguing in *Biography as Theology* when he wrote, "theology is drawn by its biographic material to face a challenge not only to its propositions, but also to the selfhood of its practitioners."[65] This is not true for much philosophy following "the Cartesian moment," for which propositions not only can but must prove valid independent of proponents' biographies.[66] This may mean that Foucault has more in common with theology than contemporary analytic philosophy because he very much doubted the validity of any truth claim separate from its instantiation. Or more precisely, for Foucault a claim was true only as its instantiation, as its face, linking claims to biographies (we might speak of his often invoked "dispotif" as the biography of a claim; the biography of a claimant;

the biographies of links between claims and claimants; biographies of background worlds where claims are linked with claimants; and so on) and drawing Foucault into the province of Christian theology's inescapable incarnational and sacramental epistemology.[67]

In his 1983 seminar "Discourse and Truth" on parrhesia at Berkeley, in which he takes up the question of "truth-teller or truth-telling as an activity"[68] Foucault says about the relation between utterance and truth,

> does the parrhesiastes say what he thinks is true, or does he say what is really true? To my mind, the parrhesiastes says what is true because he knows that it is true; and he knows that it is true because it is really true. The parrhesiastes is not only sincere and says what is his opinion, but his opinion is also the truth. He says what he knows to be true. The second characteristic of parrhesia, then, is that there is always an exact coincidence between belief and truth. It would be interesting to compare Greek parrhesia with the modern (Cartesian) conception of evidence. For since Descartes, the coincidence between belief and truth is obtained in a certain (mental) evidential experience. For the Greeks, however, the coincidence between belief and truth does not take place in a (mental) experience, but in a verbal activity, namely, parrhesia. It appears that parrhesia, in this Greek sense, can no longer occur in our modern epistemological framework.[69]

Foucault understood "spirituality" to indicate the inseparability between moral constitution and habits of knowledge so that the question of truth boils down to, "At what cost?"[70]

In discussing parrhesia and Christian practices of truth-telling, Craig Hovey speaks of parrhesia as confidence strong enough to endure persecution, and by its endurance deny persecution its goal, the silencing of truth-telling. For Hovey, parrhesia's endurance became its own substantiation. The question regarding parrhesia is not only what the person claims but what kind of person does the claiming, or more precisely, the coherence between the person and her claim. Hovey writes, "Parrhesia involves the morality of the agent for both knowing and telling the truth and they cannot be separated in the way modern questions tempt us to do. The Greeks were interested to know if someone was a truth-teller, not how the truth-teller could claim certainty for his beliefs."[71] It is this lack of confidence, this lack of parrhesia, that Miller's detractors, those who fall back on modern epistemologies of truthfulness, forget about Foucault: his life could sustain the truth of what he said, even against the likes of *The Passions of Michel Foucault*. What Halperin's critique lacks then is what Hovey refers to as patience,

> Patience first comes with the confidence that the truth can speak for itself. It then is further displayed in how assuredness that the truth will be victorious means that the witness cannot rush the events that lead to that victory or intervene violently to bring it about. If victory could be brought about by the timorous intervention of the witness qua protester, it would not be the truth that wins.[72]

Patience stands in the face of "the risk" of violent critique and even reprisal. Parrhesia by its nature stands on its own utterance without looking to external criterion for validation. This patience allowed the early Christians, in Hovey's reading, to assume "the risk" inherent to parrhesia:

> The words of the testimony and the boldness with which it is given are together two witnesses and not two aspects of a single witness. So in overcoming the dangers that proclaiming the gospel might entail, the very overcoming is itself part of the claim that what is proclaimed is true. Martyrs are those whose boldness—whose parrhesia—is a risk unto death but, precisely because of that risk and death, are spoken of as the paradigmatic witnesses of the Christian gospel.[73]

Part of the benefit of McClendon's earlier comment is how it reveals the force of Michel Foucault's work and life. Immediately prior to the above quote, McClendon says of twentieth-century Christian saints, as he might have said of Foucault as secular saint: "Their lives witness to their vision, even as they challenge the depth of our own. So there comes the question, not so much of the suitability of their vision to their own circumstances, but the justification of our present way of life when held against theirs."[74] If McClendon can say this to Christians regarding Christian saints then how are Christians to hold the life of Michel Foucault, whose *biography as philosophy* no doubt challenges the courage of the modern-day church's collective vision, its present-day life as held against his? For Miller the beauty of Foucault's life as art finds its most stunning articulation in its final moments, which we might liken to Hovey's patience:

> one of the things I most admire is a certain kind of heroic openness to the possibility of transforming, through philosophizing, his ethos, a noble trait perhaps most movingly displayed at the end of his life, when he faced death with what an eyewitness like Paul Veyne has described as striking serenity.[75]

Chapter 4
Writing the Self

> *Working in philosophy—like work in architecture in many respects—is really more like working on oneself.*
> —Ludwig Wittgenstein

If not biographies, perhaps Michel Foucault would have liked us to postulate trajectories that pushed in certain directions and intensities that pooled in particular spaces if only to grant that those energies were always a pushing *against* and a leaking *out*. In this way at least, we can speak of his writing at the time of his death as the continuation of a basic orientation to his work: the subject and its constitution in freedom.[1] In this chapter I characterize this intensity and orientation in terms of what Foucault called "a new kind of self" or more specifically "self-identity as referred to the problem of 'individualising power.'"[2] In the first part, "Where There Is Power, There Are Selves," I describe how disciplinary processes always and everywhere at work produce selfhood. Second, in "Surfaces of Emergence: For and against Heidegger" I attend to stylizations of the self Foucault both inherited and sought to overcome, namely the transcendental self as articulated by Martin Heidegger's phenomenological reiteration of the Cartesian ego. In "Confessing the Self" the third and final part, I return with Foucault to a pre-modern conception of selfhood, beginning with the Greeks and heading toward the early Christians. From classical Athens to early Christianity Foucault traced a line from self-mastery to self-sacrifice, from the power of possession to the efficacy of submission. Here I will attempt to align philosophy as "care for the self" with a Christian account of self-knowledge that prescinds from participation in God.[3]

In Christianity and the unexpectedly fruitful practices of confession and self-sacrifice Foucault found a genuine interruption in modernity's hagiography of the sovereign self. By pointing to this moment Foucault thought he might at least muddy modernity's trinity of self-presence, self-possession, and self-fascination.[4] And so in his history of sexuality, Foucault narrates a history of the self in order to remind us that the self *has* a history, *forward* from Greek self-mastery to Christian self-sacrifice and *backward* from modern self-interest to Christian self-sacrifice.[5] The critical transition within this two thousand year period from Antiquity to modernity is not, as might first appear, from the Greeks to Christianity and then to modernity, but rather what Foucault calls "the Cartesian moment" that drastically alters conceptions of the self.

In contrast to Descartes' transcendental ego advanced within a progressive narrative of indeterminacy, the self, Foucault thought, might speak freedom not in a key of sovereignty but rather dispersion, achieving the self by giving it up, returning the self to self-care and the critical dispositions of ethical formation.[6] For Foucault there could be no self, power, or freedom without a mutual inherence that denotes an interdependence that forfeits all three by prioritizing any one. Within this *inter*-subjectivity, the self must give itself to power or it will forfeit the ground of its production. Precisely at the moment when the self posits itself free of power (as in the repressive hypothesis portrayed in the first volume of the *History of Sexuality*) or deploys power without considerations of freedom (as in the carceral systems described in *Discipline and Punish*) it loses both, often to disastrous consequence.

It should surprise us that Foucault turned to the early Christians, but not for the reasons we might suppose. Current caricatures would suggest that a modern like Foucault—and he was too smart to believe himself anything but modern—would eschew Christianity given its historic complicities within disciplinary societies.[7] This is in part true. Foucault calls "pastoral" the innovation of uniquely Christian "techniques oriented toward individuals and intended to rule them in a continuous and permanent way."[8] Even if this modality of power transfigured into vastly different state forms (the state as its own reason) its origins stem from peculiarly Christian and Hebraic, versus Greek or Greco-Roman, sources. This has ushered in the most regrettable realities: "Among all the societies in history, ours—I mean, those that came into being at the end of Antiquity on the Western side of the European continent—have perhaps been the most aggressive and the most conquering; they have been capable of the most stupefying violence, against themselves as well as against others."[9] Yet even with this cursed inheritance, Foucault refused to dismiss Christianity as an ethical alternative to the problems he saw plaguing late modernity.[10] Indeed we might guess that within Foucault's genealogical approach, an erstwhile simulacra of Christianity insured allegiance to liberal society in all its hubris. This prejudice *against* Christianity and *for* humanism was precisely the kind of game Foucault refused to play; it was both too easy and too stupid. So knowing Foucault, we shouldn't be surprised by his turn to Christianity; indeed we might have come to expect it.

Instead, the surprising move is that amongst the various premodern alternatives available to him, he is *most* intrigued by the Christians. After all, he had the Greeks and like Nietzsche and Heidegger before him, he could have stopped there.[11] That would have been an improvement at least in the sense that going back two thousand years would have yielded some new gods.[12] But Foucault did not conclude with the Greeks but with the Christians and historically one can contend that he only went through the Greeks and the Romans to get to the Christians.[13] A simplistic explanation for this would be to surmise that Foucault's larger goal was to chart the development of sexual repression as a continuous decline from the Greeks such that modern sexual homophobia is but the destiny of Christianity's artifice of good and evil.[14] But this is precisely what Foucault was ridiculing. To be sure, in Foucault's mind the penitential rites of medieval Catholicism and the sentimentalism of Wesleyan Protestantism found its genesis in the Greeks and its culmination in contemporary sexual homogeneity. Doubtless the prolixity of fashionable confessions in the wastelands of the blogosphere finds its reasons in the Stoic admonition of self-mastery with Christianity standing in the middle as the guardian of this perpetuity. But limning this lineage was not meant to spirit in a naive teleology to the history of sexuality but rather its intervention. In reading Foucault's histories of sexuality, one is tempted to deduce a progression of increasing modes of confinement.[15] However, this is to miss Foucault's constructive content within its deconstructive form. While Foucault certainly focused on modes of disciplinarity, his growing emphasis on power in the 1970s until the end of his career increasingly fostered an account of what he called "governmentality" that meant, simultaneously, discipline imposed by others and discipline imposed by self, and most critically the latter as a hedge against the former. Power's ubiquity as a concept helped Foucault avoid positing resistance outside the terms of discipline, and so we find Foucault at this stage of his work watchful for modes of resistance within the brutal surveillance and control modern disciplinary societies enact on individuals. Foucault turned to self-care in order to salvage the self from total capitulation. Foucault discovered self-care by excavating a history of the self that understood self-care as internal to its conceptions of subjectivity. In turning to Christianity and Antiquity Foucault found what he was looking for (or at least discovered what he was still searching for). His account figures selves operating in the midst of local forms of governmentality (tutelage under teachers, submission to monastic orders, ascetic rituals, confessional self-writing, and so on) for the sake of the self, government of the self *for* the self. In contrast to one's biography written by another, one's story proscribed by another, here one writes one's own story, from biography to autobiography.

Hence it is a mistake to read Foucault's histories of sex as only chronicles toward modern-day surveillance and control. Foucault's earlier work on madness, medicine, knowledge, and prisons had already accomplished those tasks and it is doubtful Foucault thought such efforts needed further supplementing by way of even earlier histories. Rather, these histories chronicle alternatives. Rather than read governmentality as only negative confinement these histories evoke relational modes of subjectivity that come about not through absconding subjugation but by the self's submission to others, governmentality as self-care. In a later interview, Foucault said, "Care for self is ethical in itself, but it implies complex relations with others, in the measure where this *ethos* of freedom is also a way of caring for others . . . the one who cared for himself correctly found himself, by that very fact, in a measure to have correctly in relation to others and for others."[16] For Foucault one could not care for oneself without occupying care for others or being cared for by others, even as self-care animated both. Those relating to others in improper fashion (e.g., lording it over them) had not properly cared for themselves, did not properly know themselves, and had not properly exorcized one's propensities for improper care. For Foucault this was no so different for Christianity, which continues the Greek and Roman penchant for self-care through self-giving. Foucault describes asceticism, submission, and powerlessness as modes of freedom within the boundless horizon of power.[17] As Arnold Davidson writes (quoting Foucault), "the added emphasis on sexual austerity in these texts should not be interpreted in terms of a tightening of the moral code and its prohibitions, but rather in terms of 'an intensification of the relation to oneself by which one constituted oneself as the subject of one's acts.'"[18] Through these histories, which he elsewhere calls "fictions," Foucault returns to autobiography in order to retell the self's story by emplotting the lives of the Greeks, Romans, and Christians.[19] The many historians who have dismissed Foucault's work here as not properly historical have it right at least in this sense: Foucault does not so much recount the story of Seneca or Antony as much as reveal the history of the present. Though we are not Seneca or Antony, he seeks to relocate our lives in these fictions.[20]

1. Where There Is Power, There Are Selves

Infamously, Foucault declared the ubiquity of power.[21] Within modern parlance, such a claim cannot help but sound counterintuitive, even absurd. After all, if anything, power does not seem to be everywhere, and indeed the problem with power, according to the standard (for Foucault, Marxian) view, is that it is not everywhere *enough*. Rather, power seems to exist in an economy of scarcity comprised by haves and have-nots. This inequitable distribution of power raises the question of justice since those who *have* power are purportedly using it against those who *have not* power. As such, our very petitions for justice and their attending maneuverings depend on power *not* being everywhere, but somewhere alone. Within this frame, ethics is about wresting and redistributing power fairly. This standard view, Foucault thinks, is a ruse meant to disguise injustice by removing all other considerations. Rather than a distasteful reality we must confront, the standard view is a story persons tell themselves while coping with a world that is always already entrenched in power.[22] Revolutionaries or at least those who aspire to revolution can only pronounce progress after first re-inscribing biographies of world-historical significance. In other words, revolutions, as revolutionary as they appear, simply recycle the same old thing.

Nietzsche believed that those most renown for escaping power's temptations were most vulnerable to its machinations.[23] Part of what Foucault means by the ubiquity of power is that we are each everywhere caught. On the one hand, this means that none can long evade the normalizing powers of conformity no matter one's remonstrations of individualism.[24] Power surges everywhere at every juncture at every level for everyone at every moment: prisons excise deviance in the name of "public safety"; remissions of sanity get us to be more productive within Empire's monolith productivity; populations surrender to the gaze of police states because no one wants to die; discourses of truth work on us by concealing their discursivity; we voluntarily confess our sins because we have become our most watchful guardians.[25] On the other hand, and in contrast to Nietzsche, power according to Foucault only begins in these places, or rather, it only begins to show itself there. These happen to be the elements of power that we can swallow. We hold onto these because we can. We focus on these features because while monstrous they hold out the possibility for something better, namely a future after power. As long as power comes from *over there*, that *someone else* is unfairly using it, as long as we remain resilient, then we may one day escape power's orbit. After all, only to the extent that power is centralized can it be defeated; only as fixed can it be left behind. Hence this image of power is itself an effect of power, a pacifying picture that hides a much more troubling reality. This is not to say that Foucault discounts the local effects of power; for him, these were very real. It is only that he does not want us confusing these local effects with power itself, which is subtle rather than overwhelming, everywhere rather than somewhere, everyone more than someone, mollifying more than confronting, inspiring as much as depressing, energizing as much as enervating, pluriform and uniform.[26] Power makes more than it takes. It is not ultimately the self versus power. It is the self constituted by power.[27] Freedom does not shirk power but settles with it. One achieves the self in relation to power.

Writing the Self

For Foucault the givenness of power supplants cultural nostalgia for a lost golden age prior to power.[28] His juxtaposition of modernity in contrast to its many pre-modern alternatives is not meant to allude to mythical return but only to make the modest proposal, "What is, could have been otherwise."[29] Rather than primordial pure selves ensnared in the exigencies of power Foucault's claim is that selves come to be in the world.[30] Power comes to be at the same time as selves. Foucault doubtless wants to talk about persons subject to the determining effects of power described earlier and embodied in late capitalism; not only in philosophy but in his politics he gave himself to these efforts perhaps more so than any recent philosopher of significance. Foucault knew intimately the realities of power; he witnessed them in the batons of angry riot cops and his scars warned him not to mess with power. No theorist can speak with more credibility about power's imprisonment of the self. And yet for Foucault it was not the self against power but the self amidst power.[31] For Foucault self and power mutually create the conditions of the other's perception; looking at one reveals the other standing there.

Politics for Foucault means not the overcoming of power but rather its tactical deployments.[32] What persons can hope to do is understand the self's relation to power, register its deployments, comprehend its intricacies, and survey its strategies—in other words, map it.[33] As such might resistance ensue, but again, not against power but through and with it because politics for Foucault is constituted not by selves versus power but rather selves related to other selves within the ubiquity of power.[34] Foucault's lifelong work sought to envisage this relationship in multitudinous ways so that selves could be achieved and perceived in inexhaustible iterations. The problem with standard views of power is that they cannot imagine the self except as a discourse over against power and hence cannot envision its emergence except on those terms.[35] The standard view leaves the self impoverished because it sees the self through an impoverished imagination. Against the standard view, Foucault perceives selves coming into the world by first coming to have a world.[36] In this way power is no thing. But then again, neither are selves. They each achieve status—obtain "thingness"—through mutually informing intersubjectivity.[37] The various formative modalities of emergence take place, according to Foucault, amidst the processes of categorization, regulation, identification, and according to his final works, stylization that figure persons in the world. The modern period's real innovations were selves styled in terms of abstract freedom of choice over against determinacy.[38] (In a helpful essay, Andrew Cutrofello explicates how after Descartes logically reflective and determinate judgments were prioritized over aesthetically reflective and therefore indeterminate judgments. Yet the priority of the former was itself an expression of the latter. The insistence that aethetic judgments are inferior to logical judgments because one can give reasons for logical judgments unlike aesthetic judgments demonstrates a circularity that makes all judgments indeterminate judgments. All we have is style.[39]) The self's emergence takes place within the conditions of possibility of its emergence. Modern stylization is comprised by discourses of emancipation, fomenting conditions that conducted the self's emergence within webs of discipline: the mental institution, the clinic, human finitude vis-à-vis economics, natural sciences, or language. The self's coming to be within these discourses arrived through confession encoded to reason, health, value, biology, or meaning. In order to be born into this world, the self had to emerge within complexes that shaped that emergence and strictly confined its range of possibility: as insane, sick, scarce, finite, etc. This disciplinarity gained acceptability when the presumption of emancipation (for madness, health, and so on) donned a guise of benevolence, and hence countenanced whatever discipline deemed necessary to chaperone such emergences. This was the price paid for emergence from self-incurred tutelage, a confession of a prior pathos now seen, identified and cured by the terms of the emergence. For example, Chloe Taylor observes how the couplet of *mens rea* and *actus rea* in Western jurisprudence *conceives* the criminal through the process of confession. The criminal act conjoined to a malevolent intent produces a criminal. As Taylor writes, "the motivations of the criminal must be understood, and consequently the accused must answer the question: 'Who are you,'"[40] By answering, the self as prisoner comes to be. Likewise, Peter Brooks argues that the logics of contemporary juridical rationales themselves create the conditions for a viable notion of autonomy. In other words, *only within the discourse* of modern jurisprudence are individuals "free" and the intelligibility of that freedom relies on the productivity of freedom as an idiom.[41]

Such emergences can only be seen and hence resisted through a reflexivity that takes into account possible warrants bestowed by power in its structural realities so that it can coordinate itself among the capillary options available to it. It is here that Foucault begins to figure a self that honors history's hard fought emancipations while avoiding the trappings of a mythical freedom that purports to transcend that history. Foucault seeks a self constituted in freedom as the investment of a tradition. As shown through Charles Taylor in Chapter 1, complaints that Foucault ultimately repudiates freedom or eclipses the subject remain captive to the modern dichotomies of freedom and determinacy, individual and community, and reason and tradition.[42] For Foucault the self is not *only* beholden to regulation since power itself is determined by self-stylization that also regulates (recall Foucault on conduct and counter-conduct). The more stylizations imagined and enacted the more power must flex and shift and wrap itself around and seep into the various alterities selves assume. Hence by "power," Foucault means to overcome the metaphysical legacy he inherited where persons committed themselves to theorizing sovereignty. Describing a pathological need to impose totalizing narratives, Foucault writes,

> The history of thought could remain the locus of uninterrupted continuities, if it could endlessly forge connexions that no analysis could undo without abstraction, if it could weave, around everything that men say and do, obscure synthesis that anticipate for him, prepare him, and lead him endlessly towards his future, it would provide a privileged shelter for the sovereignty of consciousness. Continuous history is the indispensable correlative of the founding function of the subject: the guarantee that everything that has eluded him may be restored to him; the certainty that time will disperse nothing without restoring it in a reconstituted unity; the promise that one day the subject—in the form of historical consciousness—will once again be able to appropriate, to bring back under his sway, all those things that are kept at a distance by difference, and find in them what might be called his abode.[43]

Within that landscape Foucault witnessed too many too willing to join a smash and grab free for all around the question of power.[44] The collateral consequences of the have and the have nots follow as persons can no longer see other persons as anything but competitors in a zero-sum game of power. This severely limits possibilities, soft peddles the ethical significance of aesthetics, and relegates genuine alternatives to the underside of history.[45]

2. Surfaces of Emergence: For and Against Heidegger

In an interview near the end of his life, Foucault suggested that at the heart of his varied intellectual researches stood the same enduring topic: the subject.[46] How much Foucault can be trusted to interpret his biography is up for debate given his consternations about authorship and textuality described previously.[47] Even so it would be hard to deny that something like the subject takes deep residence within his thought. To get a sense of why this spanned the whole of his intellectual career we need to highlight a couple of different instances of that development and consider what he coined "*le sourci de soi*" that initiated Foucault's archaeology and genealogy of the modern self.[48] Theological interests properly understood do not drive Foucault's interest in Christianity; rather his curiosity organizes itself within a peculiarly modern rubric. He turns to the early church fathers to the extent they make available to him genuine alternatives to contemporary speech about subjectivity. It is this concern, rather than any theological preoccupation, which provokes Foucault's notice and lands him in the strange world of patristic theology. This is not to say that his retrieval is not theologically interesting; this book has tried to point to the theological contours of Foucault's heterodox self.

Even though Foucault's most immediate philosophical predecessor, and the thinker who determined his career in other ways, was Jean-Paul Sartre, it was Martin Heidegger and not Sartre that captured Foucault's early attention. Indeed, we might say that Foucault saw in Sartre only a pale version of Heidegger and perhaps even came to leave Heidegger behind because he presaged

Writing the Self

Heideggerian transcendental subjectivity coterminous with Sartre's transcendental existentialism. Hence, in attempting to understand the notion of the self that Foucault inherited, lived through for a time, and then came to reject, we must attend to the Heidegger of *Being and Time*.[49]

The sweeping vision of Heidegger's *Being and Time* represented for Foucault and his contemporaries a break with the self-driven ego of Cartesian reason and a way to go on that would not relinquish the goods procured by the death of God precipitated when Descartes replaced God with the human *cogito* as the source of all things.[50] The complexity in trying to untangle Foucault with his Heideggerian-influenced sources has to do with a contiguous development from Descartes to Foucault that travels through the critical projects of Kant and Nietzsche and the ways Heidegger tries to hold them together. So Foucault's relationship to his predecessors should not be thought within the simplistic terms of avowal or rejection, since any rejection will be made in ways that carry the conversation forward. For sure Foucault will offer something like a rejection of Descartes and his heirs but Foucault is himself an heir to Heidegger and even his turn to pre-Cartesian conceptions of the self are fueled by Cartesian sensibilities.[51]

For Heidegger the subject's interest in itself *as* subject defines it as subject. Unlike other creatures, humans care about their existence; they are concerned with it. This is not to say that other creatures like animals do not care about their lives. But caring about one's life differs for Heidegger from caring about one's existence and some humans are no more than animals in that while they care about their survival they lack the courage and constitution to care about their existence.[52] One of Heidegger's students Hannah Arendt would prioritize this concern as the mark of thinking and political life.[53] Heidegger was troubled by the ways in which this lack of care left humanity in an objectifying relationship to the world since insofar as one does not consider how it is that one relates to the world, one cannot help but objectify it.[54] This danger arises for Heidegger not by a lack of thinking but resides implicit to the very processes of thinking itself. Thinking for Heidegger continuously raises the specter of its own failure—within thinking, unthinking.[55] This is because humans are forever tempted to reduce existence to the ways they exist in the world, like animals, reducing existence to survival. Hence Arendt speculated that it was only at the point that humans secured their survival, when they finally stop living hand to mouth, that thinking could occur at all.[56]

Heidegger holds Nietzsche and Kant together by recognizing the death of God while seeking to retrieve a notion of transcendence.[57] However in contrast to what he saw as the Platonic legacy overrunning modern philosophy, Heidegger envisaged transcendence not in terms of an originary Idea haunting the fallen analog of temporal existence, but rather squarely within the world located in the everyday. The temporal unfolding of immanence is the very form of transcendence, the condition of its emergence and this Heideggerian account of emergence would continue through Foucault's notion of selfhood. For Heidegger, thinking is indelibly marked by time, and so thinking cannot happen outside of its temporal occurrences.[58] Because humans care about their existence, they are bound to the recognition of time; they think in terms of time, seeing the future a point of their concern, an aspect that must be taken into consideration. Hence, unlike animals concerned solely with the immediacy of survival, humans care about their survival but know that they will die. Time and its articulation in language allows humans to stand in relation to the world as "world" in a way that animals exist unmediated to world, and as such do not distinguish themselves from the open spatiality and temporality of world.[59] For humans this results in an anxiety about death. In anticipating death, humans, at least when they think, can appreciate the conditions of not only their existence, but existence in general. Embedded in time and aware of that embedding, humans must be continuously receptive to the potentiality of change given by the future as witnessed by the past. Even though the present may feel like something that endures, it is only the inter-subjectivity of past and present, revelation and concealment, that which holds and that which gives way. Because time marks the present as standing on the precipice between potentiality and actuality, living well, or what Heidegger called authenticity, entails remaining open to what the future brings. For Heidegger this means there is no present as such or past as such but only momentary agreements that subsist at the whim of the future. At any moment, no matter how seemingly permanent our arrangements may feel, selves exist within an abiding contingency that metaphysically goes all the way down.[60] Heidegger recognizes this as rightfully frightening and summons the virtues necessary to live authentically: courage, resolute anticipation, fortitude, and strength.[61] Because the being of human beings does not remain the same but changes in and as time, the person who seeks to live well must not only anticipate the changing nature of nature but learn to embrace it as the very condition of existence, speaking to an ontological horizon of change. The authentic person receives from the surfeit produced in the torsions of time. Life then is found not in an after life or a prior life but in everyday life. The difference of transcendence is itself resident within immanence if we hold to immanence as temporal existence. Here difference rises within the horizon of the same, marking the same as never only the same, but always new and yet temptingly familiar articulations of difference.

For Heidegger the everyday is made possible by living in the world as if rather than changing, beings (things like hammers, dogs and persons *and* our various conceptions about hammers, dogs and persons) are taken for granted. Rather than embracing things as constantly changing, we live in the world as if they were what Heidegger aptly describes as "ready-at-hand." In this sense, this is not only how we live in the world; it's how we come to have a world and as such Heidegger can make the seemingly strange claim that without humans there is no world; what he means is not that the world does not physically exist but rather "world" is, prior to being a physical concept, an *existential* concept. This is not to say the practical realities of the world don't matter; these have *existentelle* significance, but they are not the same as world as ontological reality and indeed for Heidegger unless one has an adequate understanding of the world ontologically one cannot have a sufficient understanding of the world ontically—get your metaphysics confused and you risk everything. So "world" comes into being in our interactions with it and in this way is involved with us phenomenologically—that is, the "truths" about the world show themselves in an unending play of world concealing and revealing, truth as *aletheia*, which is yet another way Heidegger talks about time. So the world is comprised of all the ways we imagine things ready-at-hand and act in it accordingly.⁶²

Problems arise when we reduce all of existence to the ready-at-hand existence that allows us to exist, when we confuse, as Heidegger says, beings with being, and things with the thing. Again, this is not the difference between transcendence and immanence in the Platonic and Kantian sense. Rather, our reduction for being with beings and the thing with things is our unwillingness to live into the temporal nature of our lives, to live as if change were not the truth of things. It is just very difficult, according to Heidegger, to remember that things-at-hand are primarily arrangements and agreements because of a tendency to ossify things as only things ready-at-hand. Later, Heidegger argues that when we imagine things as only ready-at-hand, things that have become too familiar by our practices and uses, then we move from a relationship with our worlds from ready-at-hand to standing-reserve as if things are simply standing around for our use.⁶³ In this sense, rather than seeing the world as the constancy of change, we make it simply our object since our use, we think, exhausts its possibilities (In the next chapter, I return to this theme by examining what Empire does with animals).

Heidegger stylizes the self within the exigencies of becoming, locating it in the processes by which world becomes world. It is precisely in the vanishing moment that persons willing to think gain the freedom to think. Again we can see these investments within Arendtian thought when "natality" occurs between past and future. In the event of thinking the self comes to be. Otherwise, she remains simply an object of the world, incapable of being anything but a thing at-hand to be handed from one moment to the next. For Arendt in the demands of work and labor selves remain caught between obligations that affix them to the needs of everyday survival. Only upon courageously willing herself no longer so determined, or no longer solely determined, can she risk the divestures of survival and move into the permanence of labor and ultimately the freedom of thought; otherwise, she surrenders to the caprice of luck.⁶⁴

Heidegger has an inverse sociality where rather than persons caught up with survival, persons for Heidegger find themselves continuously seduced by *das Man* ("the they") who give into the

Writing the Self

temptation to freeze being as standing-reserve and hence go about their lives in the banality of "idle speech."[65] For Heidegger most only work at the surface of things, never questioning being in its nature, transfixed with observing ontic things as a means to get at ontological things. For Heidegger, if one does not first risk everything in the consideration of being within the terms of *phusis* and its movements, one can get no further than a superficial understanding.[66] By "standing-reserve" (*Bestand*) Heidegger means to forcefully show how the irrepressible difference of things finally escapes even the most insistent calcifications, its own *energia* toward newness standing recalcitrant and insurgent.[67] In this dynamic selves and world self-show dialectically without sublimation.

The arch from Heidegger's rather a-political philosophy to Foucault's ineluctable power then can be traced through Arendt, conceptually if not historically, for Arendt better than any other descries the political within Heidegger's philosophically narrow Dasein. While Heidegger emphasized the dangers of idle thinking of *das Man* and hence analyzed the self's emergence from this world, he could have just as well emphasized the irreducible politicality of Dasein, since the very danger of "the they" implies a common life (*Mitdasien*) whereby idle speech becomes toxic.[68] Heidegger himself writes, "By reason of this Being-in-the-world, the world is always the one I share with Others. The world of Dasein is a with-world. Being-in is Being-with-Others. Their Being-in-themselves within-the-world is Dasein-with [*Mitdasein*]."[69] Arendt would glean from this the plurality and the "already existing web of human relationships" for which her political philosophy became known.[70] Foucault in his turn would transition from discursivity to discipline to power. Both were in their own turn following on transcendental critique, speaking of "conditions of possibility."[71] For each, selves emerged onto the world-state from the company of others.[72]

Nowhere is Heidegger's influence more apparent than Foucault's first major publication, the 1954 essay "Dream, Imagination and Existence," which appeared as an introduction to the 1930 *Dream and Existence* by Foucault's friend and colleague Ludwig Binswanger, pioneer of the existential psychiatry deeply indebted to a Heideggerian reading of Freud, appropriately entitled *Daseinsanalyse*.[73] During this period Foucault understood himself specifically within the terms of phenomenology and explicitly invokes Heidegger to make his arguments—using the language of "the conditions of appearance" in another 1954 publication—that situate him squarely within the ambit of Heidegger's thought.[74] Here, Foucault criticizes Freudian dream analysis to the extent that it repeats the Western metaphysical error of prioritizing meaning and representation. Foucault argues that rather than symbolizing certain things about the conscious world through the unconscious world of dreams, the dream approximates the world-creating processes of human existence and the index of consciousness/unconsciousness repeats the old theological error of a universal will on the ordinary structures of existence-as-world-creating.[75] In contrast Foucault's reconsideration of dream analysis is strikingly Heideggerian in its temporal imagery: "The dreams mean repetition only to the extent that the repetition is precisely the experience of a temporality which opens upon the future and constitutes itself as freedom. This is the sense in which repetition may be authentic."[76] Heidegger will help Foucault move beyond philosophies which remain beholden to a solipsistic subjectivity that envisages "world" less adequately than the imaginatively constituted "worlding" of Heidegger.[77]

Foucault, like Heidegger, focuses on the processes of emergence. Foucault leans on Heidegger's phenomenological notion of becoming, especially when he turns to discursivity. Akin to how Heidegger speaks of the heroic self emerging from *das Man* and transcendence arising within immanence, Foucault speaks of "surfaces of emergence" whereby objects arise from "the field of initial difference" and "finds a way of limiting its domain, of defining what it is talking about, of giving it the status of an object—and therefore of making it manifest, nameable, and describable."[78] And while Foucault differs from Heidegger's analytic of emergence, which spends much time describing the constitution of worlds from which emergence takes place, he follows Heidegger in denoting emergence as the origins of things.[79] In attempting to delineate an archeology of knowledge, Foucault seeks "what was being said in what was said" and he means by this, critically, not what remains hidden in language, but rather how statements are deployed for the emergence of certain objects.[80] Within discourse, objects take on an event-nature. Foucault here does not imagine objects as primordially extant until revelation through emergence. Rather, objects come to be by way of deployment of statements through certain discursive habits, what he called "dispotifs." Hence, he can claim "facts" as "constituted" through speech acts. For example, public speech about madness grants the impression of factuality and scientific discourse lends professionalization which in turn warrants respect and coercion.[81] Foucault seeks to show by way of "the history of madness" its emergence and hence its contingent status. An archaeology of madness reveals how subsequent studies of madness did not so much share a central object called "madness" as much as create and recreate madness in their respective images. It is the semantic aggregations of discourse that grant "madness" continuity since "the unity of a discourse is based not so much on the permanence and uniqueness of an object as on the space in which various objects emerge and are continuously transformed."[82] Speech—"a certain way of speaking"—about the thing, rather than the thing itself, holds together all the desperate elements of an object and grants the impression of external and internal coherence.[83] Within the interrelations of statements and practices regarding madness, we see madness come to be.[84] By archaeology Foucault seeks to survey the means by which these emergences take place necessarily within the terms of its emergence, how the field of its emergence determined its appearance,

> We do not seek below what is manifest the half silent murmur of another discourse; we must show why it could not be other than it was, in what respect it is exclusive of any other, how it assumes in the midst of others in relation to them, a place that no other could occupy. The question proper to such an analysis might be formulated this way: what is this specific existence that emerges from what is said and nowhere else.[85]

Within and around these formations Foucault wonders how a different arrangement of statements could have made equally inevitable other states of affairs. Such surveying takes on political significance because "surfaces of emergence" are policed for the sake of certain discourses and their objects. Already in *Madness and Civilization* Foucault had demonstrated how a certain notion of madness was prioritized for (and in turn produced) a certain view of the world: "let there be no misunderstanding: it is not the objects that remain constant, nor the domain that they form; it is not even their point of emergence or their mode of characterization; but the relation between the surface on which they appear, on which they can be delimited, on which they can be analyzed and specified."[86]

The context of emergence exists as the vast inter-relational patterns that seek to conserve certain grounds of emergence "established between institutions, economic and social processes, behavioral patterns, systems of norms, techniques, types of classification, modes of characterization."[87] By the time Foucault transitions from *Madness and Civilization* to his positive and productive account of power, we find him speaking about the emergence of new categories within the medico-legal discourse of psychiatry as its "conditions of possibility for the appearance, construction, and regulated use of a concept within a discursive formation."[88] Rather than prescinding from necessity or nature, such habits of speech assemble around accidents of history, which prove to be the casuistrical occasions for the formation of assemblages like psychiatry. Speaking of such accidents and their intelligibility within their discursive traditions (the dispotif's casuistry), Foucault says, "these cases do not pose a problem for criminal psychiatry as much as constitute it, or rather, they are the ground on which criminal psychiatry is able to constitute it as such."[89]

The fragility of these discursive formations demands strict policing of the fields of emergence, the world made possibly by constant repudiation and reproduction.[90] Foucault offers here a precursor to his turn to power by outlining how these discourses and their constitutive statements "are preserved by virtue of a number of supports and material techniques . . . in accordance with certain types of institutions . . . and with certain statutory modalities."[91] The givenness of these establishments moves Foucault beyond phenomenology's strictly nominalist view of things: "We can certainly say that madness 'does not exist,' but this does not mean it is nothing. All in all, it was a matter of doing the opposite of what phenomenology has taught us to say and think, the phenomenology that said, roughly: Madness exists, which does not mean that it is a thing."[92]

Writing the Self

When it comes to the objectivity of the self as subject, then, Foucault seeks to till the soil for the emergence of certain kinds of statements about selves, "to the exclusion of all others."[93] Foucault's interests here lie not on repressions but productions. For behind the notion of an a priori primordial object lays an a priori primordial subject, the magical cogito, as its ground or what Foucault calls "*the* unifying function of *a* subject." By upsetting the logic of a preexistent object, Foucault means to upset the logic of just such a subject, utilizing archaeology to unearth our presumptions: "it deprives us of our continuities; it dissipates that temporal identity in which we are pleased to look at ourselves when we wish to exorcise the discontinuities of history; it breaks the thread of transcendental teleologies; and where anthropological thought once questioned man's being or subjectivity, it now bursts open the other, and the outside."[94]

Foucault moves beyond Heidegger by placing becoming not in the context of idle thought but rather power, which we might interpret as one way of talking about the local consequences of idle thought.[95] Both carry forward the tradition of transcendental critique through recoiling questions that not only recoils against idle thought but also against the questions themselves.[96] The repressive hypothesis rightly interrogates the capillary oppressions of modern sexuality. Foucault is not denying a repressive air regarding contemporary sexual discourse. Yet the questions do not go far enough, do not question enough, and like the structuralism Foucault inherited, does not question itself.[97] It destines itself to the un-thought, a hypothesis that finally represses thinking itself, lacking the reflexivity of genuine transcendental critique. Quoting John Cassian, in whom Foucault will find an interesting interlocutor: "A bad thought brought into the light of day immediately loses its veneer. The terrible serpent that this confession has forced out of its subterranean lair, to throw it out into the light and make its shame a public spectacle, is quick to beat a retreat."[98] For Arendt the failure to question ends in monstrous banalities. For Foucault the un-thought too quickly surrenders to Empire, not only obeying biopower but more troubling internalizing it, believing in it, and giving life for it.[99]

Foucault marshals and then restates the Heideggerian vocabulary. Locating the self amidst power represents a crucial departure from situating the self over against *das Man*. In some sense, we can say that "power" names for Foucault the limits of the subject; "power" is Foucault's reconsideration of Heideggerian transcendence and the danger of positing selfhood in contradistinction to *das Man*. Power's ubiquity means no such transcending is to be had, that a hermeneutics of suspicion must first be suspicious of itself. It is always the first ruse of power to make others believe it sits "over there" in "them" and not in, with, and as us. Heidegger veers in this direction unable to resist the attraction of the heroic self.[100] When he does so, he ends up objectifying "*das Man*" as the emergent self's condition of possibility.[101]

3. Confessing the Self

Near the end of the nineteenth century an anonymous author published *My Secret Life*, which over eleven volumes documented the author's many sexual exploits.[102] In the same way that Anonymous produces volume after volume of confessions, so moderns, according to Foucault, produce voluminous talk about sex. The comical aspect to this discourse is the way it conjoins truth and pleasure by making truth and its disclosure the pleasurable catharsis of *jeau de verite*; the repressive hypothesis invents a world teeming to get out, pulsating with untapped pleasures seeping in the unmentionable crevices of society.[103] The repressive hypothesis not only demands the truth but makes its utterance pleasurable. One can glimpse a semblance of Heidegger's account of ontological difference here, where he holds to a suppression of being under the occlusions of idle speech.

Two millennia before *My Secret Life*, in his letters to his young protégé, Seneca admonishes Lucilius: "*Disce gaudere*, learn how to feel joy. I do not wish you ever to be deprived of gladness... look toward the true good, and rejoice only in that which comes from your own store [*de tuo*]. But what do I mean by 'your own store'? I mean your very self and the best part of you."[104] In his histories of sexuality Foucault traces a development from the Greeks through the early and medieval Christians, until the Reformation scatters the penitential liturgy into the many parts that obtain in contemporary medicine, pedagogy, economics, jurisprudence,

Writing the Self

behavioral science, so on and so forth.[105] Foucault revisits the past in order to offer a counterhistory that uncovers selves buried beneath these obscurations. Here Foucault discovers what the Greeks called *heautou epimeleisthai* or "care for the self" enabled by "a cultivation" (*techne tou biou*) which entails both a duty and a privilege that culminates in the Christian social imaginary, which, for Foucault, is both contiguous with the ancient and the modern ages, but is also a genuine alternative to both.[106] Foucault speaks of this care as "a whole set of occupations" by which one nurtures the self as the site of selfhood at the center of its concerns. For the pagan sources that would later inform Christian care for the self, selfhood becomes the anchor which weathers the distentions of time as the core of personhood.

By "care" Foucault does not mean the *existential* sense by which Heidegger's self experiences itself as Dasein, but rather care in the sense of *therapaea*—care as an art of life, the mixed soil of ethics as aesthetics.[107] By care do selves come into being and Foucault believes that the more modes of care available, the more selves available and so he seeks to affirm selfhood as this coming-to-presence over against a static epistemological and moral warrants of correspondence and identity. To this, Christianity contributes a politics gathered around the care of the self so that by Tertullian the Delphic *cura sui* (*epimeleia heautou*), know thyself, has morphed into *publicatio sui,* show thyself.[108] The Christian monastery advances Aristotle's *enkrateia* so that John Cassian can boldly claim, "Everything the monk does without permission of his master constitutes a theft."[109]

According to Foucault the Greeks conceptualized sex in terms of self-care. Over time these notions of decorum, which made matrimony but one among many sites of self-mastery, evolved into conceptions of mutual love and self-giving as ethical issues.[110] For Christianity similar discourses pooled around practices of confession that, for Foucault, reached their greatest literary intensity in Athanasius' desert monk Antony and what the protagonist called a "system of observation" turned inward.[111] According to Antony, in Foucault's reading, only by confession does the "unaware" come to see himself; or, as Foucault understood in terms of surfaces of emergence, the self *appears* through confession as self-showing, emerging through surfaces of the pastoral dispotif.[112]

The *Vita Antony* narrates an unending cycle of appearance and disappearance and revelation and concealment wherein the monk seeks solitude only to show himself and remains hidden only to be found by gathering up an otherwise scattered *logoi*; the more people seek after him, the more he withdraws; the more he flees the more he gathers.[113] In his speech to the pagan religious he speaks of this mystery as the church itself, the greater its persecution, the greater its witness, martyrdom the surface of its emergence into the world.[114]

Whereas the Greeks considered passivity (*aphrodisiasthenai*) unfit for the morally mature, the early Christians believed submission to right masters the end of virtue and virtue the inculcation of genuine power.[115] Antony submits himself to the powers as the demons continuously accost him. But just so, Christian faithfulness appears amidst these possessions, new selves in every event of faithfulness.[116] Against Antony, the demons' dogged temptations prove "powerless" before his resilience.[117] Introducing *The Life of Antony* Athanasius admonishes those seeking the monastic life to "emulate" Antony so that they might "emulate him in goodness."[118] This invitation to emulate, and hence submit to and participate in, the life of Antony, which itself submits to and participates in the life of Christ, is extended, Athanasius thinks, to all who would read this text.[119] Foucault writes, "Through [confessional writing], one opens oneself to the gaze of others and puts the correspondent in the place of the inner god. It is a way of *giving ourselves* to that gaze about which we must tell ourselves that it is plunging into the depths of our heart (*in pectis intimum introspicere*) at the moment we are thinking."[120] Here we see an important similarity between Christian theology and Foucault, this account of knowing by semantic participation as the Christian self's surface of emergence. The life of Antony elicits desire for a life not so much possessed as possessing. Similarly in Book VIII of *The Trinity*, Augustine speaks of the interdependence of desire and possession: "to behold and grasp God as he can be held and grasped is only permitted the pure in heart ... before we are capable of doing this we must first love by faith, or it will be impossible for our hearts to be purified and become fit and worthy to see him."[121] In a strange epistemic locution, "love by faith," Augustine articulates a Christian conception of love drastically different than that espoused after the Cartesian turn. Love requires faith because it does not yet possess its beloved, and yet because it already loves, because already possessed, it seeks after that already but not yet possessed by faith. Similarly, Foucault's knowing takes on the form of self-care that cultivates the self toward particular but unspecified ends, requiring, hence, a whole pantheon of epistemic liturgies: "That the truth cannot be attained without a certain practice, or set of fully specified practices, which transform the subject's mode of being, change its given mode of being, and modify it by transfiguring it, is a prephilosophical theme which gave rise to many more or less ritualized procedures."[122] For Foucault, this identifies philosophy as spirituality, a way of being in the world, an account of knowledge as activity. In his 1981–1982 Collège de France lectures, he discusses a "dynamic entanglement" between *gnōthi sauton* (knowledge of self) and *epimeleia heautou* (care for the self) presaged in the famous Delphic oracle. Within this spiritual epistemology, the self had to be prepared for knowledge. Knowing became an epistemic possibility only through spiritual exercises of self-care. The Cartesian turn separates the two, prioritizing *gnōthi sauton* at the cost of *epimeleia heautou*. By the modern period, *epimeleia heautou* drops out completely, knowledge as *gnōthi sauton*, a stand-alone acquisition (possession without desire). Modern epistemologies following Descartes are founded on this disappearance that makes modern conceptions of the self, as empty forms of knowing (knowing as pure indeterminacy), vulnerable to myths like the repressive hypothesis, the positing of an interior realm of being sought after through knowing as clutching after possessions (I return to clutching vis-à-vis Stanley Cavell in the following chapter).

These developments parallel a similar ecclesial shift in the practice of confession when verbal *exagoreusis* replaces bodily *exomologesis*. Over time the verbal humiliation (*erubescentia*) of confession itself takes the role of penance, the regular, continuous, and exhaustive nature of the confession exhibiting itself as the performance of contrition.[123] This prepares the ground for the sixteenth century's decline of ecclesial authority under ascending secular authority and the mutation of ecclesial authority within a new zone of scrutiny, the soul as distinct from the body. The church relinquishes political authority to the state while retaining exclusive right to the individual's everyday existence, which matters because it embodies the magisterium's last stand, the singular penitent as the lone holdout of a once glorious Christendom. This fascinating development Foucault refers to as "in-depth Christianity":

> At a time when states were posing the technical problem of the power to be exercised on bodies and the means by which power over bodies could effectively be put to work, the Church was elaborating a technique of the government of souls, the pastoral ... the enormous arsenal of rules that surround this new practice of penance, or rather, this new and formidable extension of mechanisms of discourse, examination, and analysis that are involved in the sacrament of penance. There is not so much an explosion of penance as a formidable inflation of the sacrament of penance that introduces the individual's entire life into what is more a practice of general examination than a practice of absolution.[124]

With the increased authority of the state, the body and the soul gradually become discreet sites of confession answering respective prelates, with the state cordoning one while the church remanding the other. The authority of the state does not just take over what the church hitherto commanded; instead, new zones of interrogation are discovered and claimed, which means individuals are answerable for more than ever before. "All, or almost all, of an individual's life, thought, and action must pass through the filter of confession."[125] The church had already staked ever-growing spheres of accountability that needed confession; the state demanded more still. Quickened by a newfound political authority, the state's authority "assumed an even greater intensity" during this period, amalgamating within new zones of visibility that eventually come to center on the lives of children.[126] Ironically the supposed freedom individuals gained with their bodies unfettered to the church only established greater realms of state authority; the state quickly sequestered every new freedom gained under the auspices of having achieved such freedoms in the first place. As the state granted the body's freedom, so it arrogated whatever was gained by that freedom. Moreover the network that previously granted the Christian body meaning was rearticulated within a new complex of meanings: health, hygiene, fertility, usefulness, orderliness, and so on.[127]

Though the prolixity of confession carries through the Classical and modern ages, those acts come to signify entirely different things within their respective dispotifs.[128] Toward the end of his life Foucault said, "I think that one of the great problems of Western culture has been to find the possibility of founding the self not, as it was in the case of early Christianity, on the sacrifice of the self but, on the contrary, on a positive, on the theoretical and practical, emergence of the self."[129] The transition between a sexuality determined by ecclesial powers and that determined by increasingly non-ecclesial and secular powers had to do with the productivity of bodies. Whole new discourses imaged the body as all important and so biopolitics names the emergence of the life/body into history through the manifold care of education, populace, medicine, economy.[130] Thus, for example, the eighteenth and nineteenth centuries' crusade against masturbation becomes the impetus for the modern nuclear family: "One way to coagulate the conjugal family was to make parents responsible for their children's bodies, for the life and death of their children, by means of an autoeroticism that had been rendered fantastically dangerous in and by medical discourse."[131]

And so Foucault sought to re-source the self in discourses prior to this fateful Cartesian turn. James Bernauer writes,

> Foucault was fascinated with Christianity's earliest form of penance: the public manifestation to a congregation of oneself as sinner and the dramatic renunciations of that dead soul. He was drawn to the paradox of a self-revelation that was also a self-destruction. His regard for that paradox of a self-revelation that was also a self-destruction. His regard for that paradox increased even more his distance from the modern obligation to identify with that self which was fashioned by positive truths of self-knowledge. His cry of sprit is precisely an effective resistance to the prison for the human spirit today, not the body but the soul as fundamental personal truth and ground for

self-relation. Self-possession is abandoned to a breath of life, a spirit in a spiritless, soul-filled world. His cry of spirit was commitment to passionate redefining of our relationship to the fruits of human intellect and discipline.[132]

In his final years Foucault hoped to return knowledge to its Delphic home, reintegrating knowledge of self as care for the self. In doing so, he accomplishes two things. First, he deconstructively renders visible a line of development hidden from view by voluntarist accounts of rationality (that reason obtains by willed and undetermined genius) within what he calls the "despotic Enlightenment."[133] By archiving its lineage Foucault genealogically disrupts its notions—"that the *Aufklärung* names itself the *Aufklärung*"[134]—disclosing how "enlightenment" finds its sources in pre-Enlightenment ideas and practices. Second, and more constructively, Foucault teases out a conception of self where the self's desiring (of knowledge) cannot be divorced from its possessions (by knowledge), just as the soul cannot in early Christian theology be divorced from the body. It is here that Bernauer speculates that the content of the unpublished final volume of the *History of Sexuality* would "have contrasted the modern biological concept of the body with the traditional Christian notion of the flesh":

> In exploring the flesh, [Foucault] would have come face to face with an arena of self-relationship very different from the body-soul dichotomy. The Pauline flesh was not a body but rather an entire way of existing, an embrace of the carceral and the slavish in contrast to that freedom of spirit discovered in living as children of God.[135]

Foucault understood his attempt to return the body to the province of philosophical concern as an ethical project. While his last works hardly sound like ethical arguments, that is largely the point. The Cartesian unlinking of knowledge from self-care created the impression that one's ability to know had little to do with one's ability to live well. By showing through these historical reports a traditioned interdependence between self-care and knowledge, Foucault hoped to demonstrate how knowing is always intertwined with discourses of ethical well-being. This resituates the self away from Descartes' cogito toward Augustine's ontology of love. Augustine's divine illumination parallels Foucault's arts of the self, neither of which can countenance modes of knowing that leaves desire empty of anything but its form, desire without a prior possession, the undetermined self.[136] The self's freedom does not come by shirking its formation but by living into it. Prioritizing the undetermined self mythologizes a heroic self spontaneously generated without cultivation. For Augustine such arrogance epitomizes the will's privation, stealing the will from its appropriate ends in God, as if the goal of the self was willing as such, the act of the will without proper ends.[137]

In his final lectures, Foucault spoke of an ill conceived

> desire to substitute the positive figure of man for the sacrifice which for Christianity was the condition for the opening of the self as a field of indefinite interpretation. During the last two centuries, the problem has been: what could be the positive foundation for the technologies of the self that we have been developing during centuries and centuries... Maybe the problem of the self is not to discover what it is in its positivity, maybe the problem is not to discover a positive self or the positive foundation of the self. Maybe our problem is now to discover that the self is nothing else than the historical correlation of the technology built in our history.[138]

Within the techniques of early Christianity, care of the self as a politics requires confession by which truth, as truth of the self, comes to be; there can be no access to selves that does not at the same time access truth of the self. No longer can self-care be envisaged as the solitary activity of Philo's "banquets of silence" but must be adjoined to practices of confession and listening as the interrogative form of Aristotle's ethics.[139] For Foucault Christianity introduces an interdependence between the self and its coming to be in knowledge and power.[140] Achieving the self, what Foucault calls "nothing less than the shaping of the self," is made possible by confessing it.[141]

Early Christians endowed the inheritance of the Greeks by bequeathing a Hebraic self through ascetic confession. Confessing sin simultaneously negates and affirms the self (recall Foucault on writing and authorship) since Christians hold that amidst sin confession becomes the manner whereby selves come into the world (recall Antony on confession). The self-showing of confession *shows* the self's worth, that it is something worth confessing. As Augustine demonstrates better than any other, persons discover themselves in the processes of confession, almost as if there were no self or at least a different self prior to confession; almost as if in the self's dying, it is reborn; almost as if in crucifixion resides the power of resurrection. Through confessing one comes to have a world, inscribing its plentitude in the verities of life as *poiesis*.

According to Foucault's reading of John Cassian, the confessant's "permanent examination" requires the aptitude of what the Romans called *discretio* and the Greeks, *diacrisis*.[142] Foucault configures Christian confession as modalities that underscore its aptitude through skills of self-giving. *Exomologesis* bespeaks the self's emergence through dramatic expression, penance as public manifestation. *Exagoreusis* on the other hand utilizes discursive examination and confession.[143] As Andrew Cutrofello describes, "In both exomologesis and exagoreusis, confession is 'a way of renouncing self and no longer wishing to be the subject of the will', but in the former case the renunciation of self is tied to a practice of *showing*, while in the latter it is a question of *saying*."[144] Through these acts of penance sin is "published" and "written" on the body of the penitent who is made "public" through these speech acts, *showing* the truth of the matter. The donning the hair shirt or the shaving of the head display sin and repentance, manifesting truth as if to say, through the event of self-writing, "By confessing, *I become* a Christian." Here the Christian enacts the death of sin and the rebirth of repentance for the church as public witness. Repentance denotes the political shape of Christian salvation and its opposite, sin and disobedience. As sin took place in private, away from the community of believers, penance takes place with the church as its condition of possibility; not only does the penitent appear here, but also the church. Where there is embodiment, there is truth.

For the Christian ascetics, embodied most fully in the martyrs, one gives of self not to achieve the self, but rather to reclaim it.

Writing the Self

In giving the self, the church believes persons become genuine selves. This is a Christological claim. Christ's humility does not seek to usurp worldly power by some other means, but repudiates that power by avowing power of another kind. The Nicaean affirmation of the fullness of Christ's humanity and divinity holds that self-giving is not a divine tactic that ushers in pagan guilt and subjugation. Rather, Christ's full divinity means that self-giving reveals the fullness of God, the ontological character of God translated into the world. As Sarah Coakley comments, "It is not for nothing that it is Gregory of Nyssa who memorably insists that the *kenosis* of the Incarnation is the sign *of* supreme divine power, not of the loss of it."[145] The fullness of Christ's humanity displays how self-giving indicates not only what it means to be fully divine but also what it means to be fully human. Without Christ's full humanity Christ's submission would only be a ploy for power (as Nietzsche supposed). However, the fullness of Christ's humanity evinces that to be weak is to be fully human and to be fully human is to be more like God in God's freedom to choose humanness. Locating creaturely self-giving in God's own self-giving emanated in a ready articulation of power in the meekness of the martyrs. Their quiet confidence in the face of persecution and death spoke forcefully to a world desperate for power as the preemption of suffering. To the extent that the martyrs believed their own suffering participant in Christ's crucified body, they endured suffering as continuous with God's own life and hoped that as they took their share of suffering they might share in Christ's resurrection. Hence Athanasius' Antony speaks of dying daily as an enactment of Christ whose death makes possible his faithfulness.[146] Through his daily dying Antony emerges as, within Athanasius' dispotif, "Antony the Great."

Though this is a Christological claim, it is also a Foucauldian claim. By repudiating the notion of power and knowledge figured as sovereign selves, Foucault changes our perceptions of power, rendering visible what had been obscured by theories preoccupied with sovereignty. Foucault's ubiquity of power allows one to see power employed by everyone everywhere. Those who seemed powerless according to the standard view can now be seen in a new light. Illuminated by Foucault, one can *see* power in the hair shirt and ashes borne by the prostrate penitent in Tertullian's account or the tears and nakedness of the female confessant Fabiola in Jerome's. Foucault's ubiquity of power scripts martyrdom as if God mattered, that is, theo-logically, because it avails selves within the optics of becoming. One fails to understand Foucault if one sees martyrdom as masochistic capitulation to systems that cannot be overthrown, resistance as simply resignation. The tyrant who kills the martyr believes he alone holds power; from the tyrant's point of view, execution and torture *force* the martyr's submission to tyrannical power. And yet, though the tyrant thinks her powerless, by suffering gladly the martyr exercises her *own* brand of power (counter-conduct), but in a manner unintelligible within the impoverished imagination of the tyrant whose power renders him conceptually blind. In contrast the martyr dies joyfully in the radiance of her just cause. In that joy, which the patristic writers took pains to relate, the tyrant witnesses his powerlessness, his use of power frustrated. At this moment, witnessing the church as church the world discovers itself as world. The tyrant uses violence to get done what he cannot through the truthfulness of submission, as Antony keeps saying about the demons. This reversal refuses regression to sovereign power insofar as it does not deny the tyrant a kind of power—for martyrdom to be martyrdom, some power must granted the tyrant. This is the opposite of capitulation and resignation and requires active canvassing of power in order to tacitly deploy it otherwise. Again, the patristic writers went to great lengths to recount the joy the martyrs *showed* at death and how much this joy further provoked the tyrants, as if testifying to the breaking of tyrant's monopoly on power.[147] Situated within these matrices of power, the martyr's obedience to God foments great power; Foucault helps this comes to view. Perceiving the order of things along these lines is made possible by a hermeneutics bequeathed by Heidegger and carried forth in Foucault's thought. The tyrant cannot see it and so in frustration can only lash out in the same way that the ascetic can only praise God for granting her martyrdom; that one smiles while the other shakes his fist highlights a Heidegerrian notion of truth as *aletheia*. The tyrant and the martyr mutually enact power, produced and reproduced in performances that can be endlessly staged and re-staged. Again Coakley, "the 'vulnerability' that is its human condition is not about asking for unnecessary and unjust suffering (though increased self-knowledge can be indeed be painful); nor is it a 'self-abnegation'. On the contrary, the special 'self-emptying' is not a negation of self, but the place of the self's transformation and expansion into God."[148] Hence the Christological struggles of the fourth and fifth centuries were never simply theoretical arguments about the metaphysical status of Christ's two natures but the attempt to speak well about the church's ascetic practices as genuine political power.

Combining these Foucauldian *and* Christological claims unfolds in an account of ethics that surpasses the conceptions that currently circumscribe political theory. When Foucault claims no "outside to power" he means to signal its infinite possibility.[149] Because power courses through every social space ethics must be thought of within the complexes of those spaces and political agency cannot be figured devoid of relational influence nor imagined beyond social contexts. Because orthodox Christology imagines no *other* place for the expression of Christian faith, it provides an alternative to an unmediated Platonism that holds anxieties for the material and the social. In this way, the martyr acts *into* the faithfulness of the tradition not only regardless but for the sake of political consequence. Material eventualities follow (angering or converting the tyrant are both possibilities) but are not the goal of such faithfulness. The either/or of political liberalism refuses options beyond those inscribed within political space so cannot help but cast aside the martyr option.[150] The Christian need not be tempted by this political vision to the extent that she understands worship as genuinely political; after all Christ's body, as the gathered body in its corporeal and ecclesial expressions, incarnates a mutual co-existence of divine and human power. The either/or temptation then finds its theological origins in the church's early anathemas against Manichaeism (as Foucault understood) and the Christian pronouncements of Christ's full humanity anoint all body space as politically relevant. There is no exodus from power; there is the tyrant's power in relation to the martyr's power, which inhere in relationship to one another (they are not only socially *situated* but also socially *constituted*).[151] The subject cannot be figured autonomously in a field of pure indeterminacy but rather as an actor who allows herself conducted by (*se laisse conduire*) and who herself conducts (*conduire*). Government by self and others remains a problem only from the vantage point of sovereignty. From the vantage of Foucault's ubiquity of power, it is simply politics.[152]

Chapter 5

Self-Care: The Case of Animals

Knowing oneself is the capacity for placing-oneself-in-the-world.
 —*Stanley Cavell*

Jonathan Safran Foer's recent book *Eating Animals* contends that the eating habits of late capitalism produce a culture increasingly unable to *see* animal life, a fitting appraisal given our depiction of Empire in Chapter 2. What is particularly striking in Safran Foer's portrayal is the way eating can encourage fidelity by engendering a certain kind of attentiveness, without which eating portends in the opposite direction, blindness, or what the J. M. Coetzee character Elizabeth Costello calls "willed ignorance," the sustained effort to render invisible the frighteningly cruel processes of animal production. Stanley Hauerwas has coyly stated that capitalism produces shitty people; we might extend that to the observation that capitalism produces shitty people who produce shitty foods that produce shitty people.[1] The question becomes, quite literally in the case of factory farming, is there any way out of the shit?

Seeking after new forms of subjectivity within such a context is quite likely, for Michel Foucault, to take the form of suicide. The capitalist strictures that produce shitty persons are astoundingly formidable. Sometimes the freedom most available amidst these pressures is the freedom to die by one's own hand. Because biopower seeks to determine how we live (through inducements like how we eat) resistance may resemble death. Thus Foucault announced, "I'm in favor of a true cultural combat in order to teach people again that there is no conduct that is more beautiful, that, consequently, deserves to be considered with as much attention as suicide. One should work on one's suicide all one's life."[2]

In this chapter I interpret what Arnold Davidson refers to as "one of Foucault's most disquieting acclimations" as his greatest proximity to Christianity, which Hauerwas has called "extended training in how to die early." That Hauerwas likens early death to "dying well" indicates that Christianity's attempt to return subjectivity to God cannot help but sound strange. That Foucault considered suicide a form of self-care indicates the totalizing world of late capitalism. Davidson comments, "If counter-conduct at the end of life can be decisively shocking, we should not underestimate its more everyday occasions."[3] I speak in the following of one such occasion, the everyday practice of eating, and eating as an occasion for self-care that may resemble cultural death within an ethos consumed with consuming. The chapter positions itself both sympathetic to Safran Foer's concern for animal welfare but suspicious of his rather naïve, given the totalizing burdens of Empire, presumptions about the ethical benefits of vegetarianism. In contrast to what will be considered a mythic vegetarianism (recall the repressive hypothesis), I suggest that the moral good of not eating meat has less to do with making things better for animals (though that is not without consideration) than the attempt to gain some purchase on one's humanity, to care for oneself within morally damaging capitalist economies, and to not be consumed, one might say, by consuming.

The argument here turns on a recent conversation between philosophers Cora Diamond and Stanley Cavell regarding ordinary language as a kind of moral and religious activity akin to Foucault's self-care. Both scholars of the later Wittgenstein, Diamond and Cavell zero in on something Diamond calls "the difficulty of reality" which she thinks contemporary philosophy unable to grasp, or even notice. By this difficulty, Diamond means the inexorable nature of bodied existence that resists analysis yet remains critical parts of who we are as persons: "experiences in which we take something in reality to be resistant to our thinking it, or possibility to be painful in its inexplicability, difficult in that way, or perhaps awesome and astonishing in its inexplicability."[4] Diamond believes these elements get covered over in every attempt to systematize humanness, which in turn suffers the blunderings of analytic clumsiness. For Diamond, inattentiveness to these realities creates blind spots in the purview of much philosophical ethics, which explains why controversies like war or abortion achieve the status of "hot button issues" while everyday practices like eating warrant almost no scholarly consideration whatsoever. When philosophers

Self-Care: The Case of Animals

do turn to animals Diamond notices other tendencies toward evasion as evidenced by animal rights language. Like Diamond, Cavell is troubled by how animals are not considered morally serious and why many, including Cavell by his own admission, remain largely indifferent to the ethical status of animals and the moral importance of eating. Cavell's philosophical genius has developed along the lines of a crucial insight, that our commonality as persons who share linguistic worlds also supplies the conditions of a loneliness that can be abided, but never shed, by something he calls companionship. If the gap between persons who share language remains formidable then the distance between human animals and non-human animals borders on the tragic. And yet we share a common life with animals, most forcefully displayed on the dining table. How might we understand this relationship both within the terms of tragedy that helps us see animal suffering along with our reliance upon that suffering and yet beyond the claims of reason that cannot help but see separateness as necessarily tragic? Might we, using Cavell's notion, foster companionship with the animals we eat?

I am especially interested in the ways we can share lives with animals by inhabiting the differences that separate us, and so in concluding the chapter and book, I turn to Eucharistic presence and absence. I have already spoken of presence and absence while discussing biography and its seeming inability to honor absence. In speaking of "seeing" animals I will need to steer clear of seeing in terms of the gaze's surveillance that renders all commodity. By relating seeing to companionship, I mean seeing that honors difference as that which continuously exceeds our attempts to possess. In the first chapters, I explained how Hardt and Negri construed Foucault's quasi-metaphysicalism as a horizontal transcendence that does not close the door on moreness as the composition of immanence. I spoke of that moreness as Foucault's availability. By seeing, I mean remaining watchful for that moreness, what William Connolly referred to as "concentrating on how otherness appears when it is presented." Such concentrated watchfulness contrasts the gaze's surveillance which does not endeavor toward difference but only sameness conditioned by exclusion. In this final chapter I appropriate this watchfulness to watchfulness for God witnessed in the plentitude of creation. We have seen

Foucault argue that the Christian pastoral's watchful care resulted in individuation and control. Foucault is correct that such results often follow, but here I argue that individuation as control fails the pastoral's vocation which watches not for the sake of control but for that which cannot be controlled. Watchfulness as control equals watchfulness as exclusion, yet exclusion precludes that which the Christian pastoral watches *for*: God. The *Christian* pastoral concentrates on how this otherness appears when it is presented. This shares at least a family resemblance to what Foucault means when he labors to talk about the pastoral's eschatological expectations as counter-conduct over against the pastoral's exclusions. While Foucault's "total atheism" only grants him a horizontal transcendence, theology appropriates that horizontal transcendence as God's incarnational presence in the world as witnessed in the church's sacramental life. In what remains, I argue that the Eucharist trains seeing as ready anticipation for that which can be hoped for but not possessed. While God is not present in animal life in the same ways God is present in the Holy Meal, the Eucharist does help us see animal life (and the animals we eat) as an abiding realm of divine mystery that holds off capitalist impulses toward possession.

Relating Cavell's ordinary language philosophy to Foucault, David Owen writes,

> both are fundamentally concerned with the character and prospects of human freedom, where freedom is not to be identified with an individual's possession of a causal power to initiate action by an act of will in some way independent of antecedent causal conditions but with a certain kind of self-relation.[5]

Foucault and Cavell share a notion of selfhood as precessional without teleological identity. The self's perfection is a process rather than an end, especially since for Cavell and Foucault the self is best indicated by habits of care.[6] As discussed in the previous chapter, by the later Athenians and the ascetic Christians, the self transitions from a positive to a negative conception (something to be disciplined rather than cared for), but the pivotal turn for Foucault is when care is not simply overshadowed by discipline, but entirely forgotten—"obliterated" even—under the rubric of the transcendental ego began in Aristotle, intensified in Aquinas, articulated in Descartes, and come home to roost in late capitalism.[7] Hitherto, access to truth came about by care of the self which prepared one for truth, the practices of moral formation that trained one in disposition to truth. As Pierre Hadot writes, "Above all, the work, even if it is apparently theoretical or systematic, is written not so much to inform the reader of a doctrinal content but to form him, to make him traverse a certain itinerary in the course of which he will make spiritual progress."[8] The Cartesian turn marks the shift where formation becomes a barrier to truth, and exit from such prior dispositions now proves the new point of departure for knowledge, as if knowledge can stand alone: *Cogito ergo sum*. In his 1981–1982 Collège de France lectures Foucault says,

> I think the modern age of the history of truth begins when knowledge itself and knowledge alone gives access to truth. That is to say, it is when the philosopher (or the scientist, or simply someone who seeks the truth) can recognize the truth and have access to it in himself and solely through his activity of knowing, without anything else being demanded of him and without him having to change or alter his being as subject.[9]

I differ with Owen's earlier comparison, not with his reading of Cavell and Foucault on perfectionism and self-care, but rather with the kind of teleological architecture he characterizes as Christian. To be sure, Christianity's account of moral goodness has ends in sight as well as an ontological presumption along the lines of participation. However, Christian conceptions of participation presume God's eternality as the lifehood of the Trinity which knows no end. Sure, the ethical life of Christianity aims toward its return to God as the origin and goal of its existence—"You made us for yourself, and our hearts are restless until they rest in you," Augustine prays to God[10]—but return does not equal completion. Only God is complete. The Christian sojourns to God without completion because "home" names for Christian theology the moreness of God's inexhaustible goodness. The difference between Christian theology and the likes of Foucault and Cavell is ontological.

This difference, however, does not result in an account of selfhood any less boundless or processional; indeed, to the extent that it locates procession eternally within the divine life itself, its pilgrimage witnesses to a broader horizon, making known to the Christian not simply the distance between her and perfection, but more importantly, between her and God. Like Foucault's and Cavell's respective ethical games, such processing can be spoken of as love.

This chapter unfolds with three texts. First, I attend to *Eating Animals*' general depiction of factory farming. Second, presuming Safran Foer's portrayal, I turn to J. M. Coetzee's *Elizabeth Costello*, where the aging writer Elizabeth artlessly compares the "stupefying suffering" of factory-farmed animals to the Holocaust. Third, I consider *Philosophy and Animal Life*, a volume that includes Cavell's and Diamond's reconsiderations of animals beyond questions of suffering and rights, instead weighing in on Elizabeth's strange claim that she chooses vegetarianism as the desire to save her soul. In contrast to what I characterize as Safran Foer's naïveté, I advance Diamond and Cavell's conversation about ordinary language and companionship toward an account of Christian self-care where eating cultivates attention to God's presence and absence.

1. Eating Animals

Explicitly Jonathan Safran Foer's *Eating Animals* does not argue for vegetarianism; directly he states, "A straightforward case for vegetarianism is worth writing, but it's not what I've written here."[11] Still it is hard to imagine the book's current ending in anything but some kind of vegetarianism, which he eventually concedes.[12] And this is the book's force. Taking an overbearing vegetarianism off the table gets Safran Foer in the door, allowing the moral obligation of vegetarianism to slowly surface. His irenic approach develops the shock, compassion, anger, contrition, and conviction necessary for vegetarianism's moral imagination. This is no small achievement given the relative inconceivability of not eating meat for most Americans. So he wisely takes his time. The argument goes something like this:

Self-Care: The Case of Animals

In times past, enjoying meat was commensurate with its ethical production, namely the equitable treatment of animals. We no longer live in those times. Today, approximately 99 percent of all meat produced and consumed in America comes from factory farms, where the opposite of equitable treatment takes place on a harrowingly massive scale. We can go on, as we currently do, eating meat but only by trading on inequitable animal suffering. In other words, eating meat is no longer, given the suffering entailed by its production, enjoyable. Ergo: Since it is so much less enjoyable, we might as well give up eating meat.

Two immediate questions come to mind. First, what does inequitable animal suffering mean? For certainly, even in good times—i.e., those times when enjoyment and equitability were congruent—animals suffered. This will be developed further, but the main difference I gather from Safran Foer is that while in the past one's relationships with animals at least warranted concern for their suffering and hence avoidance of unnecessary suffering, today no such concern arises, while other overriding considerations—market profitability or what Foucault called the population's maximum advantage—almost guarantee unnecessary suffering. In other words, suffering as a concern has given way to suffering as an unending reality.[13]

Second, what about those unbothered by the suffering produced for their eating? What about those who enjoy meat no matter animal suffering? Here, Safran Foer has seemingly divided his (potential) audience into two categories: virtuous and vicious readers. Regarding the former, his argument presumes one would not knowingly enjoy products gained through illicit means. For them, showing how animal production is unethical and then implying the kinds of abstinence that might follow can make the case. Even if caught unawares, these people, Safran Foer presupposes, would rethink their ways once shown the collateral damage. Some may downplay such suffering and others may disagree about possible responses, but still they would be people for whom personal gratification would not justify unethical behavior. *Eating Animals* directs its efforts to these kinds of readers—those for whom ignorance is bliss—and hence presumes the kinds of virtue necessary for hearing, deliberating upon, and responding to evidence. Regarding the vicious, Safran Foer has little time for readers whose enjoyment is unaffected by inordinate suffering. For these, ignorance is not the issue, but rather character because for them recognition will not curtail enjoyment of animal meat. These are people for whom ignorance is itself only a cover for a vicious preoccupation with pleasure, or their distorted versions of it. Such bliss guarantees ignorance and no amount of reasoning (even when expressed in native terms) will do anything for them. We might characterize these as persons whose souls are not sufficient for truthfulness. It is hard to tell how many such people there are, but I'm assuming they are not entirely uncommon given the pressures of capitalism; this is what I think Hauerwas means by "shitty people"—these are shitty people. Acknowledging them as shitty people is not meant to dismiss them as people but simply to dismiss the possibility that Safran Foer's tactics will seriously impact their ways. For them, something else will need to happen before a significant change of course becomes possible, and here we are reminded of Johannes Climacus' opposing Socratic awakening to salvific conversion.[14] These people would need something akin to conversion before the kinds of Socratic awakening Safran Foer plots would become realistic. This second class of *Eating Animals* readers is not unimportant for our purposes, but only later in my argument will it become apparent how.

So what about eating meat? Through *Eating Animals*, I discovered that the meat I have readily consumed my whole life comes from animals and that those animals in almost every case are brutalized for my satisfaction. The latter discovery will come as some surprise for most Americans, even though the former shouldn't. Yet there is a connection here in a way that many Americans forget that meat comes from animals. This is because the process that produces 99 percent of all meat, a process known as factory or mechanized farming, disguises its identity as animal. In order for those animals to *become* meat they must be caged, cordoned, corralled, crowded, prodded, pushed, plucked, often kicked, manipulated, driven insane, torn away from familiar social patterns, branded, battered, broken, beaten, burned, scalded, starved and stuffed, dehydrated and pumped, castrated and inseminated, and all this occurs long before they ever get to the slaughter house to die painful, terrifying, humiliating, and too often, slow deaths. The miserable process from animal to meat remains largely unacknowledged by the vast majority of meat eaters and so the last violation the animals suffer on the way to satiating our appetites is one of the worst: forgotten. No one wants to remember that their hamburger or chicken nuggets were once creatures with lives of their own; or more precisely, no one wants to remember that their meat was once a creature that never had a life of its own. They were bred, born, bullied, and butchered for one purpose only, to serve our seemingly inexhaustible appetite for meat.

As I said, I only recently discovered this. Hitherto over the course of what must now be thousands of meals, I ate meat as if it came readymade like manna from heaven. What disturbs me about my recent discovery isn't just the misery the animal-to-meat process imposes, or that I didn't know. What disturbs me is that I never cared to know. I suppose at the corner of my mind I've always implicitly understood—given late capitalism's tendency to wound everything it touches—that the process that produces meat must be rather awful. Given how much I liked meat, I didn't want to know (and even feared to know). In my case, ignorance *was* bliss. And yet as a theologian, and more importantly as a Christian committed to the ethical materiality of the Gospel, I had never given it more than a passing thought. I had published on topics ranging from the suffering of the handicapped to the criminalization of immigrants to the care of children; I had even penned a cover story on the global sex trade for a major Christian publication. My writings covered topics from war to forgetting to the ubiquity of power.[15] And yet, when I ate turkey I ate with abandon. Nor am I a stranger to believing that eating relates to faith; for years now, I have regularly fasted and understand such disciplines integral to the Christian life.[16] I simply did not see animals as related to any of this; I merely saw them as things to be eaten. In an amazing act of willed ignorance, I did not see them at all.

Given Empire's dominance, I'm guessing my blindness in this regard is not entirely unique. The same industry that produces meat simultaneously pulls a huge vanishing act that makes that meat palatable, literally disappearing animals in the process. Still given my researches on forgetting and disappearance, I should have known better. My claim at this point isn't that eating meat is wrong on Christian grounds since one can anticipate any number of theological arguments for killing and eating animals.[17] My concern regards the ways these animals are hidden so that no such theological reflection takes place. Safran Foer puts it this way:

> Why would a farmer lock the doors of his turkey farm?
> It can't be because he's afraid someone will steal his
> equipment or animals. There's no equipment to steal in the
> sheds, and the animals aren't worth the herculean effort it
> would take to illicitly transport a significant number.
> A farmer doesn't lock his doors because he is afraid his
> animals will escape ... so why? In the three years I will
> spend immersed in animal agriculture, nothing will
> unsettle me more than the locked doors.[18]

While most Christians hold at least semblances of positions on issues like abortion or war, regardless of where they stand, most do not think of eating animals as one of those issues. And yet, while abortion and war are monumentally important ethical issues for Christians, abortion and war will not directly touch the daily lives of most American Christians. They will however eat meat. They will desire it, shop for it, spend money on it, prepare and cook it, cut it, chew it, swallow and digest it. They will do so two, often three times a day every day of every week of every month of every year of every one of their lives, save the occasional diet or fast. The overflow of all this eating inevitably leaks into any number of other ethical issues: many of the most distressing diseases of recent years are byproducts of industrial farming practices; the production of meat contributes to global warming on levels comparable to automobile usage; factory farming drains natural resources like land, water, and grain, placing massive strains on global economies leading to increased competition, tension, and warfare across boundaries due to the political results of poverty; the deplorable conditions in most meat processing factories rely on and exploit undocumented labor; pharmaceutical-agricultural conglomerates run roughshod over local economies; etc.. How is it possible that we have become blind to so many of these realities? In such a context, excusing this as ignorance too easily lets us off the hook, for any willing person can easily discover the truths hidden in the foods we eat. According to J. M. Coetzee's character Elizabeth Costello, our ignorance is something much more intentional, even egregious, a "willed ignorance."

Since reading *Eating Animals* I have abstained from eating most meat. Surprisingly, the transition was much easier than I expected, and this is what I meant earlier when I suggested that practices like not eating meat are internal to ways of seeing (just as, conversely, practices habituate ways of seeing). The power of Safran Foer's book is that it helps us imagine a world where eating animals is un-enjoyable. Again, quite an accomplishment. A few years back, I gave up meat for Lent and found that experience difficult. Lent invites and even requires such difficulty ("self-denial" traditionally one of the four activities comprising the *Quadragesima*) in order to help Christians see Christ's journey to the cross. Lent does not seek to deplete enjoyment but rather the opposite, utilizing enjoyment as the footing by which Christ's sufferings draw closer; Lent is supposed to be difficult. Safran Foer's book goes in the other direction; it wants to make vegetarianism easy by making meat enjoyment hard. Here, the graphic images Safran Foer deploys do their job, after which one cannot eat without their coming to mind, making meat eating distasteful, even disgusting. Again, this is different than the previously discussed ascetical practices of self-giving (Lent being just one) which seek not to obviate desire (at most they render temporal pleasures *relatively* un-enjoyable compared to eternal ones) but rather order desire so that all desires are fulfilled in God; one delays gratification in order to more deeply fulfill it (e.g., "O taste and see that the LORD is good, happy are those who take refuge in him" Ps. 34.8) while the other wants to rid us of the desire for meat altogether. Safran Foer's book is as effective as its abilities to do the latter.

2. The Claims of Vegetarianism

At the end of *Eating Animals,* Safron Foer foists several heavy-handed assertions about eating animals and the moral necessity of vegetarianism as a way of staving off animal suffering.[19] These claims overestimate one rendition of suffering while underestimating the breadth of suffering produced by capitalist economies. By overestimating suffering I don't mean to diminish the extreme brutality suffered by animals through the cruel practices of factory farming. Instead, Safran Foer's efforts presume the questionable proposition that ethical decisions should be determined by a calculus of suffering (sharing a sense with R. M. Hare's preference utilitarianism as employed by Hare's student Peter Singer in his animal liberation efforts). According to this rationale, animal suffering alone warrants vegetarianism. In this vein, Safran Foer strategically deploys in-your-face portraitures of suffering animals (with diminishing returns I might add, mimicking the very emotional desensitizing he complains about) in order to force certain moral judgments, the results of a transitive logic where vegetarianism is ethical because it alleviates suffering.

There can be little doubt that this tactic is effective, as long as one's ethics is determined by the goal of ending suffering. However, this overestimates the role suffering qua suffering should play in determining ethical deliberation. By its own lights, the moral project of ending suffering, and what Gerald McKenny calls the human condition, is largely what drove (and still justifies) the very capitalist economies that produced factory farming in the first place.[20] If the ethics of eating is decided on the issue of suffering alone, I would argue that no eating of any kind could be deemed ethical, at least consistently so. If Christians are going to think well about animals, they will need to do so within a theological framework of creation and its concomitant accounts of suffering, which frames suffering by imagining a horizon, and hence an ethics, that appropriately addresses suffering without undermining the irreducibly contingent conditions of creaturely life.[21] This is not to say that issues of suffering should play no part in moral deliberation but only that suffering can overrun how we think about moral questions (as if the avoidance of suffering ought to be primary) if not ordered to broader constellations of meaning (as if "suffering" possessed some kind of standalone meaning).

Conversely, by narrowing the scope for what counts as suffering (i.e., animal suffering), *Eating Animals* underestimates suffering as it ignores how non-animal food as well entails suffering in its production. The prevalence of slave-like conditions and the depletion of whole ecologies for the sake of mono-cultural plant production also exact great tolls of destruction and suffering since the very capitalist modes of dominance that mistreat animals treat laborers and land with no more regard in non-animal food industries. If the ethics of eating gets locked on the horns suffering then we will be forced into the absurd game of comparing suffering. On this score, a healthy dose of Foucault would help Safran Foer recognize how Empire's totalizing powers mean there is no easy way out, that vegetarianism will not eliminate suffering but only relocate it to less obvious sites of the biopolitical economy.[22] Safran Foer has written a compelling book about how animals suffer under market capitalism; he could as well have written a book about migrant workers toiling in cabbage farms or the role chattel slavery played in colonial era molasses production. Putting the question in terms of suffering has the unfortunate effect of positing animal welfare in competition with human welfare, a false dilemma that gets us nowhere. I concur with Safran Foer regarding some kind of abstinence, but not with his reasons, which I believe rely on a thin humanism that quickly undercuts its purposes. Instead, I think the good that is vegetarianism has less to do with the heroic will to end suffering and more with self-care or what the Coetzee character Elizabeth Costello describes as "a desire to save my soul."

I do not understand suffering as the moral impetus for vegetarianism. Rather, I see vegetarianism as a means of gaining some purchase on our lives within capitalist economies. It is rather like an attempt, however meager, to avoid being consumed by consumerism, that within a culture that encourages us to eat everything, to choose not to eat some things, including some things that bring us pleasure, and even joy. The reason I like Elizabeth Costello's way of putting it—that she doesn't eat meat as the desire to save her soul—is because it avoids a measure of the self-righteousness that comes with the pretension that we have escaped and even outsmarted an economy that seeks to colonize every aspect of our lives. I have no illusion that I have somehow chosen out of choosing. Indeed, vegetarianism in our meat-saturated dietary culture comes as a rather intentional choice.[23] I don't foresee much benefit in the outcomes of my refraining, as if the sum total of those who refuse to eat meat will someday reform the titanic meat industry (though that would be a beneficial if unlikely consequence).

As I have already described in terms of Empire, capital seeks to commodify everything, to consume everything in the endless task of consuming. Standing against this, etching out self-care within it, entails in part refusing to be so commodified. This brings us back to Foucault's later work on self-writing and subjectivity. Discussing Alcibiades' training under Socrates, Foucault speaks of caring for one's soul, somewhat like Elizabeth's concern for her soul's salvation. Denoting a "dialectical moment" Foucault says, "You have to worry about your soul—that is the principle activity of caring for yourself."[24] This dynamic of self-care travels through Christian patristic literature where it comes to reconfigure care in relation to self-giving. Here renunciation will not come to mean, as is sometimes supposed by Foucault, disparagement of the body, for that is after all part of the soul's good, the index by which self-care is measured, but rather disciplining the body so that it becomes the site of the soul's care and demonstration of its health. Hence asceticism in this ancient sense does not seek after bodily suffering but understands that suffering—which will sometimes resemble suicide—may be one of many paths traversed on the way to the soul's salvation. Part of self-care in a world dominated by late capitalism is then guarding the soul as the animating principle of the body against the effects of capitalism, a dominance which happens to be readily evident on the body as display of that dominance. Today abstaining from foods produced for capitalist markets speaks to similar modes of bodily integrity. These are ascriptions of how one imagines one's body as if not possessed by Empire. These are stylizations of the self that witness to the plentitude of God's creation even within the material conditions of the world in which we find ourselves. Hence when Foucault says, "the renunciation of the self distinguishes Christian asceticism" and then concludes by distinguishing Stoicism as "not renunciation but the progressive consideration of self, or mastery over oneself, obtained not through renunciation of reality but through the acquisition and assimilation of truth" he misses how Christianity's renunciation *is* the mode through which it acquires and assimilates truth.[25] In this way, the forms of both asceticisms (e.g., Christianity's so-called renunciation and Plutarch's "mortification of the flesh") look the same, though the content of the self and the self's truth differs.

Self-Care: The Case of Animals

Hence, unlike Safran Foer, I do not see the animals as the primary beneficiaries of my abstaining, because that way of putting it too easily pits humans in contradistinction to creatures. Rather, I do it for myself, a creature. By further lights, I do it for God. There is a family resemblance between Elizabeth Costello's vegetarianism and the Christian asceticism I differentiated from *Eating Animals* earlier, to the extent that asceticism does not disavow the self but maximally affirms it, following Chalcedon's insistence that abstinence expresses both divinized bodies and bodies fully human.[26] With their standing Platonic imaginaries, early church ascetics did not see much sense in delineating between divine and human benefits, since for them what was good for one was good for the other; the self's good and God, as the arche and telos of the self, are coextensive.[27] Hence, I choose abstinence for God, but that is not much different than saying I choose it for myself, a self that desires God but finds itself too readily consumed by things other than God, consumed by consuming.

3. Coming to Terms

In J. M. Coetzee's novel *Elizabeth Costello*, the title character, a celebrated if somewhat passed over writer, presents a visiting lecture series entitled, "The Lives of Animals."[28] Elizabeth gives the lectures at the twilight of her life and career, when she has become somewhat a novelty within the contemporary literary world, her public appearances mainly occasioned by honorific celebrations of her earlier work. After the lectures, which prove to be quite controversial, she has the following conversation with her son (an assistant professor at the college hosting the lectures) about his wife Norma, an analytic philosopher with little patience for her mother-in-law's severe views about animals or the imposing ways she carries them.

> "I'm sorry about Norma," he says, "She has been under a lot of strain. I don't think she is in a position to sympathize. Perhaps one could say the same for me. It's been such a short visit, I haven't had the time to make sense of why you have become so intense about the animals business."

She watches the wipers wagging back and forth. "A better explanation," she says, "is that I haven't told you why, or dare to tell you. When I think of the words, they seem so outrageous that they are best spoken into a pillow or into a hole in the ground, like King Midas."

"I don't follow. What is it you can't say?"

"It's that I no longer know where I am. I seem to move around perfectly easily among people, to have perfectly normal relations with them. Is it possible, I ask myself, that all of them are participants in a crime of stupefying proportions? Am I fantasizing it all? I must be mad! Yet every day I see the evidences. The very people I suspect produce the evidence, exhibit it, offer it to me. Corpses. Fragments of corpses that they have bought for money.

"It's as if I were to visit friends, and to make some polite remark about the lamp in their living room, and they were to say, 'Yes, it's nice, isn't it? Polish-Jewish virgins.' And then I go to the bathroom and the soap wrapper says, 'Treblinka—100% stearate.' Am I dreaming, I say to myself? What kind of house is this?

"Yet I am not dreaming. I look into your eyes, into Norma's, into the children's, and I see only kindness, human kindness. Calm down, I tell myself, you are making a mountain out of a molehill. This is life. Everyone else comes to terms with it, why can't you? *Why can't you?*"

She turns to him a tearful face. What does she want, he thinks? Does she want me to answer her question for her?

They are not yet on the expressway. He pulls the car over, switches off the engine, takes his mother in her arms. He inhales the smell of cold cream, of old flesh. "There, there," he whispers in her ear, "There, there. It will soon be over."[29]

Elizabeth cannot find words appropriate to the disturbances she experiences regarding animal cruelty nor can she adequately state the convictions she has come to hold in relation to those disturbances. Coetzee has Elizabeth express these slippages by the lectures' simultaneous brilliance and befuddlement; what Elizabeth is getting at both exceeds the lectures and remains hidden within them, rendering even that which is brilliant befuddling. The most

Self-Care: The Case of Animals

troublesome part of the lectures compares factory farming to the Holocaust (an analogy Elizabeth continues in the passage above), yet this evocation so tenuous it lands Elizabeth in hot water with the university faculty, some of whom have good reason to be offended by the discomfited comparison. The best we might say for Elizabeth Costello is that at least she recognizes this, that even as she offends to make a point she understands she has still to discover what her point is, failing to get to the heart of the matter. And what is the heart of the matter? It is unclear Elizabeth knows. If her point is that factory farming is like the Holocaust then the implication she must come to terms with is that most people, including her children and grandchildren, are "participants in a crime of stupefying proportion." Yet she cannot reconcile that conclusion with what she senses as their evident humanity. At one point in the lectures, Elizabeth asks her audience, "What is it like to be a bat?"[30] The upshot of her bizarre question is that instead of imagining ourselves into the being of animal (underscoring what Cora Diamond deems "the animal's independent life"[31])—a task humans with their amazing conceptual abilities are perfectly capable of doing—that's all most of us can do is eat them—vitiating the same amazing conceptual abilities to the point of stupidity. Yet is *that* what her grandchildren are doing when they eat the chicken set before them at dinner? And is such eating akin to participating in the slaughters of Treblinka, indeed even worse "in that ours is an enterprise without end"?[32]

Rather than using Elizabeth as a mouthpiece for his own stringent views about animals, I think Coetzee is trying to get at a more interesting difficulty: the ways our convictions set us off in the universe. I mean this in two senses. First, our convictions set *us* off, granting us handles on our lives by demarking what it is I believe, or don't, in relationship to what you do and don't; convictions integrate us into a common world by which agreements and disagreements gain significance, emplacing us with *the lives of others*. Secondly, our convictions set us *off*, sending us away from others as the momentum of our convictions, if we have but the courage, carry us off. (Most of us don't have the requisite parrhesia, recognizing how alienating it might be if one followed the conclusions of one's beliefs: i.e., believing one's grandchildren complicit in something like Treblinka.) Such setting off cannot help but puzzle about the world in which one finds oneself, "What kind of house is this?" The burden of one's convictions strains under the weight: Why can't I come to terms with it?

These are some of the questions raised by vegetarianism. Not simply the question about whether or not one eats animals, but more precisely how one holds one's beliefs about animals in a world where lots of people eat animals. Most have tired of animal advocates who pit animals against people. This will simply not do in making a case for animals. But the benefit of those kinds of certainties is a consistency Elizabeth surely lacks. She finds herself unable to at once hate the ways meat is produced and hate the people who enable that production. Safran Foer I think recognizes this tension and hence waxes poetically about family meals and traditions, yet at the end of the day, wants it both ways, convictions without the estranging effects. Elizabeth recognizes she can't have it both ways and hence wonders about the house she has made for herself, weeping all the while her son ominously assures her, "It will soon be over."

Immediately following the lecture in which she asks the audience to imagine the being of a bat and compares factory farming to the Holocaust, Elizabeth has the following conversation with the lectures' host, university president Garrard.

> "But your own vegetarianism, Mrs. Costello," says President Garrard, pouring oil on troubled waters: "it comes out of moral conviction, does it not?"
>
> "No, I don't think so," says his mother, "It comes out of a desire to save my soul."
>
> Now there truly is a silence, broken only by the clink of plates as the waitresses set baked Alaskas before them.
>
> "Well, I have a great respect for it," says Garrard. "As a way of life."
>
> "I'm wearing leather shoes," says his mother. "I'm carrying a leather purse. I wouldn't have overmuch respect if I were you."
>
> "Consistency," murmurs Garrard. "Consistency is the hobgoblin of small minds. Surely one can draw a distinction between eating meat and wearing leather."
>
> "Degrees of obscenity."[33]

Self-Care: The Case of Animals

Elizabeth's convictions not only alienate her from others but moreover from herself. It is this alienation that begins to trace the difficulty with which we carry moral commitments, commitment to animal welfare being one among many. When Safran Foer recommends vegetarianism as *the* way forward, he might do well to qualify such recommendations: "Don't have overmuch respect" because the inconsistencies that need to be ignored for our moral commitments to hold much weight in the context of Empire are multiple. Again, this is not to diminish the reality that our moral actions, as well as immoral ones, have good, and bad, consequences; yet, amidst the contingencies that constitute our lives, what Hannah Arendt aptly named "plurality" in the world of action, we had best be careful with our certainties, or at least carry them with the irony I have spoken of.[34] Elizabeth recognizes the caprice by which we hold our most profound, trusted, and certain convictions in shallow, unfamiliar, and warped ways, at once delivering a diatribe about how meat consumption makes us complicit in something as horrifying as the Holocaust while outfitted in the latest animal products. These are paradoxes we are not consistently able to avoid. This doesn't mean we quit trying (especially in the way President Garrard conveniently allows). It does mean our moral efforts will be undertaken within a world where relations with others greatly complicate the matter, that any good to be had will be had in the company of others, not elsewhere (this is what I take to be Foucault's great lesson). Safran Foer and Elizabeth are both sure that vegetarianism is preferable to eating meat. Both consider factory farming morally indefensible. And both offer lives that are, in contrast to the moral problems of factory farming, morally praiseworthy (at least President Garrard thinks so of Elizabeth and I do of Safran Foer). But whereas Safran Foer concludes with an unapologetic endorsement of vegetarianism, Elizabeth can only apologize for herself. This is an important difference, one that needs to be considered even while ruminating over their respective admonitions regarding vegetarianism. The problem here is not just the problem of eating animals or wearing leather shoes, but the problem of *not* eating animals *and* wearing leather shoes, of overmuch respect for unrespectable things; it is not even just the challenge of an encroaching capitalism that seeks to envelop the world within a panoptic gaze valuated by profitability, but the challenge of coming to terms squarely with that world.

Coming to terms, that is the rub. Elizabeth has come to terms, with her convictions and contradictions, her public and private alienations, and so lacks the words (a writer no less!) to describe the world she lives in. Is this tragic? Only if one presumes that we are supposed to have such words. Maybe this is simply a difficulty that marks us as persons. Undoubtedly there are tragic things about us as people—in this case, that we rely on a manner of suffering in order to be fed. But supposing estrangement itself tragic succumbs to the guilt Martin Heidegger believed incumbent upon persons who fear humanness in the first place.[35] This isn't tragic, but life, what the philosopher Cora Diamond calls "the difficulty of reality" we come to discover in discovering our words fail to capture the terror we often feel, and sometimes create: "the difficulty of reality, the difficulty of human life in its relation to that of animals, of the horror of what we do, and the horror of our blotting it out of our consciousness." In an essay reflecting on "The Lives of Animals" Diamond presses further, claiming that Elizabeth's *use* of the Holocaust demonstrates her own difficulty, an "understanding of our relation to animals [that] seems to throw into shadow the full horror of what we do to each other, as if we could not keep in focus the Holocaust as an image for what we do to animals without losing our ability to see it, and to see what it fully shows us of ourselves. So there is a part of the difficulty of philosophy here that is not seen by Costello: so far as we keep one sort of difficulty in view we seem blocked from seeing another."[36] A difficulty wounds Elizabeth as difficulties scar humanity, intimating how Coetzee's larger comment here speaks to the wounding we suffer in a factory-farming world, a wound commensurate to that borne by animal life for our eating.

I understand Elizabeth's desire to save her soul as commentary on the difficulties that comprise life as we know it within the capitalist logics of late modernity, an attempt to come to terms with its difficulties with as little pretension as one can muster—which we recognize, given her chafed alienation from her own kin, as no easy matter. The desire to save one's own soul bespeaks the attempt to say: "Here I am. I think your inability to imagine yourself into the being of a bat and your ability to eat all kinds of animals repugnant. And I wear leather shoes. The difference between us as persons is at best degrees of obscenity." Elizabeth's desire to save her soul has to do with how apropos it is that our moral convictions recoil upon themselves, going ever deeper, reaching further toward a vanishing horizon of endless humility.[37] It is to admit that the relentlessness of global political economies can be matched only by equally far-reaching, equally dogged moral fortitude. And that it will still not be enough. It will never be moral like we would hope it would be, and even when moral, or more precisely especially when moral, it will often come at the price of alienating those around us, even those we love most. The desire to save one's soul is the desire to be okay with this, to come to terms with it, to get a handle not in the sense that one's self can be handled, but in the sense that we come to see reality. What is the "it" that we become okay with, what is the reality I speak of? It is that we have not the language to know how to speak about our inconsistencies, to know how to think about our violence toward animals and one another as human animals. It is that we have made our relating to animals simply an issue, a topic of books where certain intellectual ratiocinations can be made for and against, where suffering can be deployed as a strategy, "and in so doing reveals the characterization I just offered (of our responsibilities to animals as an 'ethical issue') to be a kind of evasion of a problem that is not so easily disposed of" to quote Cary Wolfe's comments on "The Lives of Animals."[38] This is a far more difficult reality, the much needed and entirely eerie stillness of this disquiet.

4. The Difficulty of Reality

Cora Diamond's "The Difficulty of Reality and the Difficulty of Philosophy" (quoted earlier) continues a conversation within contemporary philosophical skepticism which Stanley Cavell, one of Diamond's subjects and conversations partners in the essay, is at the forefront. For our concerns, Diamond's essay later became the subject of the responses collected in *Philosophy and Animal Life*. Here, I will attempt to convey Diamond's claims in order to deepen my discussion of animals.

Diamond has written previously about animals, herself a practiced vegetarian who has occasionally dealt with philosophical questions of animal welfare through the lens of Wittgenstein.[39] In this essay Diamond takes a bit more of an elliptical approach as she tries to reveal a tendency, present in both our treatment of and speech about animals, she calls "deflection." Diamond believes academic philosophy tends to conflate conceptual difficulties with actual ones. This is not to say that the problems philosophers consider are not real problems; it is not evasion in *this* way. Rather they "characteristically" take real problems, or what they take to be real problems, and, in lieu of treating the subject offer analyses that deflect away; instead of the initial subject, what is dealt with is analytic proxy. Carried by this momentum, the subject matter sometimes becomes simpler, sometimes more complex; either way, *the problem about* the thing replaces *the thing itself* (the allusion to Kant here is intended). Hence, in responding to Diamond John McDowell is in part correct to infer that animals are not directly the "problem" treated in Diamond's essay.[40] However, McDowell is not entirely right because if cruelty to animals as a difficulty of reality is not the point in *some* way then surely Diamond would be committing the very deflection she identifies, making a difficulty of reality only a difficulty of philosophy. Diamond is interested in talking about the difficulties of animal life, especially that kind of animal life that tends to get tripped up by its peculiar mode of animality: "Philosophy characteristically misrepresents both our own reality and that of others, in particular those 'others' who are animals . . . we are moved from the appreciation, or attempt at appreciation, of a difficulty of reality to a philosophical or moral problem apparently in the vicinity." We do this, Diamond surmises, because certain realities (including things we do to animals) overwhelm us: "To attempt to think it is to feel one's thinking come unhinged. Our concepts, our ordinary life with our concepts, pass by this difficulty as if it were not there; the difficulty, if we try to see it, shoulder us out of life, is deadly chilling." Diamond says of philosophy's knack for dealing with animals as "issues" (e.g., "vivisection" or "Do animals have rights?" and so on): "Philosophy knows how to do this. It is hard, all right, but that is what university philosophy departments are for, to enable us to learn how to discuss hard problems, what constitutes a good argument, what is distorted by emotion, when we are making assertions without backing them up ... the hardness *there*, in philosophical argumentation, is *not* the hardness of appreciating or trying to appreciate a difficulty of reality."[41]

Diamond's consternation about deflection presupposes the ability to do better, that humans possess equipment—namely language—that allows them to generatively situate themselves in the world. Diamond's Wittgensteinian sensitivities aid her analysis of animals, and her work there constitutes the flip side of her work here. Human animality issues in part as an aptitude for envisaging the lives of other animals, even bats. Other animals may or may not do this, but for certain they do not do so in the ways humans do; if animals speak language, they do so in ways unrecognizable to our speaking. Other animals, as far as we can tell, don't spend their time conceptualizing human suffering, nor do they utilize those concepts as deflection. Humans, in both their engaged and deflecting moods, are rather extraordinary this way. But Diamond worries that this faculty (call it the metaphysical faculty) can also get us off subject. It can trick us into believing we are talking about *something* when we are only just talking (call this the metaphysical error). By "just" I don't mean to disparage talking, as if getting past the sign to the referent is the point. The problem is not with language, but with us, the way we sometimes use our concepts to avoid rather than meet the world. This is the problem with philosophy, what is called "deflection," the strong proclivity toward inattentiveness regarding things. This proclivity is strong and strong in its consequences, for Elizabeth, Holocaust strong.

These are intuitions for Diamond shared and somewhat bequeathed by Stanley Cavell. Cary Wolfe characterizes the matter for Cavell: "we find ourselves in a position that is not just odd but in fact profoundly unsettling, for philosophy in a fundamental sense then fails precisely insofar as it succeeds. We gain knowledge, but only to lose the world."[42] Wolfe helps us locate Cavell's larger philosophical concern and encounters it, along with Diamond's, loosed from a mass of epistemic anxieties (recall the earlier allusion to Kant):

> These fundamental challenges for (and to) philosophy are sounded by Cavell in his reading of the philosopher most

important to him, Ralph Waldo Emerson, who writes in his most important essay, "Experience": "I take this evanescence and lubricity of all objects, which lets them slip through our fingers then when we clutch hardest, to be the most unhandsome part of our condition." For Cavell, this moment registers the confrontation with skepticism, certainly, but it also voices an understanding of how philosophy must change in the wake of that confrontation: For the "unhandsome" here names not just the Kantian *Ding as sich* but also, Cavell writes, "What happens when we seek to deny the stand-offishness of objects by clutching at them; which is to say, when we conceive thinking, say the application of concepts in judgments, as grasping something." When we engage in that sort of "deflection," we only deepen the abyss—*"when we clutch hardest"*—between our thinking and the world we want to understand. The opposite of clutching, on the other hand, what Cavell will call "the most handsome part of our condition"—is facing the fact that "the demand for unity in our judgments, that our deployment of concepts, is not the expression of the conditionedness or limitation of our humanness but of the human effort to escape our humanness."[43]

This slippery-when-clutched feature sometimes finds expression in painful discoveries: "one is in a certain sense alone, profoundly unknowable by others."[44] If estrangement is indigenous to those who share language, then—and here is how Diamond's essay *is* about animals—it is doubly present in our relations with those with whom we share no language. Diamond and Cavell reveal our lives with animals as ineluctably tragic—cruelty to animals across the divide of non-language—in a way that our linguistic lives with one another is only accidentally so. In other words, tragedy obtains not due to language but when no common world is gathered by language.

Yet tragedy also subtends the moral force of Diamond's and Cavell's skepticism (the ability that Diamond's lament presupposes): animals do not share linguistic worlds with us; they have lives of their own. Minding the distance between humans engenders the regard necessary for noticing the many differences between humans and animals. Our faculties serve us exactly here, if not atrophied by neglect (capitalism is shitty this way). Even though, or better still, *because* we do not share linguistic worlds with animals, language beckons us to see animal life (e.g., the being of a bat), if only to see difference, to honor separateness. Difference held together by similarity; similarity opened up by difference.[45] These critical differences and similarities are most readily discovered amidst companionship, sharing already a common life. Alasdair MacIntyre thinks that for certain species of non-human animals, the shared task of living toward common ends (even ones as limited as survival) requires dependent forms of life strikingly similar, in his view, to human animals.[46] For Christians, commonality is similarly drawn from ends but those which encompass human *and* non-human animals alike—namely those ends conveyed within the story Christians call "Creation" (e.g., Rev. 5.13). Relating to creatures (including eating them) without acknowledging this story or the company it describes grossly distorts the modes of participation the story envisions. It is this type of common life that locked turkey farms avoid, and indeed prohibit. How might we be companions to the animals we eat? It might look like living with them, and possibly even walking with them in their dying. If we have to eat animals, perhaps we might participate in their lives, including those parts of their lives that end in slaughter.[47] Companionship at such times and places may just yet grant us acknowledgment that our eating them means a critical distance between their dying and our enjoyment, their dying for our enjoyment.

5. Seeing

Recall earlier my distinction between virtuous and vicious readers of *Eating Animals*. Some will be disturbed by what we do to animals, disturbed to the point of reconsideration. Others won't be bothered, their enjoyment unaffected by suffering. I speculated the former Safran Foer's target audience, the latter (shitty as they are) not worth his time. I also said that listing the latter as "shitty" was not to dismiss them but only the likeliness that they would be impressed by vivid accounts of animals suffering like those offered in spades by Safran Foer. The issue is one of seeing.[48] *Eating Animals* presumes a ready disposition to seeing things as Safran Foer does, bothered to the point of change by inordinate suffering. The book does not (or at least it should not) think it can convince everyone, not because it lacks sufficient evidence but just because conviction relies on first seeing, then knowing, or seeing and knowing as mutually informing. We know as we see. Or as Wittgenstein famously quipped, the world of a happy man is different than that of a sad man.[49] Happy people see the world as such, know it uniquely, understand it eventualities accordingly, happily versus sadly. Virtuous readers will pick up quickly on Safran Foer's message, even if they don't go all the way with it. Vicious readers won't get that far. For them, little is at stake because they simply do not see anything at stake. Capitalism produces this shittiness, as it inculcates a way of seeing. Return to my prior point for a moment. I said that recognizing the slippages that attend human language might sharpen our ability to see critical differences between humans and animals (including difficult realities like our killing them for meat). Seeing one aids seeing the other. (Yet again why a zero-sum analysis that pits human welfare against animal welfare won't do.) Capitalism does not encourage this kind of seeing. Indeed, it encourages the opposite. For capitalism, there is nothing other to see. It does not want to believe that anything has a life of its own, convinced that any distance can be closed, any thing possessed. It does not honor borders or boundaries, difference or independence.[50] It seeks to make everything its own (or someone's own). Colonizing everything, it is no respecter of mystery, believing everything belongs to the market. It clutches hardest.

Yet clutching, according to Cavell's Emerson, fails at capturing everything. Something escapes. As reviewed in Chapter 4, Heidegger labeled this "standing-reserve" (*Bestand*): our machinations toward damming the Rhine (the attempt to render it only *Bestand*) cannot hold it; moreness (*Bestand*) remains and surges forth.[51] But comportment to moreness, "the standoffishness of objects" as Cavell puts it, requires a particular kind of seeing. Consider turkeys. Ian Hacking brings up *M. gallopavo*, or the unnamed turkey we regularly eat. Hacking informs us that the breeding of this particular species has been so overdone that these birds can no longer survive on their own, their grotesque hormone-engorged bodies too massive for mating. In this case, these animals literally have no lives of their own; they exist solely for (and are sustained by) human use. How do we *see* this state of affairs? Rather than being troubled, might some marvel at this innovation of modern agricultural technology, an animal manufactured exactly to the specifications of American dietary needs? Must we be bothered?[52] What encourages us to look behind the doors Safran Foer unlocks, and upon looking *see* there something worthy of compassion and not, as profound on some registers, the genius of the factory farm? Might compassion speak to *Bestand*'s plentitude; might *M. gallapavo* self-show in excess of what's been made of her?[53]

Elsewhere, Diamond writes, "The capacity to respond to injustice depends, not on the category to work out what is fair, but on the capacity really to see, really to take in, what it is for a human being to be harmed. This is not easy for us; it requires a recognition of our own vulnerability, and there are no comparable demands on us in thinking about deprivations of rights."[54] Diamond's intimation of the vulnerable nature of moral judgments touches on the allure of animal rights language. Rights say, "Regardless of how you see, this is what you will do." Rights are universal this way. At least they are for Peter Singer who advances a version of his teacher R. M. Hare's preference utilitarianism (in short, a utilitarianism appropriated to Kant's concept of duty, permitting *hypothetical* imperatives) I mentioned earlier.[55] If human rights are universally binding regardless of one's way of seeing humans, the primary work to be done is to show how animals are similar to humans, or at least similar in terms of warranting rights; the demonstration of equality requires, based on an assessment of fairness, the associated moral respect. According to this argument human rights legitimizes animal rights and one cannot trample on animal rights without also trampling on at least the notion of human rights.

In "Eating Meat and Eating People" Diamond shows confused (and corrupt) Singer's case, which she characterizes as "the obtuseness of the normal arguments."[56] This approach, Diamond writes, "makes it hard to see what is important *either* in our relationship with other human beings *or* in our relationship with animals."[57] Such delineations are attracted to metaphysical legitimation largely because of an anxiety about the provincial and even provisional nature of moral judgment which Diamond readily acknowledges: "In the case of the difference between animals and people, it is clear that we form the idea of this difference, create the concept of the difference."[58] This explains her attraction to Elizabeth Costello, who rather than fleeing to the self-legitimating realm of rights portrays her arguments about animals as bearing a wound. For Diamond, appeals to "an abstract principle of equality" that seeks to skirt the critical difference between humans and animals undermine the ground that grants that difference moral traction: "if we appeal to people to prevent suffering, and we, in our appeal, try to obliterate the distinction between human beings and animals . . . there is no footing left from which to tell us what we ought to do . . . moral expectations of other human beings demand something of me as other than an animal," and the conclusion to this line of thought is critical: "we [*as* humans] do something like imaginatively read into animals something like such expectations when we think of vegetarianism as enabling us to meet a cow's eyes."[59]

Responding to Diamond, Cavell states:

> In an essay from 1978, which she entitles "Eating Meat and Eating People", Cora Diamond identifies herself as a vegetarian and specifies her motive in writing about the question "How might I go about showing someone that he had reason not to eat animals?" as that of attacking the arguments and not the perceptions of philosophers who express the sense of "the awful and unshakable callousness and unrelentingness with which we most often confront the non-human world?" The arguments, familiarly in terms of animal rights, she finds not just too weak, but the impulse to argument at this level to be itself morally suspicious. I have I think felt this way when, in response to my expressing doubt that there are moral truths for whose certainty moral theory should undertake to provide proofs, philosophers more than once have proposed "It is wrong to torture children" as a certain truth to which moral theory has the responsibility of providing an argument, and at least one philosopher added: an argument strong enough to

convince Hitler. In *The Claim of Reason* I reply to this train of thought by saying that morality is not meant to check the conduct of monsters.[60]

In *The Claim of Reason*, Cavell problematized naturally causal relationships between criterion and judgments, maintaining instead that what counts as criteria for the certainty of judgments grow out of the rough and tumble world where disagreements come to matter in the first place.[61] As Diamond and Cavell have learned from Wittgenstein, one cannot argue with monsters just as one cannot talk to lions; as different as the world of a happy man from the world of an unhappy man is "the awful and unshakable callousness and unrelentingness" of meat eating from those who cannot imagine doing so.[62] One can question oneself and others about eating habits, but it will not work to oblige "the impulse to argument" beyond the terms provided by those habits. This gets at what I understand Cavell to be hinting at in admitting, "I have sometimes felt vegetarianism to be a way of declaring a questionable distance from the human animal," that imposing the moral obligation of vegetarianism on meat eaters too often ensues as a denial of their biographies and hence shared humanity.[63] At its best, *Eating Animals* tries to enjoin the biographies of its readers to its author's, hoping that virtuous readers might come to find distasteful factory farming; at its weakest, when it has given up on that more difficult endeavor, it reverts to moral injunctions about suffering.

6. Companionship with Animals: Eucharistic Seeing

In *The Claim of Reason*, Cavell writes, "those capable of the deepest personal confession (Augustine, Luther, Rousseau, Thoreau, Kierkegaard, Tolstoy, Freud) were most convinced they were speaking from the most hidden knowledge of others." Cavell opposes confession with contemporary analytic philosophy which "fails to take this gap seriously as a real, a practical problem. It has either filled it with God or bridged it with universals which insure the mind's collusion with the world; or else it has denied, on theoretical grounds, that it *could* be filled or bridged at all." For Cavell, realism and idealism spring from the same moral deficit, though in different directions. The certainty of or against knowledge of the world "originates in an attempt, or wish, to escape (to remain a 'stranger' to, 'alienated' from) those shared forms of life, to give up the responsibility of their maintenance."[64] By confession, Cavell means knowledge of the world that refuses to trade on certainty in its various forms. In his book about Cavell, Peter Dula observes that while Cavell's work is neither explicitly Christian nor is his philosophy theological in any straightforward manner, it is curious that in admonishing confession, most of those he invokes understood themselves to be Christians of some sort.[65] While I suspect it is unclear what is meant by Cavell's passing references, I would like to conclude with Eucharistic confessions of divine presence and absence that are "companionable" in ways witnessed in Diamond and Cavell.

For Diamond, companionship makes thinkable the "difficulty of reality," helping us see how beauty like horror often escapes our understanding, even our language: "In the case of our relationships with animals, a sense of this difficulty may involve not only the kinds of horror felt by Elizabeth Costello in Coetzee's lectures, but also and equally a sense of astonishment and incomprehension that there should be beings so like us, so unlike us, so astonishingly capable of being companions of ours and so unfathomably distant. A sense of its being impossible that we should go and *eat* them may go with feeling how powerfully strange it is that they should be capable of incomparable beauty and delicacy and terrible ferocity; that some among them should be so mind-bogglingly weird or repulsive in their forms or in their lives."[66] In order to get to this kind of life with animals, Diamond borrows Cavell's notion of "exposure": "Our 'exposure' in the case of animals lies in there being nothing but our own responsibility, our own making the best of it. We are not . . . in what we might take to be the 'ideal' position. We want to be able to see that, given what animals are, and given also our properties, what we are like . . . there are general principles that establish the moral significance of their suffering compared to ours, and we could then see what treatment of them was and what was not morally justified. We would be *given* the presence or absence of moral community (or thus-and-such degree or kind of moral community) with animals. But we are

Self-Care: The Case of Animals

exposed—that is, we are thrown into finding something we can live with, and it may at best be a bitter-tasting compromise."[67] Diamond contrasts exposure with the kinds of evasions characteristic of philosophy's disavowals of this very thing, chasing after rationales that follow on the order of "because": "because animals are this kind of being, or because they are that kind of being, thus-and-such is their standing for our moral thought." These deflections are what Diamond thinks Cavell helps us out of, "the desire for something better than what we are condemned to (as the kind of animals we are."[68]

My attraction to Foucault like my attraction to Cavell and Diamond and both as readers of the later Wittgenstein are the ways they see the world, or at least speak about seeing the world. Hence, Cavell's "ordinary language philosophy" intimates a kind of activity, a sort of attention and attunement. The problem with certain modes of philosophy for Cavell and Diamond is the attempt to evade reality while working on reality. In an early essay Cavell attests, "For Wittgenstein, philosophy comes to grief not in denying what we all know to be true, but in its effort to escape those human forms of life which alone provide the coherence of our expression."[69] For certain, there is no one way of seeing the world. Clearly, there are many, just are there are many ways of eating. Factory farming is one, Safran Foer's vegetarianism another. I am less concerned here with any one way of seeing the world than with *ways* of seeing that grant us the kind of attention Cavell admonishes and what Connolly called "concentrating on how otherness appears when it is presented" and what I believe to be at the heart of the church's liturgical life.

Capitalism is "shitty" in that it inculcates a way of seeing the world, namely the world as commodity. The unfortunate reality for animals is that the invisible hand of the market remains necessarily blind to animal life in its own right; when productivity hogs the show, the being of a bat simply doesn't warrant consideration. It trains the opposite of seeing in the Cavellian sense; instead of imagining animal life, we can only eat them, and eat them in ways that render them unavailable to us as what Cavell names companions and Christians name creatures.[70]

In contrast, I have been concerned in this chapter with speaking of companionship akin to a distinction that Richard Sorabji makes that gets at what I understand as a biblical conception of animals as fellow creatures: they belong *with* but not *to* us.[71] Animals as fellow creatures belong with us in our creaturely lives; they do not, however, belong to us; they are not, as Diamond says, simply "props in our show."[72] As Diamond and Cavell offer ordinary language philosophy and Foucault offers self-care, the church offers a liturgy where animals might be made available by seeing, akin to Diamond looking into the eye of a cow or Elizabeth into the being of a bat or Connolly "concentrating on how otherness appears when it is presented." For Christians, this seeing is learned through the sacramental liturgy of the church. It is critical to remember that the church's sacramental liturgy does not, as Foucault sometimes thought, get us to another world; rightly stated, the sacraments get us more fully into *this* world, mining its depths and tasting its plentitude. Sacraments are exposure as Diamond says and witness as I have been saying. The sacramental vision I speak of is Christological as such, and hence can only itself be received in the elements as an already but not yet realization of the eschatological seeing of creation.[73] This is different than requiring that animals possess rights-bearing status because God created them. Rather, it is to say that we do not completely know what status animals bear; that is yet to be seen, which is why a certain kind of attention is needed (and why imposing rights becomes alluring).[74] Ben Quash writes,

> When Christians don't know what a thing is, or what to do with it, they go back to where it figures in the Eucharist to find out. In this case, contra the Manicheans, they learn that because of God's direct and loving relationship to his creation, both human and non-human, and because Christ is present by the power of the Spirit in the communion of all created things, they just have the same sort of hope for it as they have for themselves.[75]

The church has been given pictures of a reconciled creation, where animals no longer eat animals, evident in passages like Gen. 1.19, Isa. 11.6–9, Rom. 8.19–21 and Rev. 5.13–14. The narrative structure of Christian theology (its unavoidably telic orientation) tells us that we interpret the beginning in terms of the end, what it was in the beginning by what it will be fulfilled and this story as recounted in the liturgy. Moreover, Stephen H. Webb believes that Christians learn how to eat at the one meal that orders their lives, the Eucharist. For Webb, it is no accident that while the invocation speaks of Christ's body and blood, it is a vegetarian meal, as if to say the one given body of Christ *is* the final animal sacrifice, the bread and wine themselves proleptically anticipating the restoration of God's created order: we have been once and for all nourished by flesh; we are now nourished by bread and wine. A bloodless meal follows Christ's bloodied body, as if to say, "It is finished."[76] Webb writes, "Think about how inappropriate it would be to receive meat with the wine ..." poignantly highlighting the incongruity of a killed animal on the occasion inaugurating the peacable kingdom.[77] The completion of sacrifice ends the requirement of sacrifice and restores creation to its edenic state, where animals were not eaten and yet creation named good and exceedingly provided for. This meal orders, or *should* order, Christian eating; how Christians eat meat here (in a way that they need no longer eat meat) ought to imaginatively shape their eating habits elsewhere.[78]

The already but not yet realities of creation unfold, or more precisely, are held in tension in the presence of Christ in the elements, signifying an absence that is yet to be filled by Christ's final coming. Until then, the Eucharist marks the already present reality of God in the world, and the not yet fulfillment of that presence—both a presence and an absence, presence as a placeholder for absence *and* a future presence. Denys Turner develops this line of thought:

> The Eucharist is not yet the kingdom of the future as it will be in the future. It points to it *as absent*, not because, as a sign, it is in the nature of signs to signify in the absence of the signified, but because by means of the Father's action this human sign of eating and drinking acquires a depth, an "inwardness" of meaning which realises the whole nature of our historical condition: what, in its essential brokenness, the Eucharist haltingly and provisionally signifies, can be fully realised only by its abolition in the kingdom itself. The Eucharistic sign thus caught up in this eschatological

two-sidedness becomes thereby and necessarily a two-sided sign: it is affirmation interpenetrated by negation, presence interpenetrated by absence: *that* is what is made "real" in the Eucharist.[79]

And so the presence/absence of God in the elements conditions a way of seeing: *watching* for God in creation. We are exposed here. Again, my argument is not one of moral status; the presence of God is not meant to consign moral value to animals. Rather, it is the opposite; it is to envision the entire creation as an abiding landscape of divine mystery, where God's presence does not guarantee moral status but rather blunts the presumption of status as anything *we* can bestow on things. All thing are God's and are returning to God. We cannot presume to name things except as God's. Creation subsists as the altar of God's presence and absence and while God is not present in creation in the same ways God is in the bread and the wine, receiving and consuming the bread and wine cultivate seeing creation within these tensions and expectations. What is needed is a kind of patient looking in order to see God. Since God can be so present *in* the elements (can be present in creaturely things) this looking is a looking *for*, a patient expectation that God will arrive and so imagining the beings of creatures as theophanies of this arrival. This attunes one to the world and its powers in a tension-filled way, where the expectation of epiphany expresses itself as desire, longing for that which will come, looking for that which has already come. None of this requires vegetarianism but it does summon certain kinds of seeing.

Within this Eucharistic way of seeing, it is possible to fashion an account of companionship that involves eating animals beyond the capitalist terms of possession and the like. What will be harder, given the prevailing investitures of capitalism (e.g., 99 percent of all meat comes from factory farms), is gaining access to relations with animals that makes good on this way of seeing. The art of self-care then may include refraining from meat because one refuses inculcation into cultural habits that steal one's soul toward seeing animals as just things to eat. I imagine these determinations can only be made provincially and rather provisionally, negotiated according to the resources immediately available that make possible styles for being in the world. As Hardt and Negri suggest,

Self-Care: The Case of Animals

"We can pursue a line of flight while staying right here, by transforming the relations of production and mode of social organization under which we live."[80] Saving one's soul involves this attentive work, rigorous resistance else one's soul gets consumed. This locality is always the case anyhow with sacramental power; they are always performed in this place at this time with these elements given by God's providential ordering. One learns such things by regular attendance and attention, an ordering of the world that reveals it as God's.

Postscript

In the late 1970s Michel Foucault put his considerable influence behind the Iranian revolution that eventually established the totalitarian Islamicist regime of the Ayatollah Khomeini. Writing for *Corriere della Sera* and *Le Nouvel Observateur* Foucault ventured a short jaunt as a news correspondent that included two trips to Iran and even a face-to-face visit with the Ayatollah in Paris. Foucault's public support of the revolution raised the ire of the French intelligentsia especially on the issues of women's liberation and human rights. Foucault's limited and even naïve prognostications regarding the "political spirituality" of Iran's Shi'ite Islam angered many who were proven right when the Ayatollah's victory eventuated in the public execution of homosexuals and the brutal suppression of human rights. Much like the young Hegel's enthusiasm for the French Revolution and Heidegger's for the Nazis Foucault's support of the Ayatollah seemed a tremendous mistake.

Yet how do we interpret this mistake? Is it, as some of his defenders have suggested, only a diversion from his more central politics and writings? Or is it, as others have claimed, internal to the trajectory of Foucault's attempt to find a non-Western modernity? Or, might his efforts here be yet another one of James Miller's so-called limit-experiences with death and subjectivity?[1]

These questions are relevant to the current study insofar as I have argued for a certain appropriation of Foucault toward a Christian version of self-care. In the same way that Foucault found himself fascinated and even seduced by Islamic extremist martyrdom, I have claimed that Christian martyrdom enacts a novel form of subjectivity, self-care by self-giving. As well, I have argued that Foucault found an alternative to modern modes of selfhood in ancient Christian selfhood, even while recognizing how Christianity played a central role in instituting control, discipline, and normalization. If, as I have suggested, Foucault found "a new kind of self" within the same Christianity that produced the disciplined self, then need I also endorse Foucault's turn to extremist Islam?

These are important questions and ones I am hardly qualified to answer being that I am no expert on Islam, Iran, or the Iranian Revolution. I do want to problematize the depiction of "extremist" religion given how such descriptions are politically hedged. As well, I want to make two dissociations. First, I want to distinguish between Iran and Iran's human rights violations. Especially, I would want to search every community for resources that help persons, especially women, minorities, and so-called deviants, flourish. I may not find much to be praised in the Ayatollah's Iran, but also want steer clear of the prejudice that nothing of value can be found. Second, I want to make sure our reading of Foucault's interpretation of that particular stripe of Shi'ite Islam is not indicative of Islam as such. And here I see in Foucault during this period a consistency that remains throughout his long career of political activism and writing. Namely, Foucault refused to believe the condemned were as demonic as the condemnation asserted. Foucault's activism concerned itself with the demonized and his intellectual thought concerned itself with the process of demonization; in both cases, Foucault found demonizing to say more about those doing the condemning than the condemned. In other words, Foucault was amazingly wrong about the Iranian revolution but his suspicions were spot on. Most importantly, he was quite right to seek after any available lights in his long search for modes of human subjectivity that might help us think our way out of the present. For Foucault this frequently meant turning to the demonized: the mad, the deformed, the disordered, the over-sexed, the self-flagellating, the sadomasochistic, so on and so forth. The fact that the liberal French intelligentsia sought to demonize him for the path his search had taken him tells us more about them than Foucault, who had at least remained consistent in his suspicions, brilliance, and naiveté.

My guess is that to the extent that I espouse a self-giving version of Christian discipleship, liberal humanists will find less troubling my particular vision of the church. This has to do with what liberals might suppose to be a Christianity easily fitted to secular humanism, as the Christianity I have offered in this book may sound less threatening than the Ayatollah's Islam. But this can only be so by drastically underestimating the ways I believe Christianity, and its accounts of freedom, personhood, and witness, offers not only an alternative but an end to capitalism's dominance, and hence an undermining of the social orders of humanism. Another way of saying this is to say that secular humanism's remarkable ability to conscript Foucault into its ranks comes at the cost of underestimating Foucault.

Notes

Introduction

1 James Bernauer, SJ, "Cry of Spirit" in Michel Foucault, *Religion and Culture*, ed. Jeremy R. Carrette (New York: Routledge, 1999), xi–xvii (xvi). Bernauer references the conversation as Document D250 (7) of the Foucault Archive, Paris, 21 April 1983 discussion between M. Foucault, and P. Rabinow, B. Dreyfus, C. Taylor, R. Bellah, M. Jay and L. Lowenthal, 32 pages, 11.

2 For example, see John McSweeney, "Foucault and Theology," *Foucault Studies* 2 (May 2005), 117–44 and Stephen Carr, "Foucault Amongst the Theologians," *Sophia* 40:2 (2001) 31–45. McSweeney offers a helpful survey of three appropriations, the third of which (consisting of the individual and joint work of James Bernauer and Jeremy Carrette) proves most beneficial, McSweeney argues, because it follows on the latest publication of Foucault's work on sexuality and selfhood and hence most forcefully allows Foucault to inform theology on his own terms. McSweeney admits difficulty at times in distinguishing between Bernauer and Carrette, but ultimately finds the contribution of the former situating Foucault toward Christianity in a way that aligns Foucault with "negative theology" and the latter situating Christianity toward Foucault, and hence opening zones of religious experience within political space. Sweetney concludes by turning to the recent work of J. Joyce Schuld and Henrique Pinto. See James Bernauer SJ, *Michel Foucault's Force of Flight: Toward an Ethics of Thought* (Atlantic Highlands: Humanities Press International, 1990); James Bernauer SJ, "The Prisons of Man: An Introduction to Foucault's Negative Theology," *International Philosophical Quarterly* 47:4 (December 1987), 365–80; Jeremy R. Carrette, *Foucault and Religion: Spiritual Corporality and Political Spirituality* (London: Routledge, 1999); Jeremy R. Carrette, "Prologue to a Confesson of the Flesh," in Michel Foucault, *Religion and Culture*, ed. Jeremy R. Carrette (New York: Routledge, 1999), 1–47; James Bernauer SJ and Jeremy R. Carrette, ed., *Michel Foucault and Theology: The Politics of Religious Experience* (Burlington: Ashgate, 2004); J. Joyce Schuld, *Foucault and Augustine: Reconsidering Power and Love* (Notre Dame: University of Notre Dame Press, 2003) and Henrique Pinto, *Foucault, Christianity and Interfaith Dialogue* (New York: Routledge, 2003).

3 Paul Veyne, "Final Foucault and His Ethics," *Critical Inquiry* 20:1 (Autumn, 1993), 1–9 (3).

4 See the documentary "The Possibility of Hope" directed and produced by Alfonso Cuarón, in the DVD *Children of Men* (Universal Pictures, 2006).

Notes

Chapter 1

1. Cf. Michel Foucault, *The Order of Things: An Archaeology of the Human Science* (New York: Vintage, 1994), xv–xxiv.
2. Michel Foucault, "The Political Technology of Individuals," in *Technologies of the Self: A Seminar with Michel Foucault*, ed. Hugh Gutman, Patrick H. Hutton and Luther H. Martin (Amherst: The University of Massachusetts Press, 1988), 145–62 (146).
3. Michel Foucault, "The Ethics of Care for the Self as a Practice of Freedom: An Interview with Michel Foucault on January 20, 1984," in *The Final Foucault*, trans. J. D. Gauthier, SJ, ed. James Bernauer, SJ and David Rasmussen (Cambridge: The MIT Press, 1991), 1–20 (10).
4. Michel Foucault, "Politics and the Study of Discourse," in *The Foucault Effect: Studies in Governmentality with Two Lectures by and Interview with Michel Foucault*, ed. Colin Gordon and Peter Miller and Graham Burchell (Chicago: The University of Chicago Press, 1991), 53–72 (55). Emphasis original.
5. Michel Foucault, *Abnormal: Lectures at the Collège de France 1974–1975*, ed. Arnold I. Davidson, trans. Graham Burchell (New York: Picador, 2003), 323; see also ibid., 1–42; 118–24.
6. Michel Foucault, *The Birth of Biopolitics: Lectures at the Collège de France 1978–1979*, ed. Arnold I. Davidson, trans. Graham Burchell (New York: Picador, 2008), 3.
7. Foucault, "The Ethics of Care for the Self," 11, 12. In a late lecture, Foucault filled out his notion of power as relation: "Power is not a substance. Neither is it a mysterious property whose origin must be delved into. Power is only a certain type of relation between individuals. Such relations are specific, that is, they have nothing to do with exchange, production, communication, even though they combine with them. The characteristic feature of power is that some men can more or less entirely determine other men's conduct— but never exhaustively or coercively. A man who is chained up and beaten is subject to force being exerted over him. Not power. But if he can be induced to speak, when his ultimate recourse could have been to hold his tongue, preferring death, then he has been caused to behave in a certain way. His freedom has been subjected to power. He has been submitted to government. If an individual can remain free, however little his freedom may be, power can subject him to government. There is no power without potential refusal or revolt." Michel Foucault, "*Omnes et Singulatim*: Towards a Criticism of 'Political Reason'" The Tanner Lectures on Human Values, Delivered at Stanford University, October 10 and 16, 1979, 225–54 (253) www.tanner-lectures.utah.edu/lectures/documents/foucault81.pdf.
8. Ibid.
9. Ibid., 11, 12.
10. Rux Martin, "Truth, Power, Self: An Interview with Michel Foucault October 25, 1982," in *Technologies of the Self: A Seminar with Michel Foucault*, ed. Hugh Gutman, Patrick H. Hutton and Luther H. Martin (Amherst: The University of Massachusetts Press, 1988), 9–15 (11).

Notes

11 Rux Martin, "Truth, Power, Self," 15.
12 Michel Foucault, "*Society Must Be Defended*": *Lectures at the Collège de France 1975–1976*, ed. Arnold I. Davidson, trans. David Macey (New York: Picador, 2003), 7.
13 Michel Foucault, *Power/Knowledge: Selected Interviews & Other Writings 1972–1977*, ed. Colin Gordon. (New York: Pantheon, 1980), 72–73.
14 Ibid., 186.
15 Ibid., 102. Foucault writes, "I am well aware that I have never written anything but fictions. I do not mean to say, however, that truth is therefore absent. It seems to me that the possibility exists for fiction to function in truth, for a fictional discourse to induce effects of truth, and for bringing it about that a true discourse engenders or 'manufactures' something that does not as yet exists, that is, 'fictions' it. One 'fictions' history on the basis of a political reality that makes it true, one 'fictions' a politics not yet in existence on the basis of a historical truth" (Ibid., 193). To say that there is little distinction between history and fiction is not to deny history of certain goods, such as truth. Such a view champions history as a methodological uncovering of truth in a way that relegates fiction to the arbitrary, subjective, and power-laden. Rather, history and fiction speak of an author. More importantly, as Foucault's work shows fiction is not devoid of truth claims, the engendering of truths and regimes of truth. Fiction creates imaginary worlds but those images proliferate imaginative ways of interpreting and existing in the world. The distinction between history and fiction is not the distinction between "the real world" and imagination, but between imaginations and the worlds engendered.
16 Ibid., 102. Obviously, given Foucault's nominalist tendencies, "the state" for Foucault has no ontological substance, but rather, like the self, comes to be: "What if the state were nothing more than a way of governing? What if the state were nothing more than a type of governmentality? What if all these relations of power that gradually take shape on the basis of multiple and very diverse processes which gradually coagulate and form an effect, what if these practices of government were precisely the basis on which the state was constituted?" Foucault, *Security, Territory, Population: Lectures at the Collège de France 1977–1978*, ed. Arnold I. Davidson, trans. Graham Burchell (New York: Picador, 2007), 248.
17 Foucault, *Power/Knowledge*, 97.
18 Foucault comments, "if you ask me, 'Does this new technology of power take its historical origin from an identifiable individual or group of individuals who decided to implement it so as to further their interests or facilitate their utilization of the social body?' then I say 'No'. These tactics were invented and organised from the starting points of local conditions and particular needs. They took shape in piecemeal fashion, prior to any class strategy designed to weld them into vast, coherent ensembles. It should also be noted that these ensembles don't consist in a homogenization, but rather of a complex play of supports in mutual engagement, different mechanisms of power which retain all their specific character" (ibid., 159).

Notes

19 Ibid., 142.
20 Ibid., 107.
21 Foucault, *Discipline and Punish: The Birth of the Prison*, trans. Alan Sheridan (New York: Vintage, 1995), 195.
22 Ibid., 195, 196.
23 Ibid., 205.
24 Ibid., 280.
25 Ibid., 201.
26 Ibid., 207, 222.
27 Foucault, *Abnormal*, 48. "It seems to me that essentially there have been only two major modes for the control of individuals in the West: one is the exclusion of lepers and the other is the model of the inclusion of plague victims" (ibid., 44).
28 Foucault, *Discipline and Punish*, 198.
29 Ibid.
30 Ibid., 196.
31 Ibid., 197, 198; 199.
32 Foucault, *Abnormal*, 47; Foucault, *Discipline and Punish*, 200.
33 Ibid., 205.
34 In *The Birth of the Clinic*, Foucault speaks most directly to power's use of medicine as a means of control and production through objective gaze. "The sight/touch/hearing trinity defines a perceptual configuration in which the inaccessible illness is tracked down by markers, gauged in depth, drawn to the surface, and projected virtually on the dispersed organs of the corpse" (The Birth of the Clinic, 141). For Foucault, modernity characteristically involves disciplinarity through biotechnologies implemented by physicians as "priests of the body" (32).
35 Foucault, *Discipline and Punish*, 214.
36 Foucault, *Security, Territory, Population*, 33. Emphasis added.
37 Foucault, "*Society Must Be Defended*," 25.
38 Ibid., 35–36.
39 Foucault, *Security, Territory, Population*, 12.
40 Ibid., 322.
41 Ibid., 173, 180.
42 Foucault, "*Society Must Be Defended*," 245.
43 Foucault, *Security, Territory, Population*, 62–63. "A constant interplay between techniques of power and their object gradually carves out in reality, as a field of reality, population and its specific phenomena. A whole series of objects were made visible forms of knowledge on the basis of the consititution of the population as the correlate of techniques of power. In turn, because these forms of knowledge constantly carve out new objects, the population could be formed, continue, and remain the previledged correlate of modern mechanims of power" (ibid., 79).
44 Foucault, "*Society Must Be Defended*," 36.
45 Michel Foucault, *The History of Sexuality: Volume I An Introduction*, trans. Robert Hurley (New York: Vintage, 1990), 144.

Notes

46 Foucault, "*Society Must Be Defended,*" 62. "Racism is, quite literally, revolutionary discourse in an inverted form" (ibid., 81).
47 Foucault, *The History of Sexuality*, 137.
48 Foucault, "*Society Must Be Defended,*" 52, 190.
49 Foucault understands "liberalism" to be the practice of government that overtook its predecessor political culture—*raison d'État*—by undermining the idea that the state's *raison d'être* can be self-legitimating, but rather must directed by "the internal rule of maximum economy." Foucault, *The Birth of Biopolitics*, 318.
50 Foucault, *The History of Sexuality*, 156.
51 Ibid., 147.
52 MicFoucault, *Security, Territory, Population*, 2.
53 Foucault, *The History of Sexuality*, 86.
54 By emanations, I mean those specific discourses which inculcate and perpetrate certain forms of life. In his essay, "Foucault Revolutionizes History," Paul Veyne shows how Foucault means by discourse more than "what is said" and reads Foucault like the later Wittgenstein, rejecting "dualist muddles" in favor of the interrelation of language and practice. Paul Veyne, "Foucault Revolutionizes History," in *Foucault and His Interlocutors*, ed. Arnold I. Davidson (Chicago: The University of Chicago Press, 1997), 146–82.
55 Foucault, *History of Sexuality*, 6.
56 Ibid., 7.
57 Ibid., 19.
58 Ibid., 97.
59 Ibid., 9.
60 Michel Foucault, *Power/Knowledge: Selected Interviews and Other Writings 1972–1977*, ed. Colon Gordon (New York: Pantheon Press, 1980), 73, 131.
61 Ibid., 11
62 Ibid., 83.
63 Ibid., 82.
64 Ibid., 59.
65 Ibid., 96, 187.
66 Foucault, *History of Sexuality*, 56.
67 Foucault, *Power/Knowledge*, 186.
68 Describing "Panopticism" Foucault writes, "It is polyvalent in its applications; it serves to reform prisoners, but also to treat patients, to instruct schoolchildren, to confine the insane, to supervise workers, to put beggars and idlers to work. It is a type of location of bodies in space, of distribution of individuals in relation to one another, of hierarchical organization, of disposition of centres and channels of power, of definition of the instruments and modes of intervention of power, which can be implemented in hospitals, workshops, schools, prisons." Foucault, *Discipline and Punish*, 205.
69 See Thomas Flynn's "Foucault's mapping of history," in *The Cambridge Companion to Foucault*, ed. Gary Gutting (Cambridge: Cambridge University Press, 1994), 28–46.
70 Foucault, *History of Sexuality*, 93.

Notes

71 Foucault, *Power/Knowledge*, 71.
72 Foucault, *History of Sexuality*, 147.
73 Ibid., 61
74 Foucault, *Power/Knowledge*, 185.
75 Consider Foucault's "The Thought of the Outside" in which Foucault argues interiority/exteriority dichotomies emanate from ontological prioritizations of the subject. Foucault here speaks about a subject-less textuality that brings forth a type of "infinite outside" by way of desire: "reflexive patience, always directed outside itself, and a fiction that cancels itself out in the void where it undoes its forms intersect to form a discourse appearing with no conclusion and no image, with no truth and no theatre, with no proof, no mask, no affirmation, free of any center, unfettered to any native soil; a discourse that constitutes its own space as the outside toward which, and outside of which, it speaks. This discourse, as speech of the outside whose words welcome the outside it addresses, has the openness of a commentary: the repetition of what continually murmurs outside. But this discourse, as a speech that is always outside what it says, is an incessant advance toward that whose absolutely fine-spun light has never received language." Michel Foucault, "The Thought of the Outside," in *Aesthetics, Method, and Epistemology: Essential Works of Foucault 1954–84*, ed. James D. Faubion (New York: The New Press, 1998), 153–54.
76 Foucault, *History of Sexuality*, 108.
77 Ibid.
78 For an account of the self's constitution through modern dialectics of depth and confession, see Romand Coles's *Self/Power/Other: Political Theory and Dialogical Ethics* (Ithaca: Cornell University Press, 1992), 55–64.
79 Michel Foucault, *The Use of Pleasure: The History of Sexuality Volume 2*, trans. Robert Hurley (New York: Vintage, 1990), 6.
80 Foucault, *History of Sexuality*, 92
81 Ibid., 142.
82 Ibid.
83 Ibid., 62.
84 Foucault, *Discipline and Punish*, 148.
85 Foucault, *History of Sexuality*, 86.
86 Foucault deals most directly with the gaze in *The Birth of the Clinic: An Archaeology of Medical Perception*, trans. A. M. Sheridan Smith (New York: Vintage, 1994).
87 Charles Taylor, "Foucault on Freedom and Truth," *Political Theory* 12:2 (May 1984), 152–83 (163).
88 As Taylor characterizes Foucault, "there is no order of human life or way we are or of human nature that one can appeal to in order to judge or evaluate between ways of life," and "This regime-relativity of truth means that we cannot raise the banner of truth against our own regime. There can be no such thing as a truth independent of it, unless it be that of another regime. So that liberation in the name of 'truth' could only be the substitution

Notes

of another system of power for this one," then, "There has to be a place for revolt/resistance aided by unmasking in a position like Foucault's, and he allows for it. But the general relativity thesis will not allow for liberation through a transformation of power relations. Because of relativity, transformation from one regime to another cannot be a gain in truth or freedom" Ibid., 175, 176.

Consider a similar concern raised by Foucault's friend and ally Gilles Deleuze:"if there is a truth of power, it must have as a counterstrategy a kind of power of truth, against powers. Hence the problem of the role of the intellectual in Michel and his manner of reintroducing the category of truth. Since he rejuvenates it completely by making it depend on power, will he find in this rejuvenation a material that can be turned against power? But here I do not see how." Deleuze worries, with a very different posture than Taylor, that Foucault's conflation of truth and heterogeneity appears "to block the exits as much as it opens one up." Gilles Deleuze, "Desire and Pleasure," in *Foucault and His Interlocutors*, trans Daniel W. Smith, ed. Arnold I. Davidson(Chicago:The University of Chicago Press, 1997), 183–92 (188).

89 Taylor,"Foucault on Freedom and Truth," 181.
90 William Connolly, "Taylor, Foucault, and Otherness," *Political Theology* 13:3 (August 1985), 365–76 (372).
91 Ibid. Answering Connolly,Taylor states that Foucault's meta-level arguments are too "obfuscating and issue-foreclosing" such that "Rhetorical hijinks come just where we should be deploying the most responsible arguments." Though he seems to understand Connolly's concerns, he responds to them obliquely by way of reiterating his complaints about Foucault ("confusion defending itself with confusion").The exchange between the two is a striking example of how Nietzsche (vis-à-vis Foucault in this case) proliferated powerful if also often intractable positions, and how in the wake of the questions of identity and difference he helped spawn, we, as Taylor eloquently observes, "lack at present an adequate language." Charles Taylor, "Connolly, Foucault, and Truth," *Political Theory*, 13:3 (August 1985), 377–85 (380, 381, 383, 379). Over the balance of his remarkable career, Taylor has gotten only slightly more attentive to the otherness Connolly thinks witnessed in Foucault. See for example the review of Taylor's celebrated *A Secular Age* (Belnap/Harvard, 2007) by Romand Coles, a former student of Connolly. Stanley Hauerwas and Romand Coles,"'Long Live the Weeds and the Wilderness Yet': Reflections on *A Secular Age*," *Modern Theology* 23:3 (July 2010), 349–63.
92 Michel Foucault,"The Ethics of Care for the Self as a Practice of Freedom: An Interview with Michel Foucault on January 20, 1984," in *The Final Foucault*, trans. J. D. Gauthier, SJ, ed. James Bernauer, SJ and David Rasmussen (Cambridge:The MIT Press, 1991), 1–20 (17).
93 Thomas R. Flynn, "Partially Desacralized Spaces: the Religious Availability of Foucualt'sThought," in *Michel Foucault and Theology:The Politics of Religious Experience*, ed. James Bernauer, SJ and Jeremy R. Carrette (Burlington: Ashgate, 2004), 143–55 (152).

Notes

94 Michel Foucault, "The Political Technology of Individuals," in *Technologies of the Self: A Seminar with Michel Foucault*, ed. Hugh Gutman, Patrick H. Hutton, and Luther H. Martin (Amherst: The University of Massachusetts Press, 1988), 145–62 (163).

95 Taylor mentions reductivists "who don't have much time for my ontology, and who think I belong in the Middle Ages," taking comfort in knowing the same reductivists would disqualify Foucault even faster. Taylor, "Connolly, Foucault, and Truth," 385. See Taylor's discussion of "best account available" in his classic *Sources of the Self: The Making of Modern Identity* (Cambridge: Harvard University Press, 1992).

96 Foucault, "Politics and the Study of Discourse," 65. The Taylor-like question: "Does a mode of thought which introduces discontinuity and the constraints of system into the history of the mind not remove all basis for a progressive political intervention" (ibid., 53).

97 Foucault, "*Society Must Be Defended*," 7.

98 Ibid., 126.

99 Foucault, "Politics and the Study of Discourse," 59.

100 Foucault, "*Society Must Be Defended*," 70.

101 Michel Foucault, *Security, Territory, Population*, 157, 183, 184.

102 Ibid., 193. See also Foucault's discussion of "dissidence" on 200–1.

103 Ibid., 201–2.

104 Ibid., 204–14.

105 Ibid., 204–8. I return to this in some detail in Chapter 4.

106 Ibid., 197, 209.

107 Ibid., 228, 199. Even though Arnold Davidson reads Foucault as offering a "perfectly transparent criticism of the Communist Party" he also relates Foucault's undiminished search for "styles of life" that might approximate such political societies (ibid., 220, *fn*24). See for example Foucault's delineation of counter-conduct as "the formation of communities" over against the pastoral's individuation and its "most radical form" in Foucault's reading of the Protestant Reformation (208–12, 228).

Chapter 2

1 Dani Rodrick in his even appraisal of globalization's benefits and challenges centers his analysis around the statement: "the most serious challenge for the world economy in the years ahead lies in making globalization compatible with domestic and social political stability—or to put it even more directly, in ensuring that international economic integration does not contribute to social *dis*integration." Dani Rodrik, *Has Globalization Gone Too Far?* (Washington, DC: Institute for International Economics, 1997), 2. Rodrick offers fine empirical analysis for why and how disintegration often *does* occur whenever states incur the imported pressures of international economic integration and how government attempts to curb the effects of those pressures (e.g., social security spending and the like) make

Notes

such interventions increasingly difficult (e.g., decreased abilities to tax in order to finance social security spending). Ibid., 55–67. While acknowledging its difficulties, Rodrick, one of globalization's most articulate critics, has no interest in offering an alternative. Instead, he discusses how nation-states might "selectively delink" vis-à-vis institutional "escape clauses" allotted through organizations like the World Trade Organization. How such complexities should be negotiated require creative pragmatic thinking, what he calls "an exciting intellectual challenge" (ibid., 73).

2 Michael Hardt and Antonio Negri, *Empire* (Cambridge: Harvard University Press, 2000), 22.
3 John Milbank, *Theology and Social Theory: Beyond Secular Reason* (Oxford: Blackwell, 1993), 278–325.
4 Michael Hardt and Antonio Negri, "Afterward," in *Evangelicals and Empire: Christian Alternatives to the Political Status Quo,* ed. Bruce Ellis Benson and Peter Goodwin Heltzel (Grand Rapids: Brazos, 2008), 307–14 (311). They respond specficially to Mark Lewis Taylor's "Empire and Transcendence" in the same volume (201–17).
5 Michel Foucault, "Politics and the Study of Discourse," in *The Foucault Effect: Studies in Governmentality with Two Lectures by and Interview with Michel Foucault,* ed. Graham Burchell, Colin Gordon, and Peter Miller (Chicago: The University of Chicago Press, 1991), 53–72 (65).
6 Richard Rorty along with Cornel West, Stanley Hauerwas, and Jeffrey Stout, "Pragmatism and Democracy: Assessing Jeffrey Stout's *Democracy and Tradition*," Jason Springs, ed., *Journal of the American Academy of Religion* 78:2 (June 2010), 413–48 (420).
7 Michael Hardt and Antonio Negri, *Commonwealth* (Cambridge: The Belknap Press of Harvard University Press, 2009), vi.
8 Following Spinoza, they write, "The plane of immanence is the one on which the powers of singularity are realized and the one on which the truth of the new humanity is determined historically, technically, and politically. For this very fact, because there cannot be any external mediation, the singular is presented as the multitude." Hardt and Negri, *Empire*, 73. See also ibid., 78–92.
9 Michel Foucault, *The Birth of Biopolitics: Lectures at the Collège de France 1978–1979,* ed. Arnold I. Davidson, trans. Graham Burchell (New York: Picador, 2008), 3.
10 Hardt and Negri, "Afterward," 313.
11 Ibid.
12 Ibid. Also see Hardt and Negri's discussion of universalism's passage through particularity in Hardt and Negri, *Commonwealth*, 120–21.
13 Hardt and Negri, *Commonwealth*, 317; ibid., xiii.
14 Hardt and Negri, *Empire*, 377.
15 Hardt and Negri, "Afterward," 314.
16 "The Possibility of Hope" directed and produced by Alfonso Cuarón, in the DVD *Children of Men* (Universal Pictures, 2006); Sheldon S. Wolin, *The Presence of the Past: Essays on the State and the Constitution* (Baltimore: The Johns

Notes

Hopkins Press, 1989), 1. For similarities between Wolin and Foucault, see Wendy Brown, "Democracy and Bad Dreams," *Theory & Event* 10:11 (Baltimore: The Johns Hopkins University Press, 2007), http://muse.jhu.edu/journals/theory_and_event/v010/10.1brown02.html. For my extended treatment of Wolin's account of radical democracy, see my *The Vietnam War and Theologies of Memory: Time and Eternity in the Far Country* (Oxford: Wiley-Blackwell, 2010).

17 Hardt and Negri, *Empire*, 332.
18 Martin Albrow offers the following, "There is a sense today of a deep transition taking place, but the diagnoses are products of the older period, either modernity or nothing. For the making of one world has arisen neither out of the progress of reason nor from a single world empire. It is not the triumph of universalism. It has come about when the Modern Project has found its limits in the globe. The result is a fragmentation of modernity and a shape to the world which few anticipated, but is not the end of history." Martin Albrow, *The Global Age: State and Society Beyond Modernity* (Stanford: Stanford University Press, 1997), 77. Albrow's suggestions are significant both because they, like Hardt and Negri, prognosticate a "deep transition" and because in the midst of this transition "taking place" he argues that the diagnostic tools are not sufficient for the task, namely that the hermeneutic lenses utilized by modernity prove to be inadequate to interpret anything but modernity. Modernity, by its nature, finds it difficult, and quite unnecessary, to image something other exactly because its presumptions cannot imagine an other as legitimate. To fully understand what is at stake, one needs to consider the totalizing effects of modernity's discourse of history. Albrow writes, "Modernity is then a nexus of ideas and power sited in institutions, in which the new, the up to date, is associated with the expansion of rationality" (ibid., 26). Inherently, modernity involves temporal claims, situating human being within the context of time and Albrow shows how within modernity the agency of time as a movement is none other than the dialectic materiality of rationality. History "moves forward" as the rationality colonizes ever-new territories, from economies to modes of education to political discourse. Thus, modernity could honestly speak of an "end to history" to the extent that the rationalizing process of history could reach an end in the colonization of everything. Implicit to Albrow's characterization is that modernity held both a vision of what it meant to be human, rational, but also a pogrom for the imperial expansion of that vision of humanness. By its nature, modern rationality both spatially (colonizing) and temporal (teleological) expands. This became the very idea of history, the narrative idea of the West, and the political justification of its destiny.
19 Michael Hardt and Antonio Negri, *Multitude: War and Democracy in the Age of Empire* (New York: The Penguin Press, 2004), 83.
20 Hardt and Negri, *Empire*, 332.
21 Ibid.
22 Ibid., 332–33.

Notes

23 David Harvey, *The Enigma of Capital and the Crises of Capitalism* (New York: Oxford University Press, 2010), 40, 47.
24 Hardt and Negri, *Empire*, 326.
25 Ibid., xii.
26 Ibid., 44. See Hardt and Negri's list of particular grievances: inequitable representation, violations of rights and justice, economic inequality, and biopolitical exploitation. Hardt and Negri, *Multitude*, 270–85.
27 Hardt and Negri, *Empire*, 319.
28 Michel Foucault, *The History of Sexuality: Volume I An Introduction*, trans. Robert Hurley (New York: Vintage, 1990), 62.
29 Hardt and Negri, *Empire*, 309–14.
30 Ibid., 309.
31 Ibid., xii.
32 Ibid., 384.
33 Ibid., 310.
34 Ibid., 334. Also see Hardt and Negri, *Commonwealth*, 281.
35 Hardt and Negri, *Empire*, xv.
36 Consider, "The poverty of the multitude . . . does not refer to its misery or deprivation or even its lack, but instead names a production of social subjectivity that results in a radically plural and open body politic." Hardt and Negri, *Commonwealth*, 38.
37 Michael Hardt and Antonio Negri, *Multitude: War and Democracy in the Age of Empire* (New York: The Penguin Press, 2004), 285.
38 Hardt and Negri, *Empire*, 45. Emphasis original.
39 Hardt and Negri, *Commonwealth*, 176.
40 Ibid., 82. Just before, Hardt and Negri write, "We should not think power as primary and resistance a reaction to it; instead, paradoxical as it may sound, resistance is prior to power" (ibid.). This is not quite right from a Foucauldian perspective which would refuse sequencing that emplots either before the other. Rather, power and resistance come to be simultaneously given power's approximation to relations. Hardt and Negri are correct insofar as they cast power as repressive; power as productive precedes power as inhibiting (See for example Hardt and Negri, *Empire*, 361.) One could not say, however, that resistance precedes power in the basic sense that I discussed in Chapter 2 and return to in Chapter 4, because power like subjectivity is not a substance but a relation.
41 Hardt and Negri, *Multitude*, 94; 151–52.
42 Hardt and Negri, *Empire*, 357.
43 Ibid., 299.
44 Hardt and Negri, *Commonwealth*, 278.
45 Ibid., 230.
46 Ibid., 127.
47 Hardt and Negri, *Multitude*, 99–101.
48 Hardt and Negri, *Empire*, 214.
49 Hardt and Negri, *Commonwealth*, 112.

Notes

50 Hardt and Negri, *Empire*, 361.
51 Hardt and Negri, *Multitude*, 356.
52 Hardt and Negri, *Empire* 362.
53 Ibid., 397.
54 Ibid., 318.
55 Hardt and Negri, *Commonwealth*, 151.
56 Ibid., 169. Emphasis original.
57 Alasdair Macintyre, *After Virtue: A Study in Moral Theory* (Notre Dame: University of Notre Dame Press, 1984), 263.
58 Hardt and Negri, *Commonwealth*, 95.
59 Hardt and Negri, *Empire*, 413. See also their construal of martyrdom as resistance in *Multitude*, 346–47.
60 Hardt and Negri offer their own "war against war" by suggesting that the multitude does not rebut Empire's impositions and injustices in dialectical form, but rather by making use of its production of new forms of life finds other ways beyond violence to respond. Hardt and Negri, *Multitude*, 342–47. In other words, war as response denotes a lack of creativity and remains stuck in a sovereign understanding of authority and power. This does not mean that Hardt and Negri rule out war in principle. They allow something called "defensive violence" and "new weapons" which do not, unlike just wars, require justification. They only rule war out as the multitude's *only* option.

Chapter 3

1 Michel Foucault, *language, counter-memory, practice: selected essays and interviews*, ed. Donald F. Bouchard, trans. Donald F. Bouchard (Ithaca: Cornell University Press, 1977), 118–19. Cf. Michel Foucault, *The Order of Things: An Archaeology of the Human Sciences* (New York: Vintage, 1994), 27.
2 David Macey, *The Lives of Michel Foucault* (London: Hutchinson, 1993), 415. Macey reports that more than anything else, Foucault's frequenting the Saulchoir had to do with convienence and suitability for his research topic.
3 James Miller, *The Passion of Michel Foucault* (New York: Simon & Schuster, 1993).
4 Lynn Hunt, "The Revenge of the Subject/The Return of Experience," *Salmagundi* 97, (Winter 1993), 45–51 (45).
5 David M. Halperin *Saint Foucault: Toward a Gay Hagiography* (New York: Oxford University Press, 1997), 145.
6 "A Symposium on James Miller's *The Passion of Michel Foucault*," *Salmagundi* 97, (Winter 1993), 30–99 (31). This particular quote comes from the first of two comments from Miller in this compendium. James Miller, "Foucault's Politics in Biographical Perspective," *Salmagundi* 97 (Winter 1993), 30–44 (32). Also see Miller, *The Passion of Michel Foucault*, 19–34; 105–22; 251–84.
7 James Miller, "Carnivals of Atrocity: Foucault, Nietzsche, Cruelty," *Political Theory* 18 (1990), 470–91 (470). This article serves as the theoretical

framework for Miller's "limit-experience" (though he does not use that language here) thesis in *The Passion of Michel Foucault* (see 484–85).

8 Ibid., 472.
9 Rüdiger Safranski, *Martin Heidegger: Between Good and Evil* (Cambridge, MA: Harvard University Press, 1998), 220.
10 James Miller, "The Prophet and the Dandy: Philosophy as a Way of Life in Nietzsche and Foucault," *Social Research* 65 (1998), 871–96.
11 Ibid., 876.
12 Michel Foucault, *Ethics: Subjectivity and Truth, Essential Works of Foucault Volume One 1954–1984*, ed. Paul Rabinow, trans. Robert Hurley (New York: The Free Press, 1997), 165, 163.
13 Foucault, *language, counter-memory, practice*, 115.
14 Ibid., 117.
15 Ibid., 53–67
16 Ibid., 116.
17 Miller, "Foucault's Politics in Biographical Perspective," 30.
18 Hunt, "The Revenge of the Subject/The Return of Experience," 46.
19 Ibid.
20 James Miller, "Policing Discourse: A Response to David Halperin," *Salmagundi* 97, (Winter 1993), 94–99 (97).
21 David M. Halperin, "Bringing Out Michel Foucault," *Salmagundi* 97, (Winter 1993), 69–93. Halperin is onto a much more incisive critique when he later concludes, "by so thoroughly personalizing Foucault's thought, Miller in effect depoliticizes it" (ibid., 83). "Bringing Out Michel Foucault" is a shorter version of Halperin's chapter "The Describable Life of Michel Foucault" in his aforementioned *Saint Foucault*, 126–85. Textual citations will be made to the more detailed "The Describable Life of Michel Foucault." In *Saint Foucault*, Halperin wonderfully writes, "I may not have worshipped Foucault [earlier] but I do worship him now. As far as I'm concerned, the guy was a fucking saint" (6). The other contributors of this discussion, philosophers Alasdair McIntyre and Richard Rorty, offer helpful analyses, but ones aimed more at rearticulating their own projects than getting at Miller's (in MacIntyre's case showing the incoherence of capitalist accounts of freedom and the necessity of non-metaphysically—i.e. democratically—derived moral orders in Rorty's case.)
22 Foucault, *language, counter-memory, practice*, 142.
23 Ibid., 144–46.
24 Ibid., 158.
25 Halperin, *Saint Foucault*, 140.
26 Ibid., 147.
27 Ibid., 164. Responding to Halperin, Miller utilizes a clever rhetorical strategy by invoking Foucault's words, following his plea, "Do not ask me who I am" (inscribed beginning this chapter), saying that it is up to Halperin "to see that my political papers are in order." James Miller, "Policing Discourse," 98. Foucault had written, "Do not ask who I am and do not ask me to

remain the same: leave it to our bureaucrats and our police to see that our papers are in order. At least spare us our morality when we write." Foucault, *The Archaeology of Knowledge* (London: Routledge, 2008), 19. While still pining an "accurate" Foucault, Jeremy Carrette offers a much more productive critqiue of Miller's work by showing how Miller mistook not Foucault but Foucault's conception of limit-experiences. See "Prologue to a Confession of the Flesh," in Michel Foucault, *Religion and Culture*, ed. Jeremy R. Carrette (New York: Routledge, 1999), 1–47. John Ransom, *Foucault's Discipline: The Politics of Spirituality* (Durham: Duke University Press, 1997).

28 Paul Veyne, "Final Foucault and His Ethics," *Critical Inquiry*, 20:1 (Autumn, 1993), 1–9 (6).
29 Ibid.
30 Michel Foucault, *The Order of Things: An Archaeology of the Human Sciences* (New York: Vintage, 1994).
31 Ibid., xxii.
32 Ibid., 16.
33 Ibid., xxiii.
34 Ibid., 6.
35 Jürgen Habermas, *The Philosophical Discourse of Modernity: Twelve Lectures*, trans. Frederick Lawrence (Cambridge: The MIT Press, 1987), 260.
36 Foucault, *The Order of Things*, 342.
37 Michel Foucault, *The Hermeneutics of the Subject: Lectures at the Collège de France 1981–1982*, ed. Frédéric Gros, trans. Graham Burchell (New York: Picador, 2005), 26.
38 Michel Foucault, "The Political Technology of Individuals," in *Technologies of the Self: A Seminar with Michel Foucault*, ed. Hugh Gutman, Patrick H. Hutton, and Luther H. Martin (Amherst: The University of Massachusetts Press, 1988), 145–62 (145).
39 Foucault, *The Hermeneutics of the Subject*, 240.
40 Ibid.
41 Ibid., 387.
42 Ibid., xxiii.
43 Ibid., 7.
44 Foucault, *The Archaeology of Knowledge*, 211.
45 James Bernauer, SJ "The Prisons of Man: An Introduction to Foucault's Negative Theology," *International Philosophical Quarterly* 47:4 (December 1987), 365–80 (376–77).
46 For example, Bernauer writes, "It is true that he has no post-humanist or post-modern philosophy to offer his readers . . . Foucault's enterprise is intended to be an effective resistance to humanism, not its replacement" (ibid., 377). Bernauer does shift his attention to Foucault's positive task when he speaks "on the level of action" and turns, as I do in the next chapter, toward Christian confession and submission, rivaling modern man's sovereignty and solidity, as new kinds of selves, including those kinds of selves not regimented through the description "man." Unlike Bernauer however I do not consider this a difference "on the level of action" but rather, simply the

Notes

other side of Foucault's deconstructive project. Bernauer, whose singular contribution to the theological features of Foucault's thought is indicated in this book by my frequent references to his work, has written broadly on Foucault. In his exquisite comprehensive treatment *Michel Foucault's Force of Flight: Toward an Ethics of Thought* (Atlantic Highlands: Humanities Press International, 1990), Bernauer amalgamates the deconstructive with the constructive. Quoting Foucualt, he writes, "If one side of this resitance is to 'refuse what we are,' the other side is to invent, and not discover, who we are by promoting 'new forms of subjectivity" (ibid., 166). Bernauer here quotes from Foucault's essay "The Subject and Power" included in Hubert L. Dreyfus and Paul Rabinow, *Michel Foucault: Beyond Structuralism and Hermeneutics* (Chicago: University of Chicago Press, 1983), 208–28 (212, 216).

47 Halperin, *Saint Foucault*, 136.
48 Rux Martin, "Truth, Power, Self: An Interview with Michel Foucault. October 25, 1982," in *Technologies of the Self: A Seminar with Michel Foucault*, ed. Hugh Gutman, Patrick H. Hutton, and Luther H. Martin (Amherst: The University of Massachusetts Press, 1988), 9. Related in David Macey, *The Lives of Michel Foucault: A Biography* (New York: Pantheon Books, 1993), xiv.
49 Foucault, *The Order of Things*, 5.
50 Ibid., 4–5.
51 Ibid., 6–7.
52 Ibid., 16.
53 Michael Peters, "Writing the Self: Wittgenstein, Confession and Pedagogy," *Journal of Philosophy of Education* 34:2 (2000), 353–68 (357). Thanks to Carole Baker for bringing this fine essay to my attention.
54 Halperin, *Saint Foucault*, 143.
55 Ibid., 153.
56 Ibid., 162.
57 Ibid., 167.
58 David M. Halperin, "Sexual Ethics and Technologies of the Self in Classical Greece," *American Journal of Philosophy* 107 (1986), 274–86 (277). Perhaps in criticizing Miller Halperin had forgotten he had registered the same complaints.
59 Halperin, *Saint Foucault*, 161.
60 Ibid., 146.
61 Ibid., 145.
62 Bernauer speaks of his own experience: "I felt privileged to have encountered a full spiritual presence: yes, the intellectual power which could intimidate at times, but also the emotional presence, a sense of humour, an interest in others, and a deep compassion for people especially those whom life turns into victims." James Bernauer, SJ, "Cry of Spirit," in Michel Foucault, *Religion and Culture*, ed. Jeremy R. Carrette (New York: Routledge, 1999), xi–xvii (xii). Bernauer echoes the version of saintliness I suggest above as continuity between life and thought: "For me 'cry of spirit' alluded to that legendary compassion and the unity of his philosophical life with the

Notes

worldly experience out of which his wisdom came, so different from mere academic brilliance" (ibid.).

63 See for example J. Kameron Carter, *Race: A Theological Account* (Oxford: Oxford University Press, 2008), 257–73. Carter offers an instructive contrast to Halperin's worries by posing the same concerns of biography, autobiography and being named by others in relation to the genre of slave narratives. I am thankful to Jenny Lynn Howell for reminding me of Carter's contribution on this point.

64 In the opening pages of *A Pitch of Philosophy*, Stanley Cavell writes, "there is an internal connection between philosophy and autobiography, that each is a dimension of the other" and "there are events of life that turn its dedication toward philosophy." Stanley Cavell, *A Pitch for Philosophy: Autobiographical Exercises* (Cambridge: Harvard University Press, 1994), vii. Cavell recently returned to these reflections in his autobiography, Stanley Cavell, *Little Did I Know: Exerpts from Memory* (Stanford: Stanford University Press, 2010). Cavell is considered at length in Chapter 5.

65 James William McClendon Jr., *Biography as Theology* (Nashville: Abingdon Press, 1974), 110.

66 Foucault, *The Hermeneutics of the Subject*, 14–19.

67 Reviewing Stanley Hauerwas' biography, Martin Copenhaver writes, "One reason to read this book is that Hauerwas's thought and his person have always been inseparable, and in ways that are not the case with many theologians. In his theological essays, he has always seemed comfortable writing in the first person and making reference to his own life. This is not narcissism as much as it is an invitation to be held accountable: Hauerwas contends that you cannot rightly consider someone's thought apart from that person's life; as he often puts it, 'Only ad hominem arguments are interesting.' Obviously, to write a memoir is to invite just that kind of argument." Martin B. Copenhaver, "Being Hauerwas," *Christian Century* 127:17 (August 2010).

68 Michel Foucault: "Discourse and Truth: The Problematization of Parrhesia" 6 Lectures given by Michel Foucault at the University of California at Berkeley, Oct.–Nov. 1983, Lecture 6 "Concluding Remarks to the Seminar," http://foucault.info/documents/parrhesia/foucault.DT6.conclusion.en.html. Also see Thomas Flynn, "Foucault as Parrhesiast: His Last Course at the Collège de France (1984)," in *The Final Foucault,* James Bernauer SJ and David Rasmussen, ed. (Cambridge: The MIT Press, 1991), 102–18.

69 Michel Foucault: "Discourse and Truth: The Problematization of Parrhesia" 6 Lectures given by Michel Foucault at the University of California at Berkeley, Oct.–Nov. 1983, Lecture 1 "The meaning of the Word 'Parrhesia,'" http://foucault.info/documents/parrhesia/foucault.DT1.wordParrhesia.en.html.

70 Foucault, *The Hermeneutics of the Subject*, 5, 17.

71 Craig Hovey, "Free Christian Speech: Plundering Foucault," *Political Theology* 8:1, 63–81 (70).

72 Ibid., 79. John McSweeney cautions against seamless Christian appropriations of Foucault's parrhesia, especially to the extent that there are elements of

Notes

Christianity that explicitly oppose what Foucault would undoubtedly have considered the very governmentality parrhesia seeks to undermine. John McSweeney, "Foucault and Theology," *Foucault Studies* 2 (May 2005), 117–44 (136–38).

73 Hovey, "Free Christian Speech," 75. Later in the seminar, Foucault says, "In Plato's or Xenophon's portrayals of him, we never see Socrates requiring an examination of conscience or a confession of sins. Here, giving an account of your life, your bios, is also not to give a narrative of the historical events that have taken place in your life, but rather to demonstrate whether you are able to show that there is a relation between the rational discourse, the logos, you are able to use, and the way that you live. Socrates is inquiring into the way that logos gives form to a person's style of life; for he is interested in discovering whether there is a harmonic relation between the two." Michel Foucault: "Discourse and Truth: The Problematization of Parrhesia" 6 Lectures given by Michel Foucault at the University of California at Berkeley, Oct.–Nov. 1983, Lecture 4 "The Practice of Parrhesia," http://foucault.info/documents/parrhesia/foucault.DT4.praticeParrhesia.en.html. Or consider Foucault's dictum gleaned from Deleuze and Guitarri's *Anti-Oedipus*: "the Non-Fascist Life": "Use political practice as an intensifier of thought, and analysis as a multiplier of the forms of domains for the intervention of political action." Gilles Deleuze and Félix Guattari, *Anti-Oedipus: Capitalism and Schizophrenia*, trans. Robert Hurley, Helen R. Lane, and Mark Seem (Minneapolis: University of Minnesota Press, 1983), xiv. Throughout this text, Deleuze and Guattari refer to Foucault, primarily in his early work on madness, as an expert source and so carry forth their argument as if advancing his research.

74 McClendon, *Biography as Theology*, 110.

75 Miller, "The Prophet and the Dandy," 892.

Chapter 4

1 "My objective has been to create a history of the different modes by which, in our culture, human beings are made subjects." Michel Foucault, "Afterword: The Subject and Power," in *Michel Foucault: Beyond Structuralism and Hermeneutics, ed.* Hubert L. Dreyfus and Paul Rabinow (Chicago: University of Chicago Press, 1983), 208–26 (208). See also Todd May's "Foucault's Relationship to Phenomenology," in *The Cambridge Companion to Foucault*, ed. Gary Gutting (Cambridge: Cambridge University Press, 2005), 284–311 (306). May argues that Foucault continued to be led by "who we are and who we might be" despite his own rejection of phenomenology's transcendental subject.

2 Michel Foucault, "About the Beginning of the Hermeneutics of the Self: Two Lectures at Dartmouth," *Political Theory* 21:2 (1993) 198–227 (221) and Michel Foucault, "*Omnes et Singulatim*: Towards a Criticism of 'Political Reason'," The Tanner Lectures on Human Values, Delivered at Stanford

University, October 10 and 16, 1979, 225–54 (227) www.tannerlectures.utah.edu/lectures/documents/foucault81.pdf.

3 Foucault spoke of Islam as similarly able to project a novel subjectivity. Discussing the Iranian revolution which he witnessed first hand, "when I say that they were looking for Islam to change their subjectivity, this is quite compatible with the fact that traditional Islamic practice was already there and already gave them their identity; in this way they had of living the Islamic religion as a revolutionary force, there was something other than the desire to obey the law more faithfully, there was the desire to renew their entire existence by going back to a spiritual experience that they thought they could find within Shi'ite Islam itself." Michel Foucault, "Iran: The Spirit of the World without Spirit," in *Foucault and the Iranian Revolution: Gender and Seductions of Islamism,* ed. Janet Afary and Keven B. Anderson (Chicago: The University of Chicago Press, 2005), 250–60 (255).

4 In "What is an Author?" Foucault argues that the modern conception of "the author" followed the economic development of "property" such that authorship spoke of ownership. Foucault, *language, counter-memory, practice: selected essays and interviews,* ed. Donald F. Bouchard, trans. Donald F. Bouchard (Ithaca: Cornell University Press, 1977), 124–25.

5 Foucault, "About the Beginning of the Hermeneutics of the Self," 204.

6 Michel Foucault, *The History of Sexuality: Volume I An Introduction,* trans. Robert Hurley (New York: Vintage, 1990), 122–23. See also Foucault's comments about "archaeology" in Michel Foucault, *The Archaeology of Knowledge* (London: Routledge, 2008), 146–48; 183–95.

7 See Michel Foucault, "What is Enlightenment," in *The Poltics of Truth,* ed. Sylvere Lotringer, trans. Lysa Hochroth and Catherine Porter (Los Angeles: Semiotext(e), 2007), 97–119; and Michel Foucault, *Power,* ed. James Faubion, trans. Robert Hurley (New York: New Press, 2000), 312.

8 Foucault, "*Omnes et Singulatim,*" 227. Foucault indicates the nature of this surveillance by talking about the imagery of the shepherd and an ominous "constant kindness," and here one sees not only the Hebraic-Christian "pastoral technology" but also how it differs from its predecessors: "The shepherd's role is to ensure the salvation of his flock. The Greeks said also that the deity saved the city; they never stopped declaring that the competent leader is a helmsman warding his ship away from the rocks. But the way the shepherd saves his flock is quite different. It's not only a matter of saving them all, all together, when danger comes nigh. It's a matter of constant, individualised, and final kindness. Constant kindness, for the shepherd ensures his flock's food; every day he attends to their thirst and hunger. The Greek god was asked to provide a fruitful land and abundant crops. He wasn't asked to foster a flock day by day. And individualised kindness, too, for the shepherd sees that all the sheep, each and every one of them, is fed and saved" (ibid., 229). It is the "constant kindness" that makes Christianity apiece with modern state modes of power through relationships that both totalize and individualize. For his fuller discussion of the pastoral's *omnnes et singulatim* dynamics, see Michel Foucault, *Security, Territory, Population:*

Notes

Lectures at the Collège de France 1977–1978, ed. Arnold I. Davidson, trans. Graham Burchell (New York: Picador, 2007), 128.
9 Ibid., 231.
10 For example, see Foucault's appraisal of the Anabaptists during Germany's Peasant Wars, likening them to "great popular movements against feudal lords, against the first cruel formation of bourgeois society, great protests against the all powerful control of the state." "Dialogue between Michel Foucault and Baqir Parham" in Afary and Anderson, *Foucault and the Iranian Revolution*, 183–89 (186).
11 In David Owens' reading, this is what limits Stanley Cavell's project in relation to Foucault, that Cavell, unlike Foucault, traced the best of Christianity within Greek sources and then identified and left behind the Christian appendages. Not surprisingly, Owens reads Foucault squarely in line with Nietzsche without giving account of some of their important differences, including Foucault's unwillingness to read Christianity as monolithically as Nietzsche did. Ultimately the drawback to Owen's otherwise helpful reading is that he reads Cavell, like Foucault, as a Nietzschean without recognizing Cavell's primary interlocutors, Wittgenstein and J. L. Austin. No doubt Nietzsche plays a role but circuitously through Emerson as exemplar of Wittgenstein's and Austin's ordinary language philosophy. David Owen, "Perfectionism, Parrhesia, and the Care of the Self: Foucault and Cavell on Ethics and Politics," in *The Claim to Community*, ed. Andrew Norris (Stanford: Stanford University Press, 2006), 128–55 (140). I relate Foucault and Cavell in greater detail in the next chapter where I return to Owen briefly. Interestingly Arnold I. Davidson, who has done the most to connect Foucault to Pierre Hadot and Cavell dedicated his edited volume on Foucault to Cavell and Hadot. *Foucault and His Interlocutors* (Chicago: The University of Chicago Press, 1997).
12 Friedrich Niezsche, *The Will to Power*, trans. William Kaufman and R. J. Hollingdale (New York: Vintage, 1968), 1038.
13 David Macey reports that the sequence of the sexuality series remained rather "confused" and its actual publication developed in a rather helter-skelter fashion. David Macey, *The Lives of Michel Foucault: A Biography* (New York: Pantheon Books, 1993), 457–58.
14 Foucault avers that for the Classical period the problem related to sex *para physin* (against nature) had less to do with gender than performance: playing the passive role, the penetrated, rather than the penetrator, rendered sex illicit according to a stylization that was interested much less in identities— i.e., heterosexual versus homosexual—than certain enactments e.g., the "feminized" for the Greeks and the "dominated" for the Romans. Michel Foucault, *The Use of Pleasure: The History of Sexuality Volume 2*, trans. Robert Hurley (New York: Vintage Books, 1990), 222; Michel Foucault, *The Care of the Self: The History of Sexuality Volume 3*, trans. Robert Hurley (New York: Vintage Books, 1988), 30. For another account of *para physin* and sexuality see, Eugene F. Rogers Jr., *Sexuality and the Christian Body: Their Way into the Triune God* (Oxford: Blackwell, 1999). Rogers makes two sweeping arguments:

Notes

first, by way of "unnatural" (*para physin*) gentile inclusion, gay and lesbian existence is *not necessarily* morally problematic; second, since "Christian" and "gay" are not mutually exclusive descriptions, as shown in the first argument, then gay sexual desire needs be extended the same modes of sanctification as straight sexual desire, namely the ecclesial vocations of celibacy *and* marriage.

15 Paul Veyne writes, "Foucault never saw an alternative to the Christian ethic in the Greek's sexual ethic, quite the contrary. From one age to another, problems are not similar, any more than is nature or reason. The eternal return is also an eternal departure (he had been fond of this expression of Char's); only successive valorizations exist." Paul Veyne, "Final Foucault and His Ethics," *Critical Inquiry*, 20:1 (Autumn, 1993), 1–9 (2). To trace a history of increasing confinement and hence degradation (or for that matter, increasing countenancing) of freedom from the Greeks to the modern period with Christianity to blame would be to suggest a line of continuity that can only come about through valorization. What we have are ways of speaking about things: "Each valorization of the will to power, or each discursive practice ... is a prisoner of itself, and universal history is woven of nothing but such threads" (ibid., 5).

16 Michel Foucault, "The Ethics of Care for the Self as a Practice of Freedom: An Interview with Michel Foucault on January 20, 1984," trans. J. D. Gauthier, SJ in James Bernauer, SJ and David Rasmussen, ed., *The Final Foucault* (Cambridge: The MIT Press, 1991), 1–20 (7).

17 In contrast to accounts of self-care and parrhesia Foucault takes up Kant's famous *Was ist Aufklärung?* in relation to Kant's larger critical project. Michel Foucault, *The Government of Self and Others: Lectures at the Collège de France 1982–1983*, ed. Arnold I. Davidson, trans. Graham Burchell (New York: Picador, 2010), 6–39. Here Foucault makes it a point to explicitly review Kant's denigration of tutelage and frames his lectures on the topic of "this vitiated relationship between government of self and government of others" (ibid., 30–32).

18 Arnold I. Davidson in "Ethics as Ascetics: Foucault, the History of Ethics, and Ancient Thought" in *The Cambridge Companion to Foucault, ed.* Gary Gutting (Cambridge: Cambridge University Press, 2005), 123–48 (128). Davidson quotes from Foucault, *The Care of the Self*, 41.

19 Michel Foucault, *Power/Knowledge: Selected Interviews & Other Writings 1972–1977*, ed. Colin Gordon (New York: Pantheon, 1980), 193.

20 Paul Veyne reflects, "Ancient wisdom had become personal for him in still another way; during the last eight months of his life, the writing of his two books played the role for him that philosophical writing and the personal journal played in ancient philosophy: that of a work of the self on the self, a self-stylization." Veyne, "Final Foucault and His Ethics," 1–9 (8).

21 Foucault, *The History of Sexuality*, 92–93.

22 Ibid., 83.

23 See the third treatise of *On the Geneaology of Morals: A Polemic*, trans. Douglas Smith (Oxford: Oxford University Press, 2009).

Notes

24 Ibid., 94–97.
25 Michel Foucault, *Discipline and Punish: The Birth of the Prison*, trans. Alan Sheridon (New York:Vintage Books, 1995), 75–77, 80; 195–207.
26 Ibid., 135–69. Foucault, *The History of Sexuality*, 98–102.
27 Foucault, *Discipline and Punish*, 194.
28 Consider Rudi Visker: "Behind the critique on discipline, which is an ordering of the body, but which in the process nevertheless oppresses 'the body itself,' there appears the dream of a sort of primordial spontaneity of a body that does not have to be bridled by any order—a dream that at the same time and the same vigor was always denied and criticized by Foucault." "From Foucault to Heidegger: A One-Way Ticket," in *Foucault and Heidegger: Critical Encounters*, ed. Alan Milchman and Alan Rosenberg (Minneapolis, University of Minnesota Press, 2003), 295–323 (302).Visker queries whether Foucault's notion of "ordering" has a tendency to slip into this dream at times, and suggests Foucault's texts are often working against themselves. On mythic origins, also see Judith Butler, *Gender Trouble: Feminism and the Subersion of Identity* (NewYork: Routledge, 1999).
29 Paul Veyne restated Foucault's genealogical project accordingly. *Comment on ecrit l'histoire* (Paris: Seuil, 1978), 204. Cf. Foucault, "Nietzsche, Genealogy, History," *language, counter-memory, practice*, 139–64.
30 Whether or not Foucault himself ever leaves transcendental subjectivity behind is certainly an open question, especially if we take him as I present him here, in relation to Heidegger. See Johanna Oksala, *Foucault on Freedom* (Cambridge: Cambridge University Press, 2005), 71–78, 187.
31 Foucault, *The History of Sexuality*, 60.
32 Ibid., 101–2.
33 Michel Foucault, *Power/Knowledge*, 62. Foucault, *The History of Sexuality*, 11. Foucault, *The Use of Pleasure*, 6.
34 Foucault, *The History of Sexuality*, 95–96.
35 Ibid., 136.
36 See Philip Kenneson's "come to have a world" in his description of how liturgies form imagination. Philip Kenneson, "Gathering:Worship, Imagination, and Formation," in *The Blackwell Companion to Christian Ethics*, ed. Stanley Hauerwas and Samuel Wells (Oxford: Blackwell Publishers, 2004), 54–67.
37 Foucault, *The Archaeology of Knowledge*, 43.
38 See Foucault's discussion of "a distinctive feature of philosophy as a discourse of modernity and on modernity" in Foucault, *The Government of Self and Others*, 13–14.
39 Andrew Cutrofello, "Exomologesis and Aesthetic Reflection: Foucault's Response to Habermas" in *Michel Foucault and Theology: The Politics of Religious Experience*, ed. James Bernauer SJ and Jeremy R. Carrette (Burlington: Ashgate, 2004), 157–69. Elsewhere, Foucault says critically of Habermas' communicative discourse: "The thought there could be a state of communication which would be such that the games of truth could circulate freely, without obstacles, without constraint and without coercive effects, seems to

me Utopia. It is being blind to the fact that relations of power are not something bad in themselves, from which one must free one's self." Michel Foucault, "The Ethics of Care for the Self as a Practice of Freedom: An Interview with Michel Foucault on January 20, 1984," *The Final Foucault*, 1–20 (18).

40 Chloe Taylor, *The Culture of Confession from Augustine to Foucault: A Genealogy of the "Confessing Animal"* (London: Routledge, 2009), 103.

41 Peter Brooks, *Troubling Confessions: Speaking Guilt in Law & Literature* (Chicago: The University of Chicago Press, 2000), 74, 85.

42 Foucault, *The History of Sexuality*, 70–71, 73.

43 Foucault, *The Archaeology of Knowledge*, 13.

44 Foucault, *The History of Sexuality*, 86–89.

45 In discussing the phenomena of stylization in its illimitable relationship to power, Foucault used the notion of "techniques": "analyzing the experience of sexuality, I became more and more aware that there is in all societies, I think, in all societies wherever they are, another type of technique: techniques which permit individuals to effect, by their own means, a certain number of operations on their own bodies, on their own souls, on their own thoughts, on their own conduct, and this in a manner as to transform themselves, modify themselves, and to attain a certain state of perfection, of happiness, of purity, of supernatural power, and so on. Let us call this kind of techniques a techniques or technology of the self." Foucault, "About the Beginning of the Hermeneutics of the Self," 203.

46 "I have tried to get out from the philosophy of the subject through a genealogy of this subject, by studying the constitution of the subject across history which has led us up to the modern concept of the subject." Ibid., 201.

47 "What is an author," Foucault, *language, counter-memory, practice*, 113–38.

48 Charles Taylor, *Sources of the Self: The Making of Modern Identity* (Cambridge: Harvard University Press, 1992).

49 Foucault states that he did not follow Heidegger's later developments and suggests that he never completely understood *Being and Time*. Michel Foucault, "The Return of Morality," in *Foucault Live: Interviews, 1961–1984*, ed. Sylvere Lotringer, trans. Lysa Hochroth and John Johnson (New York: Semiotext(e): 1996), 465–73 (470).

50 In one of Foucault's final public interviews, he stated, "For me, Heidegger has always been the essential philosopher . . . My whole philosophical development was determined by my reading of Heidegger . . . I have never written anything on Heidegger and I wrote only a small article on Nietzsche; these are nevertheless the two authors I have read the most." Foucault, "The Return of Morality," 470.

51 "In the years that preceded the second war, and even more so after the second war, philosophy in France and I think, in all continental Europe, was dominated by the philosophy of the subject. I mean that philosophy set as its task *par excellence* the foundation of all knowledge and the principle of all signification as stemming from the meaningful subject. The importance

Notes

given to this question of the meaningful subject was of course due to the impact of Husserl—only his *Cartesian Medications* and the *Crisis* were generally known in France—but the centrality of the subject was also tied to an institutional context. For the French university, since philosophy began with Descartes, it could only advance in a Cartesian manner." Foucault, "About the Beginning of the Hermeneutics of the Self," 201.

52 Martin Heidegger, *Being and Time*, trans. Joan Stambaugh (Albany: State University of New York Press, 1996), 40–48; 178–183; 292–308.

53 Hannah Arendt, *The Human Condition* (Chicago: The University of Chicago Press, 1958).

54 Most explicitly in Martin Heidegger, "The Question Concerning Technology," *The Question Concerning Technology and Other Essays*, trans. William Lovitt (New York: Garland Publishing, 1977), 465–73.

55 Heidegger, *Being and Time*, 150–56; 247–58

56 Hannah Arendt, *The Human Condition*.

57 "By denying us the limit of the Limitless, the death of God leads to an experience in which nothing may again announce the exteriority of being, and consequently to an experience which is *interior* and *sovereign*." Foucault, *language, counter-memory, practice*, 32.

58 Heidegger, *Being and Time*, 321–40.

59 In some ways animals are better off for this reason, especially if we remember Nietzsche's peaceful cows in contrast to Bacon's desperate humans. Friedrich Nietzsche, "On the Use and Disadvantages of History for Life," *Untimely Meditations* (Cambridge: Cambridge University Press, 2000), 59–62.

60 Heidegger, *Being and Time*, 272–82. See also Heidegger, *Introduction to Metaphysics*, trans. Gregory Fried and Richard Polt (New Haven: Yale University Press, 2000). See Carol J. White's *Time and Death: Heidegger's Analysis of Finitude*, ed. Mark Ralkowski (Aldershot: Ashgate, 2005) and John Haugeland, "Truth and Finitude: Heidegger's Transcendental Existentialism," in *Heidegger, Authenticity, and Modernity: Essays in Honor of Hubert L. Dreyfus, Volume 1*, ed. Mark Wrathall and Jeff Malpas (Cambridge: MIT Press, 2000).

61 Heidegger, *Being and Time*, 247–66.

62 Ibid., 59–108. See also Heidegger, *Introduction to Metaphysics*.

63 Heidegger, "The Question Concerning Technology."

64 Hannah Arendt, *The Human Condition* and Hannah Arendt, *Between Past and Future: Eight Exercises in Political Thought* (New York: Penguin, 1993). Cf. Foucault, "Self Writing," *Ethics: Subjectivity and Truth*, ed. Paul Rabinow, trans. Robert Hurley (New York: New Press, 2006), 207-22 (211-12).

65 One can trace a similar notion in early Foucault's psychological phenomenology as expressed by his interest in Georges Bataille: "What of us when, having become sobered, we learn what we are? Lost among idlers in the night, where we can only hate the semblance of light coming from their small talk." Foucault, *language, counter-memory, practice*, 41. Quoted from Georges Bataille, *Oeuvres completes* (Paris: Gallimard, 1973), V, 10. And yet in

Notes

the same paper, one can already sense the direction of Foucault's later work in what he calls "the shattering of the philosophical subject" (ibid., 43).
66 Heidegger, *Introduction to Metaphysics*, 15–19.
67 Heidegger, "The Question Concerning Technology," 33. Also see Hubert L. Dreyfus' unpublished "Being and Power: Heidegger and Foucault," http://socrates.berkeley.edu/~hdreyfus/html/paper_being.html.
68 Heidegger, *Being and Time*, 118–22.
69 Arendt, *Human Condition*, 184. Heidegger, *Being and Time*, xx.
70 See Seyla Benhabib, *The Reluctant Modernism of Hannah Arendt* (Oxford: Rowman & Littlefield, 2003), 51–6, 69, 104–17. According to Benhabib, the limitation of Heidegger's thought, the absence of political considerations and his failure to follow his own best insights regarding "*Mitdasein*," can each be explained by Heidegger's emphasis on Aristotle's making (*poiesis*) versus Aristotle's doing (*praxis*), which orients his philosophy much closer to teleological and, surprisingly, Platonic conceptions of being over against, as it was for the more thoroughly Nietzschean Arendt, doing. By prioritizing making as that which is directed toward its products over against doing as action and hence an end unto itself, Heidegger remains wedded to a "two-world metaphysics" without action, which later become hallmarks in Arendt's identity between doing and being and hence her notion of politics as the becoming of self-showing.
71 See Veyne, "Final Foucault and His Ethics," 4–5.
72 Arendt is surely indebted to Heidegger for this observation because Heidegger thought he saw many of the problems plaguing modern life in this nexus. The way Heidegger talked about this problem was by stating that right thinking and living requires a fundamental distinction between being and beings, the ontic and the ontological, *existential* thinking and *existentille* life, things themselves and things. In this way, Heidegger can be situated within what he considered the entirety of the Western metaphysical tradition initiated by Plato and culminating in Immanuel Kant. Within this vision, humanity is forever caught up in a basic division between transcendence and immanence. Difference would be to place on the one side the divine, eternal, unchanging nature of a presence fully present only to itself as the divine, eternal, and unchanging. On the other side sits the creaturely, temporal, and mutable materiality of bodily, animal, and human existence. This fundamental difference between God and humanity implicates all of human life and ethical existence respects this difference to the extent that truth can be mapped back onto it. Kant both intensified and transformed this distinction by speaking the epistemological, ethical, political, and aesthetic realities of it. The distinction for Kant was no longer a distinction about God and the world but rather about the ways and means of human knowing; even to get to judgments about God and the world first required an analytics of human knowing, or as it was for Kant and would become for Foucault, an analytics of finitude. This Kant deemed transcendental subjectivity through the modes of human knowing articulated as a manifold of apperception. Again, this was not driven by religious notions of the ontological difference

Notes

between God and creatures, though no doubt as a Lutheran Pietist something like this was in the back of Kant's mind. The Reformation and its messy history taught Kant and his predecessors not only that such judgments were dangerous but indeed judgments of God required first prolegomenal decisions about whether such judgments were allowable. Hence Kant, like Descartes, made room for faith by first prioritizing the human subject as the object of concern. Cf. Foucault, *language, counter-memory, practice*, 124–25. Foucault argues that while in the pre-modern period a text's place within a tradition gave its author authority, the authority of the texts came to receive authority on its own merits, which could be proven specifically by going against a tradition as a demonstration that the text could think for itself. (126) Still, the difference between transcendence and immanence continued even if Kant renamed them the noumenal and phenomenal; at the heart of his critique is the warning against the attempt to cross this divide. Nietzsche saw a continuous development from Plato to Kant and named Christianity, the tradition that links the Aristotelian notion of *akrateia hedones* to modern-day Europe, "Plato for the people" in the same way that Kant was, according to Nietzsche, only the attempt to recuperate the moral world made possible by God after the death of God, or better yet, the failure to recognize the death of God. Foucault, *The Use of Pleasure*, 43–44. Friedrich Nietzsche, *The Portable Nietzsche*, trans. William Kaufman (xx), 95–96; 124. In relation to how Focualt thinks Plato changed things: "Now Socratic-Platonic erotics is radically different: not only because of the solution it poroposed, but also and especially because it tends to frame the question in very different terms. Knowing the nature of true love will no longer be a matter of answering the question: who must one love and under what conditions can love be honorable both for the beloved and for the lover? Or at least, all these questions will be subordinated to another, primary and fundamental questions: what is love in its very being? ... For Plato, it is not exclusion of the body that characterizes true love in a fundamental way; it is rather that, beyond the apperances of the object, love is a relation to truth" (ibid., 233, 239). And it is from Plato that the Christian conception of the good and evil of sex come to be: "the tradition of thought that stems from Plato was to play an important role which, much later, the problematization of sexual behavior would be reworked in terms of the concupiscent soul and the deciphering of its arcana" (245).

73 Michel Foucault and Ludwig Binswanger, *Dream and Existence*, ed. Keith Hoeller, trans. Forrest Williams and Jacob Needleman (Atlantic Highlands: Humanity Press, 1985).

74 Michel Foucault, *Mental Illness and Psychology*, trans. Alan Sheridan (New York: Harper & Row, 1976), 60, 67. Though he seeks to dispense with an introduction which summarizes *Being and Time*, deeming unnecessary "detouring through a more or less Heideggerean philosophy" as "some initiatory rite" and instead turning his attention to Husserl's *Logical Investigations*, Foucault sounds every bit like Heidegger when he writes, "this basic opposition to any science of human facts of the order of positive knowledge, experimental analysis, and naturalistic reflection does not refer anthropology

to some a priori form of philosophical speculation. The theme of inquiry is the human 'fact,' if one understands by 'fact,' not some objective sector of a natural universe, but the real content of an existence which is living itself and is experiencing itself, which recognizes itself or loses itself, in a world that is at once the plenitude of its own project and the 'element' of its situation" (ibid., 33, 32). In the essay "Truth and Power," Foucault explains both what draws him to phenomenology and what he leads him beyond it, but again, as I suggest here, this doesn't mean that he leaves Heidegger's phenomenology behind as much as keep it true to its program, that is to historicize, which in Foucault's case means to historicize even the process of historicization, to take the phenomenological project and to wonder about the conditions of its appearance and meaning: "One has to dispense with the constituent subject, to get rid of the subject itself, that's to say to arrive at an analysis which can account for the constitution of the subject within a historical framework. And this is what I would call genealogy, that is, a form of history which can account for the constitution of knowledges, discourses, domains of objects etc., without having to make reference to a subject which is either transcendental in relation to the field of events or runs in its empty sameness through the course of history." Foucault, *Power/Knowledge*, 117,

75 "The imaginary world has its own laws, its specific structures, and the image is somewhat more than the immediate fulfillment of meaning. It has its own density, and the laws which govern it are not solely significant propositions, just as laws of the world are not simply decrees of will, even a divine will. Freud caused the world of the imaginary to be inhabited by Divine Will and Understanding: a theology of meanings, in which truth anticipates its own formulations and completely constitutes them. The meanings exhaust the reality of the world which displays that reality," Foucault, "Dream, Imagination and Existence," 35. Also see ibid., 57.

76 Ibid., 58–59. Similarly does Foucault speak of imagination, and hence the natural implication about suicide: "to imagine is not so much a behavior toward others which intends them as quasi-presences on an essential ground of absence; it is rather to intend oneself as movement of freedom which makes itself world and finally anchors itself in this world as its destiny . . . Suicide is not a way of cancelling the world or myself, or the two together, but a way of rediscovering the original moment in which I make myself world, in which space is still no more than directedness of existence, and time the movement of its history" (Foucault, "Dream, Imagination and Existence," 68, 69). I return to suicide in the chapter following.

77 One can sense as much when the early Foucault speaks of dreams: "The dream world is a world of its own, not in the sense of subjective experience defying the norms of objectivity, but in the sense that it is constituted in the original mode of a world which belongs to me, which at the same time exhibiting my solitude" (ibid., 51).

78 Foucault, *The Archaeology of Knowledge*, 46.

79 In later lectures, Foucault argues that it is Kant who for the first time posits philosophy as "becoming the surface of emergence of its own present

discursive reality." Foucault, *The Government of Self and Others*, 13. In contrast to Heidegger's *das Man*, Kant, in Foucault's reading, situates the philosopher's freedom of conscious against a overbearing past: "the question will no longer be one of his adherence to a doctrine or a tradition, or of his membership of a human community in general, but a question about him being part of a present, about his membership of a particular 'we' if you like ... This 'we' has become, or is in the process of becoming, the object of the philosopher's own reflection" (13). Just as Heidegger places thinking against "the they" so on Foucault's reading, Kant had earlier pitted the thinking of the we in the present against the tutelage-bound past.

80 Foucault, *The Archaeology of Knowledge*, 30. To clarify this statement, consider: "The analysis of statements, then, is a historical analysis, but one that avoids all interpretation: it does not quesiton things said as to what they are hiding, what they are 'really' saying, in spite of themselves, the unspoken element that they contain, the proliferation of thoughts, images, or fantasies that inhabit them; but, on the contrary, it questions them as to their mode of existence, what it means to them to have come into existence, to have left traces, and perhaps to remain there, awaiting the moment when they might be of use once more; what it means to them to have appeared when and where they did—they and no others. From this point of view, there is no such thing as a latent statement: for what one is concerned with is the fact of langauge (*language*)" (ibid., 122).

81 "The term [sexuality] itself did not appear until the beginning of the nineteenth century, a fact that should be neither underestimated nor over-interpreted." Foucault, *The Use of Pleasure*, 3.

82 Ibid., 36.
83 Ibid., 213.
84 Ibid., 37.
85 Ibid., 31.
86 Foucault, *The Archaeology of Knowledge*, 52.
87 Ibid.
88 Michel Foucault, *Abnormal: Lectures at the Collège de France 1974–1975*, ed. Arnold I. Davidson, trans. Graham Burchell (New York: Picador, 2003), 131–32.
89 Foucault, *The Archaeology of Knowledge*, 113. For a fascinating account of race discourse as assemblage along these terms, see Brian Bantum, *Redeeming Mulatto: A Theology of Race and Christian Hybridity* (Waco: Baylor University Press, 2010), 13–83.
90 For the distinctions between Foucault and structuralism see the conclusion to *Archaeology of Knowledge*, 219–32. Also see the helpful delineation in Dreyfus and Rabinow, *Michel Foucault: Beyond Structuralism and Hermeneutics*, 55.
91 Ibid., 139.
92 Michel Foucault, *Security, Territory, Population*, 118.
93 Ibid., 134.
94 Ibid., 214–15.

Notes

95 Heidegger, *Being and Time*, 235.
96 Cf. Foucault, *The Use of Pleasure*, 9–13. See Charles E. Scott, *The Question of Ethics: Nietzsche, Foucault, Heidegger* (Bloomington: Indiana University Press, 1990), 15–18.
97 "In this case—that of the *hupomnemata*-it was a matter of constituting oneself as a subject of rational action through the appropriation, the unification, and the subjectivation of a fragmentary and selected already-said; in the case of the monastic notation of spiritual exercises, it will be a matter of dislodging the most hidden impulses from the inner recesses of the soul, thus enabling oneself to break free of them. In the case of the epistolary account of oneself, it is a matter of bringing into congruence the gaze of the other and that gaze which one aims at oneself when one measrues one's everyday actions according to the rules of a technique of living." Foucault, "Self Writing," 211. Also see Hannah Arendt, *Eichmann in Jerusalem: A Report on the Banality of Evil* (New York: Penguin, 2006).
98 Foucault quotes from John Cassian, *Second Conference of Abbot Moses*, ed. Philip Schaft and Henry Wace (Grand Rapids: Eerdmans, 1955), 312–13. Foucault describes this recoiling in terms of depth: "These, whatever they are, have an unapparent origin, obscure roots, secret parts, and the role of verbalization is to excavate these origins and those secret parts." Foucault, "About the Beginning of the Hermeneutics of the Self," 220.
99 Foucault, *Discipline and Punish*, 195–230. Foucault states that his earlier work, which includes his work on panopticism, placed too much emphasis on interiorization as simply negation, not paying heed enough to its productivity: "Power consists in complex relations: these relations involve a set of rational techniques, and the efficiency of those technologies is due to a subtle integration of coercion-technologies and self-technologies. I think that we have to get rid of the more or less Freudian schema—you know it—the schema of interiorizing of the law by the self . . . the subject constitutes, the point of intersection between a set of memories which must be brought into the present and acts which have to be regulated." Foucault, "About the Beginning of the Hermeneutics of the Self," 204, 207. Cf. Foucault, *The Use of Pleasure*, 63.
100 Cf. "What is an author?" Foucault, *language, counter-memory, practice*, 119–20. In this important essay, Foucault separates himself from phenomenology on the one hand and Derrida on the other, noting his interest in breaking with the subjectivity of his own *The Order of Things*. Foucault, in asking "what is an author," asks from what perspective, other than the transcendental subjectivity, can one *see* absence.
101 The early Foucault held traces of Heidegger's notion of transgressive thought and its benefit in a society driven by objectification. See Foucault, "A Preface to Transgression," *language, counter-memory, practice*, 29–52.
102 Foucault, *The History of Sexuality*, 21–23. Anonymous, *My Secret Life* (New York: Grove Press, 1966).
103 Foucault, *The History of Sexuality*, 45–49. Foucault, *The Use of Pleasure*, 6. The confluence between pleasure and confession undermines the

trustworthiness of various (legal, analytical, etc.) confessions to the extent that the veracity of confession is equated with objectivity.

104 Foucault, *The Care of the Self*, 57, 66–67. Foucault quotes from Seneca, *Letters to Lucilius*, 23, 3–6.
105 Foucault, *The Use of Pleasure*, 48–51 and Foucault, *The Care of the Self*, 23. For Foucault population as a consideration begins with the Greeks and continues intermittently through Christian "themes of anxiety" that regulated procreation in conteporary times (ibid., 138). For Rufas of Ephesus in the Classical period, sex was by nature good as it procured survival by living on through one's own children (124). Hence, right *chresis aphrodision* toward the *energia* between right desire and right comportment required the regulation of sex toward these kinds of natural ends. So unproblematic was this nature that the Cynic Diogenes Laertius sought to do in public what he did in private (55). With the emergence of mercentile economies however you see a different kind of import given to population and sex. Later, Foucault references Galen's *On the Usefulness of the Parts of the Body* and his portrayal of an entire bodily cosmology: "For him, as for the whole philosophical tradition, the necessity of the division of the sexes, the intensity of their mutual attraction, and the possibility of generation are rooted in the lack of eternity." Foucault, *The Care of the Self*, 105. For an analysis of Foucualt and contemporary concerns of population and immigration, see my "Transgressing Borders: Genetic Research, Immigration, and Discourses of Sacrifice," *Journal of the Society of Christian Ethics* 28:2 (2008), 97–116. Similarly, the concern of medicine finds precursors in classical pagan culture and Foucault speaks of *diaite* that both share continuity with but also greatly differ from the medical gaze he had examined in *The Birth of the Clinic: An Archaeology of Medical Perception*, trans. A. M. Sheridan Smith (New York: Vintage, 1994); cf. Foucault, *The Use of Pleasure*, 100.
106 Foucault, *The Care of the Self*, 43.
107 Foucault, "Technologies of the Self," 226. Cf. Foucault, *The Use of Pleasure*, 138–39.
108 Foucault considers the first two centuries of the imperial epoch the golden age of this development. Foucault, *The Care of the Self*, 45. Michel Foucault, "The Hermeneutic of the Subject," *Ethics: Subjectivity and Truth*, ed. Paul Rabinow, trans. Robert Hurley et al. (New York: New Press: 2006), 93–106 (93); and Foucault, "Technologies of the Self," 244.
109 Foucault, *The Use of Pleasure*, 69. Foucault draws from *Nicomahean Ethics* III, 11, 1119a and later from Plato's *Republic* and the notion of *heauton kratoikizein*, "set up the government of one's soul" to describe the care of the pleasures (*Republic*, IX, 592b). Foucault, "Technologies of the Self," 246. Quoted from John Cassian, *Institutions cenobitiques*, trans. J.A. Guy (Paris: Gerf, 1965). Also see Foucault, *The Care of the Self*, 43.
110 "A long way off from the austerity that would tend to govern all individuals in the same way" in the modern period, morality takes on the form self-care in the pre-modern Classical world: "Therefore, in this form of morality, the individual did not make himself into an ethical subject by

Notes

universalizing the principles that informed his action; on the contrary, he did so by means of an attitude and a quest that individualized his action, modulated it, and perhaps even gave him a special brilliance by virtue of the rational and deliberate structure his action manifested." Foucault, *The Use of Pleasure*, 62. Also see ibid., 136 and 250–51.

111 So much so that according to the fifth century writings of John Cassian, erections became as problematic as penetration. Foucault, "About the Beginning of the Hermeneutics of the Self," 217.

112 Athanasius, 179, 177. cf. Foucault, "Self Writing," 208–9, 216. Foucault characterizes this as "a matter of constituting a *logos bioethikos* for oneself" that remains "near at hand" (ibid. 210).

113 Foucault, "Self Writing," 211.

114 Athanasius, 225.

115 Foucault, *The Use of Pleasure*, 46–47.

116 Athanasius, 141–47, 63–65; 243–45.

117 In their introduction, Tim Vivian and Apostolos Athanassakis warn against dismissing Antony's battle with the demons by linking "the powers" with other more familiar historical realities and hence likening Antony's resistance to demons as relevant to contemporary expressions of power: "As people living in an age that, incredibly, downplays the power of evil—despite the Holocaust, Cambodia, Bosnia, and Rwanda—we ought to pay special attention here" (ibid., xxxv). Also see John Howard Yoder's account of the powers in *The Politics of Jesus* (Grand Rapids: William B. Erdmann's Publishing Company, 1999), xx.

118 Athanasius, 61, 63–65, 247.

119 The Oxford classicist Simon Goldhill accuses Foucault of being so intent on a continuity to sexual thought that he passes over critical features that would undermine any unmitigated linearity. Goldhill argues that Foucault's teleological interpretation over-narrates, "like a good Christian," a contiguity from the Greeks and the early Christian and hence misses the performative play of the texts he employs. Because he focuses on what the texts *mean* rather than what they were *meant to do*, Foucault misses the subtleties of Classical talk about sex. In other words, Foucault fails to live up to his own best insights when he dispenses with the discursivity of texts, forgetting that they appear as languages-in-use. Simon Goldhill, *Foucault's Virginity: Ancient Erotic Fiction and the History of Sexuality* (Cambridge: Cambridge University Press, 1995), 102. For a different account of the "uses" of ascetic texts, see David Brakke, *Athanasius and the Poltiics of Asceticism* (Oxford: Clarendon, 1995). Brakke argues that Athanasius in his role of bishop utilized asceticism as the index of Christian unity in a time of doctrinal schism. When Christians in fourth- and fifth-century Egypt sought to emulate Antony, they would not only imitate his orthodox (anti-Arian) theology and practices, but to the extent that in Antony, one could find a continuum of faithfulness to Antony's asceticism, a diversity of possibilies could co-exist under the one umbrella of Antony's Christianity. This catholocism by proxy had a double unifiying effect: it first gathered

Notes

the asceteics back into the central body of the church and it appropriated ascetic Christianity as the gathering point for the church itself. "Withdrawal" under Athanasius' appropriation of asceticism means no longer departure but gathering.

120 Foucault, "Self Writing," 217 (emphasis added).
121 Augustine, *The Trinity*, ed. O. S. A. John E. Rotelle, trans. O. P. Edmund Hill (Brooklyn: New City Press, 1991), 246.
122 Foucault, *The Hermeneutics of the Subject*, 46.
123 Foucault, *Abnormal*, 173–75.
124 Ibid., 177–78, 182–83.
125 Ibid., 177.
126 Foucault, *Security, Territory, Population*, 231. Several major questions arise with confession's transition from the church to the sovereign state, which Foucualt summarizes as, "To what extent must whoever exercises soverign power now be responsible for the new and specific tasks of the government of men?" (ibid., 232). For how these operations transfer to suburban life with children, see my "The Otherness of Children as a Hint of an Outside: Michel Foucault, Richard Yates, and Karl Barth on Suburban Life," *Theology & Sexuality* 15:2 (2009), 191–211.
127 Foucault shows how even the notion of *laisser faire* economies had less to do with political liberty than policing populations under "natural phenomena of economic processes." Foucault, *Security, Territory, Population*, 353.
128 Foucault, "About the Beginning of the Hermeneutics of the Self," 213–23. For an extended discussion of *exomologesis* and *exagoreusis*, see Chloe Taylor, *The Culture of Confession from Augustine to Foucault*, 17–24. Taylor chronicles the development of confession as a penitial status to a penititial rite, showing the great discontinunity in its development, hence the unlikeliness that it developed univocally as disciplinary, even demonstrating the various modes of resistance at play in terms of the relationship between the clergy and the prelates and the clergy and parishoners. For Taylor this not only demonstrates a discontinuity to the meaning and practice of confession, but also displays how Foucualt's conception of capillary power and the possibilty of ethical resistance. Hence on Foucault's own terms, it would be hard to argue that confession unfolded as a disciplinary measure, either by intention or practice. The equation that confession ensues as disciplinary can only be wielded by ignoring the historical record and, on Foucauldian grounds, misses the creative enerigies of resistance always available even within disciplinary societies. Between *Discipline and Punish* and *History of Sexuality* we find Foucault attempting to limn the emergence of the subject within the terms of sociality and freedom, the same dialectic process of repression and freedom and repression again. It is within this matrix of measures and countermeasures that subjects emerge as an Heideggerean over-against-the-they, the free self not bereft of determinations but amidst them, thrown and yet free.
129 Foucault, "About the Beginning of the Hermeneutics of the Self," 222.

Notes

130 Foucault, *The History of Sexuality*, 135–57. See also Foucault, *The Archaeology of Knowledge*, 83.
131 Foucault, *Abnormal*, 265.
132 James Bernauer, SJ, "Cry of Spirit" in Michel Foucault, *Religion and Culture*, ed. Jeremy R. Carrette (New York: Routledge, 1999), xi–xvii (xiv). "I would argue that Foucault's own intellectual practice at this final stage is closer to the specific style of early Christian practice of the self than it is to the pagan" (ibid.).
133 Michel Foucault, "Introduction," in Georges Canguilhem, *On the Normal and the Pathological*, trans. Carolyn R. Fawcett (Dordrecht: Reidel, 1978), xii.
134 Foucault, *The Government of Self and Others*, 14. Foucault goes on to show how for Kant, "the [French] Revolution is actually the completion and continuation of the very process of *Aufklärung*" (ibid., 18).
135 Bernauer, "Cry of Spirit," xv.
136 Gilles Deleuze notes that a critical distinction between his work and Foucault's is Foucault's unwillingness to speak in terms of desire. Foucault told Deleuze that he could not abide the connotation of lack and oppression in notions of desire and perhaps preferred pleasure to desire. Gilles Deleuze, "Desire and Pleasure," trans. Daniel W. Smith in Arnold I. Davidson, ed., *Foucault and His Interlocutors* (Chicago: The University of Chicago Press, 1997), 183–92 (189).
137 One immediate objection between Foucault's self-care and Augustine's love of God would be located in Augustine's distance from Stoicism. Especially, consider Michael Hanby's *Augustine and Modernity* (New York: Routledge, 2003), which positions Augustine's confessional self versus Cartesian internality. Yet this objection is mitigated by remembering that Foucault is only invoking Stoicism, but he is hardly, as Pierre Hadot reminds us, a Stoic. See Hadot's "Reflections on the Idea of the 'Cultivation of the self'," in Pierre Hadot, *Philosophy as a Way of Life: Spiritual Exercises from Socrates to Foucault*, ed. Arnold I. Davidson, trans. Michael Chase (Oxford: Basil Blackwell, 1995), 206–13. Specifically Hadot writes of the Stoics, "For them, happiness does not consist in pleasure, but in virtue itself, which is its own reward. Long before Kant, the Stoics strove jealously to preserve the purity of intention of the moral consciousness" (ibid., 207). Hadot states the problematic implications of Foucault's self: "What I am afraid of is that, by focusing his interpretation too exclusively on the culture of the self, the care of the self, and conversion toward the self—more generally, by defining his ethical model as an aesthetics of existence—M. Foucault is propounding a culture of the self which is *too* aesthetic. In other words, this may be a new form of Dandyism, late twentieth-century style" (211). The "Dandyism" obtains for Foucault, according to Hadot's larger account of philosophy, because he lacks a "transcedent state" toward which the self, and the practice of the self as a philosphical mode of life, directs its care (59). There is certainly a tendency for Foucault to underread Greek and Latin practices as isomorphic (the self as a good in itself, the dandyism that

Notes

Hadot worries about) while overreading Christianity in comparison, so that whereas the Greeks were for self-care, Christianity introduced externality such that the self became less important. Yet, if we are to believe Hadot, the Stoics understood self-care as a practice internal to a larger form of life, the goods of which could be accessed by self-care. Very similarly, Christianity did not seek, as Foucault sometimes surmises, renunciation for its own benefit and neither did it believe that the goods of life were only to be found in the afterlife; these overstatements work in the same way as the understatements about Greek self-care, to valorize the two, to the detriment I would argue of more firmly grasping how Christianity offers a genuine altarnative for Foucualt. Read in this way, one can see Foucault lifting the practices of self-care and utilzing them in ways closer to Christianity than the Stoic inheritance bequeathed to Descartes and embodied of in the constellation Hadot notes. Also see Hadot's inaugural Collège de France lecture, published in English as "Forms of Life and Forms of Discourse in Ancient Philosophy" trans. Arnold I. Davidson and Paul Wissing, *Critical Inquiry* 16:3 (Spring 1990), 483–505 (494–96) Here, Hadot shows how the philosopher's *atopia* sets him at odds with unthought social convention but not for the self's own transgression against society but rather in conformity to a school's respective "form of life defined by an ideal of wisdom ... The dogmas and methodological principles of each school are not open to discussion. In this period, to philosphyize is to choose a school, convert to its way of life, and accept its dogmas" (494, 495). As with Foucault, there is a goal of transcendence but not, as seems in Foucault, for its own sake, but toward unity with an ideal often situated beyond society's conventions. For Foucault, the turn to antiquity's Platonism, Aristotelianism, Stoicism, and Epicureanism (and for that matter, patristic Christianity) were not for allegiance to those schools, but as deviation from the pantheon of modern options.

138 Foucault, "About the Beginning of the Hermeneutics of the Self," 222.
139 Foucault, "Technologies of the Self," 223–51. (New York: New Press: 2006), 236. Foucault references Philo's *La Vie contemplative*.
140 Foucault, *Discipline and Punish*, 27–28, 43–50. Foucault, *The History of Sexuality*, 5.
141 Foucault, "Self Writing," 211.
142 Foucault, "About the Beginning of the Hermeneutics of the Self," 218, 226 *fn*43.
143 Michel Foucault, "Technologies of the Self" in *Technologies of the Self: A Seminar with Michel Foucault,* ed. Hugh Gutman, Patrick H. Hutton and Luther H. Martin (Amherst: The University of Massachusetts Press, 1988), 17–49 (41). This lecture was also published as the aforementioned Michel Foucault, "Technologies of the Self," *Ethics: Subjectivity and Truth*, ed. Paul Rabinow, trans. Robert Hurley and others, 223–51. (New York: New Press: 2006).

Notes

144 Andrew Cutrofello, "Exomologesis and Aesthetic Reflection: Foucault's Response to Habermas" in Bernauer and Carrette, *Michel Foucault and Theology*, 157–69 (158). Emphasis original. In this essay Cutrofello incisively demonstrates how Habermas confuses Foucault's project as offering logically reflective and therefore determinate judgments rather than aesthetically reflective and therefore indeterminate judgments (and a backdoor devaluation of the latter), demonstrating not only a limitation of his engagement with Foucault but his account of communicative action.

145 Sarah Coakley, "Does Kenosis Rest on a Mistake? Three Kentoic Models in Patristic Exegesis," in *Exploring Kenotic Christology: The Self-Giving of God*, ed. C. Stephen Evans (Oxford: Oxford University Press, 2006), 246–64 (264). Also see her "Re-Thinking Gregory of Nyssa: Introduction—Gender, Trinitarian Analogies, and the Pedagogy of *The Song*," *Modern Theology* 18:4 (2002), 432–43.

146 Athanasius of Alexandria, *The Life of Antony*, trans. Tim Vivian and Apostolos N. Athanassakis (Kalamazoo: Cistercian Publications, 2003), 103, 61, 63–65. Athanasius offers the material emanations of divinization by describing Antony prior to his death at the age of 105: "Not one of his teeth fell out, though they had been worn down beneath the gums on account of the old man's advanced age. His feet and his hands also remained healthy. In short, he appeared more radiant, stronger, and more energetic than all those people who enjoy a wide variety of foods and baths and different types of clothing" (ibid., 257).

147 "The actions of peripheral agents in these networks are often what establish or enforce the connections between what a dominant agent does and the fulfillment or frustration of a subordinated agent's desires." Joseph Rouse, "Power/Knowledge" in *The Cambridge Companion to Foucault*, ed. Gary Gutting (Cambridge, Cambridge University Press, 2005), 96-122 (109). Rouse goes on to link Foucault with the expressive pragmatism of Robert Brandom. In this sense, one can trace a kind of Foucauldian account of power within radical democrats like Jeffrey Stout who leans heavily on Brandom's pragmatism. See Robert M. Brandom, *Making It Explicit: Reasoning, Representing, and Discursive Commitment* (Cambridge: Cambridge University Press, 1994) and Jeffery Stout, *Democracy and Tradition* (Princeton: Princeton University Press, 2004).

148 Sarah Coakley, *Powers and Submissions: Spirituality, Philosophy, and Gender* (Oxford: Blackwell, 2002), 36.

149 Foucault, *The History of Sexuality*, 98. Foucault, *Discipline and Punish*, 301.

150 Ibid., 87–91.

151 The relation between social situatedness and social constitution is explicated in Johanna Oksala's *Foucault On Freedom* (Cambridge: Cambridge University Press, 2005), 135–53.

152 It is within the dietics of pleasure that Foucault traces the development of a restrictive economy but within that understanding, which he relates to the Pythagoreans, restriction is toward the goods of the body as a small *oikos* and a microcosm of society. Foucault, *The Use of Pleasure*, 118–19, 162.

Notes

Chapter 5

1 Cornel West relates Hauerwas' remark in an interview recorded in *The Cornel West Reader* (New York: Basic *Civitas* Books, 2000), 409.
2 Arnold I. Davidson, "Introduction," in Michel Foucault, *Security, Territory, Population: Lectures at the Collège de France 1977–1978*, ed. Arnold I. Davidson, trans. Graham Burchell (New York: Picador, 2007), xiix–xxxiv (xxxi). Davidson quotes from Michel Foucault, "Conversation avec Werner Schroeter," in *Dits et écrit II, 1976–88* (Paris: Gallimard, 2001), 1076.
3 Davidson, "Introduction," xxxii.
4 Cora Diamond, "The Difficulty of Reality and the Difficulty of Philosophy," in *Philosophy and Animal Life*, ed. Stanley Cavell et al., 43–89 (New York: Columbia University Press, 2008), 45–46. Diamond's essay was previously printed under the same title in *Partial Answers* 1:2 (2003), 1–26 and originated as a 2002 symposium paper, "Accounting for Literary Language," about Stanley Cavell. Citations to this essay will come from *Philosophy and Animal Life*.
5 David Owen, "Perfectionism, Parrhesia, and the Care of the Self: Foucault and Cavell on Ethics and Politics," in *The Claim to Community*, ed. Andrew Norris (Stanford: Stanford University Press, 2006), 128–55 (143). Owen's reading of Cavell and Christianity should not only be contrasted with my particular reading here, but more significantly, that of Peter Dula's *Cavell, Companionship, and Christian Theology* (New York: Oxford University Press, 2010) and James Wetzel's forthcoming *Perplexity's Child: Augustine and the Confession of Philosophy* (Stanford: Stanford University Press, forthcoming).
6 In his memoirs *Little Did I Know*, Cavell writes, "[Foucault's later lectures'] pertinence to what I have described as perfectionism, however different in motivation (for example, I begin from a counterreading of Rawls and from a sense that Emersonian and Thoreauvian perfectionisms take on preoccupations evident throughout Western philosophical and literary culture), crosses paths at alarmingly many points with what Foucault translates and perceives as the care of the self." Stanley Cavell, *Little Did I Know: Exerpts from Memory* (Stanford: Stanford University Press, 2010), 479. I am indebted to Natalie Carnes for alerting me to Cavell's comment here.
7 Michel Foucault, *The Hermeneutics of the Subject: Lectures at the Collège de France 1981–1982*, ed. Frédéric Gros, trans. Graham Burchell (New York: Picador, 2005), 14.
8 "Forms of Life and Forms of Discourse in Ancient Philosophy" trans. Arnold. I. Davidson and Paul Wissing, *Critical Inquiry* 16:3 (Spring 1990), 483–505 (499).
9 Foucault, *The Hermeneutics of the Subject*, 17.
10 Augustine of course utters this prayer in the opening of the *Confessions*, trans. Henry Chadwick (Oxford: Oxford University Press, 1998).
11 Jonathan Safran Foer, *Eating Animals* (New York: Little, Brown and Company, 2009), 13.
12 Ibid., 203–67.

13 Referring to the experience of unending suffering, Peter Singer provocatively prologues his book on factory farming with a quote from *Paradise Lost*:

> No light, but rather darkness visible
> Served only to discover sights of woe,
> Regions of sorrow, doleful shades, where peace
> And rest can never dwell, hope never comes
> That comes to all; but torture without end . . .

Jim Mason and Peter Singer, *Animal Factories* (New York: Crown Publishers, 1980), Prologue.

14 Søren Kierkegaard, *Philosophical Fragments*, ed. Howard V. Hong and Edna H. Hong (Princeton: Princeton University Press, 1985), 23–36.

15 I refer to my following publications: "Dying with Others: Reflections on Ataxia, Suffering, and Ken's Mom," *Theology Today* 64:4 (2007), 458–468; "Transgressing Borders: Genetic Research, Immigration, and Discourses of Sacrifice," *Journal of the Society of Christian Ethics* 28:2 (2008), 97–116; "The Otherness of Children as a Hint of an Outside: Michel Foucault, Richard Yates, and Karl Barth on Suburban Life," *Theology & Sexuality* 15:2 (2009), 191–211; "Sold Into Slavery: The Scourge of Human Trafficking," *Christian Century* 124:24 (2007), 22–26; and *The Vietnam War and Theologies of Memory: Time and Eternity in the Far Country* (Oxford: Wiley-Blackwell, 2010).

16 For an elegant depiction of how eating constitutes the very form of the Christian life, see Samuel Wells, *God's Companions: Reimagining Christian Ethics* (Oxford: Wiley-Blackwell, 2006).

17 The gamut might include any number of biblical warrants, among them those New Testament passages that depict Jesus feeding the crowds with meat (Mk 8.1–9; Mt. 15.32–39), the resurrected Jesus himself eating meat (Lk. 24:41–43), and God commanding Peter to kill and eat cleansed animals (Acts 10:9–16). Within the broad tradition of Christian history, eating meat has continued with only rare comment and forms of vegetarianism would count as exceptions (monastic abstinence as *exceptional*) to the rule. For an anthology of historical texts see Andrew Linzey and Tom Regan, ed., *Animals and Christianity: A Book of Readings* (New York: Crossroads, 1988). Among major figures in twentieth-century theology, Karl Barth offers the most measured, if conflicted, allowance: "The slaying of animals is really possible only as an appeal to God's reconciling grace" (more telling, I think, is the number of significant theologians whose work never visited the question); see § 55 of Barth's doctrine of creation, *Church Dogmatics III.4*, trans. Geoffrey W. Bromiley and Thomas F. Torrance (Edinburgh: T & T Clark, 1961), 355. To be sure, none of the above makes express allowances for eating factory-farmed meat given its recent, and I'd assume hitherto inconceivable, development.

18 Safran Foer, *Eating Animals*, 86–87.

19 Ibid., 252–59. "Just how common do such savageries have to be for a decent person to be unable to overlook them? If you knew that one in two thousand food animals suffered actions like those described above, would

Notes

you continue to eat animals? One in one hundred? One in ten?" (ibid., 255).

20 Gerald P. McKenny, *To Relieve the Human Condition: Bioethics, Technology, and the Body* (Albany: State University of New York, Press, 1997), 25–38.

21 Michael Northcott's work is among the best theological treatments on the broader question of the environment, especially with its impressive range of expertise. Michael S. Northcott, *The Environment and Christian Ethics* (Cambridge: Cambridge University Press, 2001). His account of natural theology is simultaneously the book's best attribute, because it shows the "interrelatedness" of creation and the trinitarian God, and its weakest (not in the sense that it exposes the limits of Northcott's account of environmental stewardship as much as his reliance on natural law ethics). The very is-ought distinction that G. E. Moore underscored and that Northcott tries to overcome continues to haunt the argument, demonstrating that natural law utilizes ought statement by bending claims to prior judgments (and as such is best understood as retrospective casuistry). On this point his turn to Richard Hooker would help if Hooker, in Northcott's reading, offered a sufficient Christology to discipline and help interpret the relationship between the divine ordo and the natural order. His use of Thomas is instructive here: Northcott both credits Aquinas as improving on Augustine's Platonism and faults Thomas for an overdrawn distinction between humans and animals based on reason, which leads to an instrumental view of animals. Oddly, Northcott never returns to this disconnect; odd because for Thomas this delineation is critical for the very interrelation Northcott propones. Again, a Christological conception of the faculties would help here, but Northcott's reliance on the continuity between nature and grace does not help him to return to this question.

For further elaboration on Thomas' metaphysical interrelation, see William C. French's "Beast-Machines and the Technocratic Reduction of Life," in *Good News for Animals? Christian Approaches to Animal Well-Being*, ed. Charles Pinches and Jay B. McDaniel (New York: Orbis, 1993), 23–43. French speaks of Thomas portraying "a being via an examination of its multiple relations with other created beings, with its species, with the common good of creation as a whole, and with God, the cause and the Final end of God." Hence, when Thomas speaks of plants being *for* animals and animals *for* humans, his goal is more intimate than a subordinationist reading would imply; it just happens that Thomas thought of order, as any good medieval thinker would, in the terms of hierarchy and so spoke of intimacy on those terms, and so mistaken would be any attempt to interpret hierarchy on purely instrumentalist or mechanistic terms: "The Great chain of Being is a multivalent metaphor. The same metaphysical model Thomas uses to stress hierarchical gradations of value linked to the scale of being also, at other points, leads Thomas to highlight continuities and linkages throughout a conjoined cosmos pulsing with life and sustained by God's energy and love. While his stress on hierarchy generates a narrowing of direct moral concern restricted to human value and well-being, his stress upon all creatures'

Notes

participation in the broader community of creation generates an expansive vision of all beings as related to one another and to God" (37).

22 I have in mind what Foucault described as the "polymorphous techniques of power" which does not admit the kinds of mythic escape Safran Foer too easily posits as vegetarianism and the very prevalence of such myths ("freedom") underlines the problem. Michel Foucault, *Power/Knowledge: Selected Interviews and Other Writings 1972–1977*, ed. Colon Gordon (New York: Pantheon Press, 1980), 11.

23 I understand choice in the sense given by Herbert McCabe, doing what is "obvious." Herbert McCabe, *Love, Law and Language* (New York: Continuum, 2004).

24 Michel Foucault, "Technologies of the Self" in *Technologies of the Self: A Seminar with Michel Foucault*, ed. Hugh Gutman, Patrick H. Hutton, and Luther H. Martin (Amherst: The University of Massachusetts Press, 1988), 16–49 (25).

25 Ibid., 35. Still, Foucault understands that the goods purported to the Christian life (e.g., eternal life) are goods of the self, sought for the sake of self-care.

26 See Sarah Coakley's "*Kenosis* and Subversion: On the Repression of 'Vulnerability' in Christian Feminist Writing," in her *Powers and Submissions: Spirituality, Philosophy, and Gender* (Oxford: Blackwell Publishers, 2002), 3–39 and her critique of versions of kenosis, "Does Kenosis Rest on a Mistake? Three Kentoic Models in Patristic Exegesis" in *Exploring Kenotic Christology: The Self-Giving of God* ed. C. Stephen Evans (Oxford: Oxford University Press, 2006), 246–64.

27 It is not uncommon to hear vegetarianism caricatured as a privilege of middle-class elitism (a charge, ironically, leveled by middle-class elites), a prerogative of those able to choose, a luxury unavailable for those without choices, for example, the poor (though abject poverty rarely forces *meat* upon the poor, a point the complaint fails to consider), so on and so forth. Well, of course. But the ethical merit, or obligation, of a choice should not be cheapened, or inflated for that matter, because of the presence of choosing. From Antony to Macrina the Younger and her society of virgins to Francis of Assisi's rejection of Pietro's patrimony all the way to Dietrich Bonheoffer's fateful return to Nazi-occupied Germany, Christian ascetical acts often ensue as choices; that one *can* choose and yet abstains is largely the point. As Gregory of Nyssa writes of his sister's community, "Just as by death souls are freed from the body and released from the cares of this life, so their life was separated from these things." Gregory of Nyssa, *The Life of Macrina* in *Saint Gregory of Nyssa: Ascetical Works*, trans. Virginia Woods Callahan (Washington, DC: Catholic University of America Press, 1967), 170–71.

28 J. M. Coetzee, *Elizabeth Costello* (New York: Penguin, 2003). Before publishing the novel *Elizabeth Costello*, the Nobel laureate Coetzee presented "The Lives of Animals" as lectures at Princeton University. Coetzee's lectures, even before the publication of *Elizabeth Costello*, became the subject of the edited volume *The Lives of Animals*, a collection of responses by various scholars at Princeton. J. M. Coetzee, *The Lives of Animals*, ed. Amy Gutmann (Princeton:

Notes

Princeton University Press, 1999). Page references will be made from the novel *Elizabeth Costello*.

29 Coetzee, *The Lives of Animals*, 114–15. The novel ends on a surprisingly hopeful, if also ironic, note (197–225).
30 Ibid., 77.
31 Cora Diamond, "Eating Meat and Eating People," *Philosophy* 53:206 (October 1978), 465–79 (475).
32 Coetzee, *The Lives of Animals*, 64–65.
33 Ibid., 88–89.
34 Hannah Arendt, *The Human Condition* (Chicago: The University of Chicago Press, 1958), 175–247.
35 See Heidegger's discussion of "guilt" in *Being and Time*, trans. Joan Stambaugh (Albany: State University of New York Press, 1996), 279–306.
36 Cavell et al., *Philosophy and Animal Life*, 55.
37 On the recoiling nature of ethics, see Charles E. Scott, *The Question of Ethics: Nietzsche, Foucault, Heidegger* (Bloomington: Indiana University Press, 1990), 15–18 and 171–72.
38 Cavell et al., *Philosophy and Animal Life*, 3. Following Derrida, Wolfe makes an interesting observation regarding Diamond's imagining the being of a bat: "there is the suggestion in Diamond, I think, that imaginative and literary projection can somehow achieve in this instance what propositional, syllogistic philosophy cannot achieve . . . but Derrida would see this, too, as a 'deflection' or 'exposure': exposure not just to mortality but also to a certain estranging operation of language, to a second kind of finitude whose implications are enormous" (ibid., 23). While I doubt that the goals of Diamond's imaginative projections are the same as those of propositional philosophy (hence the analogy is not a straightforward one), Wolfe does pose an interesting question whether Diamond goes far enough in terms of these implications, apparently more "enormous" than Diamond may have initially considered.
39 See the chapters "Eating Meat and Eating People" and "Experimenting on Animals: A Problem in Ethics" in Cora Diamond, *The Realistic Sprit: Wittgenstein, Philosophy, and the Mind* (Cambridge: The MIT Press, 1991), 319–66. Also see Cora Diamond, "Injustice and Animals," in *Slow Cures and Bad Philosophers: Essays on Wittgenstein, Medicine, and Bioethics*, ed. Carl Elliott (Durham: Duke University Press, 2001), 118–48. Though Cavell spends most of his energies with the later Wittgenstein, Diamond reads the antimetaphysicalism of Wittgenstein's later work in continuity with his early work. See especially Cora Diamond, "Throwing Away the Ladder," *Philosophy*, 63:243 (Jan 1988), 5–27 along with *The Realistic Sprit*.
40 Cavell et al., *Philosophy and Animal Life*, 128–29.
41 Ibid., 57–58. Emphasis added.
42 Ibid., 4.
43 Ibid., 6–7. Wolfe quotes from Cavell's *This New Yet Unapproachable America* (Albuquerque: Living Batch Press, 1989), 86–87.
44 Cavell et al., *Philosophy and Animal Life*, 136.

Notes

45 In *Sexuality and the Christian Body*, Eugene Rogers writes, "Indeed, for material creatures, intimacy depends on physical boundaries. You cannot hug someone unless the two bodies have skins to press up against each other. Temporally, finitude means having a beginning and an end. You cannot hug someone unless your bodies adjoin at the same time. A sexual orientation is in part a special appreciation for the particular delights of spatial finitudes, or bodily forms ... We live in different places and at different times. This difference is not yet a fault. It is the appropriate condition of creaturely intimacy." Eugene F. Rogers, Jr., *Sexuality and the Christian Body: Their Way into the Triune God* (Oxford: Blackwell, 1999), 201. No one has developed these themes with greater power and elegance than Luce Irigaray. See her *I Love to You: Sketch of a Possible Felicity in History* (Routledge, 1995).

46 Alasdair MacIntyre, *Dependent Rational Animals: Why Human Beings Need the Virtues* (Chicago: Open Court, 1999). MacIntyre writes about animals who "flourish only because they have learned how to achieve their goals through strategies concerted with other members of the different groups to which they belong or which they encounter. The similarities between their strategies in pursuing their goals and the strategies of human beings have been obvious to human observers at least since Aristotle" (ibid., 22).

47 Consider the extraordinary work and life of Temple Grandin, whose autism has allowed (encouraged) her to imagine the slaughterhouse as a cow or pig might, envisaging the being of an animal on its way to death. Grandin's efforts have resulted in a number of improvements in American slaughterhouses. See Temple Grandin, *Thinking in Pictures: and Other Reports from My Life with Autism* (New York: Vintage, 1995) and Temple Grandin and Catherine Johnson, *Animals in Translation: Using the Mysteries of Autism to Decode Animal Behavior* (New York: Scribner, 2005).

48 Coetzee registers his concern with seeing by noting the following John Berger quote in the original published manuscript of "The Lives of Animals": "Nowhere in a zoo can a stranger encounter the look of an animal. At most, the animal's gaze flickers and passes on. They look sideways. They look blindly beyond. They scan mechanically ... That look between animal and man, which may have played a crucial role in the development of human society, and with which, in any case, all men had always lived until less than a century ago, has been extinguished." The Tanner Lectures on Human Values, 111–66, Princeton University, October 15 and 16, 1997, 132. John Berger, *About Looking* (New York: Pantehon, 1980), 26.

49 Ludwig Wittgenstein, *Tractatus Logico Philosophicus*, trans. D. F. Pears and B. F. McGuinness (London: Routledge, 2001), 87.

50 Consider William Easterly, *The Elusive Quest for Growth: Economists' Adventures and Misadventures in the Tropics* (Cambridge: The MIT Press, 2002) and *The White Man's Burden: Why the West's Efforts to Aid the Rest Have Done So Much Ill and So Little Good* (Oxford: Oxford University Press, 2007); Dani Rodrik, *Has Globalization Gone Too Far?* (Washington, DC: Institute for International Economics, 1997) and *One Economics, Many Recipes: Globalization, Institutions, and Economic Growth* (Princeton: Princeton University Press,

Notes

2008); Martin Albrow, *The Global Age* (Stanford: Stanford University Press, 1997); and Atilio A. Boron, *Empire and Imperialism: A Critical Reading of Michael Hardt and Antonio Negri*, trans. Jessica Casiro (New York: Zed Books, 2005). For a shockingly unabashed display of capitalism's arrogance and aims, see http://www.scribd.com/doc/6674234/Citigroup-Oct-16-2005-Plutonomy-Report-Part-1. For globalization's false promises see William T. Cavanaugh, *Theopolitical Imagination: Discovering the Liturgy as a Political Act in an Age of Global Consumerism* (London: T & T Clark, 2002), 97–122.

51 Martin Heidegger, *The Question Concerning Technology and Other Essays*, trans. William Lovitt (New York: Garland Publishing, 1977), 3–35. Barry Lopez's fiction carries the same sensibilities. His stories show how attempts to domesticate wildness often end badly. See Barry Lopez, *Light Action in the Caribbean: Stories* (New York: Vintage, 2001).

52 Cavell et al., *Philosophy and Animal Life*, 148.

53 See Martin Heidegger, *Introduction to Metaphysics*, trans. Gregory Fried and Richard Polt (New Haven: Yale University Press, 2000), 14–19. In the third installment of their "Empire" trilogy, Michael Hardt and Antonio Negri construe fundamentalism (in its religious, political, and economic varieties) as an intense fixation on bodies that gives way to abstract transcendental theorization, in turn visiting upon bodies a vengeful and compensating contempt. For Hardt and Negri, the failure to maintain the immanent moment, the inability to keep one's eyes fixed on bodies, comprises, by its character, what fundamentalism *is*. Yet, along with identifying the fundamentalist threat, they presage how the visible body—when seen but for a moment—might also ignite biopolitical powers that explode fundamentalist boundaries by awakening previously enervated senses, enlivening the body by and to the presence of other bodies. Quoting Marx, they write, "Labor, freed from private property, simultaneously engages all our senses and capacities, in short all our 'human relations to the world—seeing, hearing, smelling, tasting, feeling, thinking, contemplating, sensing, wanting, acting, loving.'" Michael Hardt and Antonio Negri, *Commonwealth* (Cambridge: The Belknap Press of Harvard University Press, 2009), 38. Hardt and Negri quote from Karl Marx, *Early Writings*, trans. Rodney Livingstone and Gregor Benton (London: Penguin Press, 1975), 351.

54 Diamond, "Injustice and Animals," 120–21.

55 While I am unmoved by Hare's admixture of utilitarian and deontological argumentation, I find attractive the clarity and sobriety with which he analyzes "demi-vegetarianism." See his *Essays on Bioethics* (Oxford: Clarendon Press, 1993), 219–35. Hare names Singer specifically as drawing his attention to animal welfare (221).

56 Cora Diamond, "Eating Meat and Eating People," *Philosophy* 53: 206 (at 1978), 465–79. See Singer's classic *Animal Liberation* (New York: New York Review, 1975) along with his edited collaboration with Tom Regan, *Animals Rights and Human Obligations* (Englewood Cliffs: Prentice-Hall, 1976). For a Christian presentation of animal rights, with the attending problems, see Andrew Linzey's *Animal Rights: A Christian Assessment of Man's Treatment of*

Notes

Animals (London: SCM, 1976) and *Christianity and the Rights of Animals* (London: SPCK, 1987).
57 Diamond, "Eating Meat and Eating Animals," 467.
58 Ibid., 470. For comment on what is at stake epistemologically here, that is in seeing animals beyond the terms of the purported objectivity of rights, see Alice Crary, "Humans, Animals, Right and Wrong," in *Wittgenstein and the Moral Life: Essays in Honor of Cora Diamond,* ed. Alice Crary (Cambridge: The MIT Press, 2007), 381–404.
59 Diamond, "Eating Meat and Eating Animals," 478. See also Diamond, "Experimenting on Animals," 351–52.
60 Cavell et al., *Philosophy and Animal Life,* 101–2.
61 For example, "the phenomena which constitute the criteria of something's being so are fully *in the nature of things*—they are part of those very general facts of nature or of human life against the background of which our concepts mean anything at all, and in particular, mean something about which we call 'the nature of things' or 'the world'," *The Claim of Reason: Wittgenstein, Skepticism, Morality, and Tragedy* (Oxford: Oxford University Press, 1979), 106.
62 Ludwig Wittgenstein, *Philosophical Investigation,* trans. G. E. M. Anscombe (Englewood Cliffs: Prentice Hall, 1958), 223. Cavell often quotes Wittgenstein's aphorism about legitimation: "If I have exhausted the justifications I have reached bedrock, and my spade is turned. Then I am inclined to say: 'This is simply what I do'" (ibid., 85).
63 Cavell et al., *Philosophy and Animal Life,* 122.
64 Cavell, *The Claim of Reason,* 109 (emphasis original).
65 Peter Dula, *Cavell, Companionship and Christian Theology* (Oxford: Oxford University Press, 2010), 66–7. Dula quite aptly appraises Rowan Williams "the most Cavellian of contemporary theologians" (ibid., vii).
66 Cavell et al., *Philosophy and Animal Life,* 60–61.
67 Ibid., 72.
68 Ibid., 71.
69 Stanley Cavell, "The Availability of Wittgenstein's Later Philosophy," in *Must We Mean What We Say? A Book of Essays,* (Cambridge: Cambridge University Press, 1976), 44–72 (61).
70 Diamond, in "Experimenting on Animals," observes how the "ethics" of animal experimentation is reduced to the question of physical pain. Notice the double reduction: animals are thought of only in terms of pain; humans are shorn of all faculties other than an ability to measure animal pain. Diamond, "Experimenting on Animals," 354–55.
71 Richard Sorabji, *Animal Minds and Human Morals: The Origins of the Western Debate* (Ithaca: Cornell University Press, 1993).
72 Diamond, "Injustice and Animals," 136.
73 See Paul F. Bradshaw's discussion of the Jewish *Birkat ha-mazon*—"We give thanks to you, Lord our God, that you have caused us to inherit a good and pleasant land, the covenant, the Law, Life and food"—as cultic antecedent to the Holy Meal blessing. *Eucharistic Origins* (Oxford: Oxford University Press, 2004), 32–42. Bradshaw differentiates the eschatological and revelatory

Notes

emphases of early Eucharistic prayers contained in the *Didache* from those quoted in the Mishnah.

74 This is how I interpret Stanley Hauerwas and John Berkman in their quibble with those who refer to creation as "nature," a notion that strips nature of its creaturely form, which is narratival in structure. Stanley Hauerwas and John Berkman, "The Chief End of All Flesh," *Theology Today* 42:2 (1992), 196–208 (204). "To say that creation is an eschatological notion is to say that the universe is part of the drama that is not of its own making. That is, creation is part of a story Christians learn through being initiated into a community that has learned to live appropriately to that story" (206–7). See Stephen H. Webb's critique of Hauerwas and Berkman in *On God and Dogs: A Christian Theology of Compassion for Animals* (Oxford: Oxford University Press, 1998), 35–38.

75 Ben Quash, "Offering: Treasuring the Creation," in *The Blackwell Companion to Christian Ethics*, ed. Stanley Hauerwas and Samuel Wells (Oxford: Blackwell, 2004), 305–18 (314). I would qualify Quash's comments by saying that language learning, that is, learning to see the world, is more primitive than Quash suggests. We do not return to the Eucharist in order to learn something we realize we do not know; rather these processes are always already underway. If we did not know how to describe a thing we would probably fail to see it at all. This seems to me to be the problem with factory farming, not that we see such practices and don't know what to do with them, but by the available terms of capitalism, we have already been taught how to see (not see) them. What is required is not a Christian liturgy in order to fill in the blanks, but rather as a rival set of descriptions that might replace a prior way of seeing. Quash is right that the Eucharist helps us to see creation eschatologically in this way, as tutelage for what things are by what they are to be. Quash makes his argument within the larger context of Christian worship, specifically as related to the offering, where stewardship might orient us to the world in a more wondrous way. I think this is a helpful corrective, which if more richly ornamented in church liturgies might offer alternative modes of seeing. On the primitive nature of moral sentiments, see Rush Rhees, *Moral Questions*, ed. D. Z. Phillips (New York: St. Martin's Press, 1999), 109–27.

76 For example consider the end of blood sacrifices ascribed in Hebrews 9.

77 Stephen H. Webb, "The Lord's Supper as a Vegetarian Meal" in *Christian Ethics: An Introductory Reader*, ed. Samuel Wells (Oxford: Wiley-Blackwell, 2010), 303–5. See Webb's fuller treatment *Good Eating* (Grand Rapids: Brazos, 2001), as well as *On God and Dogs: A Christian Theology of Compassion for Animals* (Oxford: Oxford University Press, 1998), the latter likely the most theologically astute of recent studies.

78 It's obviously the case that for many the Eucharist has little to no effect on their eating habits. I take this disconnect not as a problem with the Eucharist per se, but rather indication of its embedding within a whole complex of competing and complimenting practices, discourses, and imaginaries. These sorts of limitations on the Eucharist's formative powers are the whole point of this chapter's use of Coetzee, Cavell, and Diamond. And, to be sure, the

Notes

Eucharist is more than its formative powers, indeed, expression of God's sufficiency in the face of those limitations.

79 Denys Turner, "The Darkness of God and the Light of Christ: Negative Theology and Eucharistic Presence," *Modern Theology*, 15:2 (April 1999), 143–58 (157).
80 Michael Hardt and Antonio Negri, *Commonwealth* (Cambridge: The Belknap Press of Harvard University Press, 2009), 153.

Postscript

1 For one interpretation, see Janet Afary and Keven B. Anderson, *Foucault and the Iranian Revolution: Gender and Seductions of Islamism* (Chicago: The University of Chicago Press, 2005). The book is helpful in that it offers for the first time full English tranlations of Foucualt's writings and interviews on the question (ibid., 179–277). For reviews of Afary and Anderson's somewhat contorted interpretation, see the following: Jonathan Rée, "The Treason of the Clerics" in *The Nation* (August 15, 2005) http://www.thenation.com/article/treason-clerics; Valentine M. Moghadam, "Review" in *Perspectives in Politics* 5:1 (March 2007), 141–42; Babak Rahimi, "What is Happening" in *H-Gender-MidEast* (October 2006) http://www.h-net.org/reviews/showrev.php?id=12437; Lois McNay, "Book Reviews" in Constellations 14:1 (February 2007), 292–301; and Michael J. Thompson, "Review" in *Democratiya* (Summer 2005), 20–24.

Index

Albrow, Martin 172n. 18, 203n. 50
Alcibiades 138
animals 2, 103–4, 106, 185n. 59
   animal rights (language) 127, 151–2
   and Eucharistic 128, 153–9
   and factory farms 131, 137, 144
   and farming practices 134
   and Holocaust 130, 141–4, 147
   and imagination 130, 135, 142, 144, 147, 149, 152, 153
   and language 147–9
   and philosophy 127, 139, 145–9
   production of meat 132
   and suffering 131, 133, 135, 136–9, 148, 149
Antony 97, 113–14, 120–2, 192n. 117, 192n. 119, 200n. 27
Aquinas, St. Thomas 129, 199n. 21
archaeology 40, 102, 109, 111, 180n. 6
Arendt, Hannah 103–4, 106–7, 111, 143, 186n. 70, 190n. 97
Aristotle 68–9, 113, 119, 129, 186n. 70, 187n. 72, 195n. 137, 202n. 46
asceticism 12, 46, 97, 138–9
Athanasius 113–14, 121
Aufklärung 36, 38, 118
Austin, J. L. 181n. 11
Ayatollah Khomeini 160–2

Barth, Karl 182, 198n. 17
Bataille, Georges 185n. 65
Being and Time 71, 103, 187n. 74
Benhabib, Seyla 186n. 70
Benjamin, Walter 53

Berger, John 202n. 48
Berkman, John 205n. 74
Bernauer, James, SJ 1, 81, 117, 118, 163n. 2, 176n. 46, 177n. 62
Binswanger, Ludwig 107
biography 2, 67–92, 96–7, 102, 127, 178n. 63
biopolitics 30–3, 45, 67–92, 117
biopower 13, 23, 26–34, 45–6, 49, 57, 111, 125
   and plague 26–33
Boron, Atilio 203n. 50
Bradshaw, Paul F. 205n. 73
Brakke, David 192n. 119
Brooks, Peter 100
Butler, Judith 183n. 28

capital, capitalism 2, 5, 6, 7–12, 14, 203n. 50, 205n. 75
   and America 56
   and animals 125, 137, 155, 158
   and biopower 57
   capitalism myth 12
   capitalist societies 2, 23
   as Empire 49
   logic of 11
   and nation-states 48, 53–5
   scarcity and 6, 28–9, 97
   and shittiness 125, 132, 149, 150, 155
   totalizing effects of 2, 98, 126
Carr, Stephen 163n. 2
Carrette, Jeremy 163n. 2, 176n. 27
Carter, J. Kameron 178n. 63
Cassian, John 111, 113, 120, 190n. 98, 192n. 111
Cavanaugh, William T. 203n. 50

207

Index

Cavell, Stanley 2, 115, 125–30, 145–56, 181n. 11, 205n. 78
Children of Men 163n. 4, 171n. 16
Christianity
　and biography 88–9
　Christendom 62–3, 116
　"in-depth Christianity" 116
Climacus, Johannes *see also* Søren Kierkegaard 132
Coakley, Sarah 121–2
coercion 20, 25, 30, 109
Coetzee, J. M. *see also* Elizabeth Costello 125, 130, 135, 137, 139–44, 154, 200n. 28, 202n. 48, 205n. 78
Coles, Romand 168n. 78, 169n. 91
companionship 2, 127, 130, 149, 153–9
Comte, Auguste 81
conduct (conduire) 45–6, 124
confession (exomologesis/exagoreusis) 28, 31, 37–8, 45, 93, 95–6, 100, 111, 112–24, 190n. 103, 193n. 128
Connolly, William 41–3, 127, 155–6, 169n. 91
Copenhaver, Martin 178n. 67
criminal/criminality 18–19, 27, 100, 110, 133
Cutrofello, Andrew 100, 120

Dasein 107, 113
Davidson, Arnold 97, 125–6
Deleuze, Gilles 2, 51, 169n. 88, 179n. 73, 194n. 136
Derrida, Jacques 67, 190n. 100, 201n. 38
Descartes, René (Cartesian) 90, 93–4, 100, 103, 115, 117–19, 129, 185n. 51, 187n. 72, 194n. 137
Diamond, Cora 2, 126–7, 130, 141, 144, 145–56
Discipline and Punish 13, 18, 26, 38, 70, 94
　Damiens' execution 70
Dula, Peter 154

Easterly, William 202n. 50
Elizabeth Costello *see* Coetzee, J. M.
Emerson, Ralph Waldo 148, 150, 181n. 11, 197n. 6
Empire 48–63, 106, 111, 125–6, 138, 143
enlightenment *see also* Aufklärung 3, 10, 23, 35–6, 39, 118
epistemes 42, 75–7
Eribon, Didier 86–8
Eucharist 127–8, 153–9, 204n. 73, 205n. 75, 205n. 78
exceptionalism 27
exclusion 18, 21–2, 27, 40–4, 111, 127–8

Fabiola 122
faithfulness (Christian) 2, 3, 5, 63, 114, 121, 123
family 37, 117
Flynn, Thomas 43
Francis of Assisi, St. 62, 200n. 27
French, William C. 199n. 21
Freud, Sigmund 75, 107–8, 153, 188n. 75, 190n. 99

genealogy 8, 21, 37, 40, 45, 50, 61, 102
globalization 48–9, 51, 61
Goldhill, Simon 170n. 1
governmentality 45, 47, 96
grammar 17, 73, 79–80
Grandin, Temple 192n. 119
Gregory of Nyssa 121, 200n. 27

Habermas, Jürgen 78, 196n. 44
Hacking, Ian 150
Hadot, Pierre 129, 181n. 11, 194n. 137
Halperin, David 69, 75, 78, 82, 86–91, 175n. 21
Hanby, Michael 194n. 137
Hardt, Michael and Antonio Negri 47, 48–64, 127, 158
Hare, R. M. 136, 151, 203n. 55

208

Index

Harvey, David 54
Hauerwas, Stanley 4, 125, 132, 178n. 67, 205n. 74
Hegel, G.W. F. 81
Heidegger, Martin 13, 50, 68–9, 71, 93, 95, 102–12, 122, 144, 150, 184n. 49, 186n. 70, 186n. 72, 188n. 74, 189n. 79, 190n. 101, 193n. 128
Hitler, Adolf 153
Hobbes, Thomas 22, 28
Hooker, Richard 199n. 21
Hovey, Craig 90–2
Hunt, Lynn 74, 88–9

imagination 52, 99, 122, 130, 183n. 30, 188n. 76
irony 8, 40, 72, 75, 78
Islam 160–2, 180n. 3

Jerome 122

Kant, Immanuel/Kantian 3, 8, 79, 81, 103–4, 106, 146–8, 151, 182n. 17, 186n. 72, 188n. 79
Kenneson, Philip 183n. 31
kenosis 121
Kierkegaard, Søren 153
King Philip IV 77–8, 85
Klein, Naomi 61

Las Meninas see Velázquez 77–8, 81, 85
liberalism (political) 61–2, 123, 167n. 49
Locke, John 22
Luther, Martin 48, 153

Macey, David 86–8
MacIntyre, Alasdair 62, 74, 149, 175n. 21
McCabe, Herbert 200n. 23
McClendon, James 89, 91–2
McDowell, John 146
McKenny, Gerald 136
McSweeney, John 163n. 2, 179n. 72

madness 18, 70, 96, 100, 109–10, 179n. 73
Malthusian Economics 28
Martin, Rux 164n. 10, 164n. 11
Marx, Karl/Marxism 7–8, 55, 203n. 53
historical materialism 10
May, Todd 179n. 1
Milbank, John 50
Miller, James 69–76, 78, 83–4, 86–92, 160, 175n. 21, 176n. 27
Moore, G. E. 199n. 21
multinational corporations 25, 56
multitude, the 38, 52–3, 57–63
My Secret Life 112

nation-state 22, 25, 53–61, 171n. 1
Negri, Antonio *see* Hardt, Michael
Nietzsche, Friedrich 8, 17, 40–1, 50, 67, 74, 76, 78, 81–2, 95, 98, 103–4, 121, 168n. 91, 181n. 11, 184n. 50, 185n. 59, 187n. 72
Nietzschean genealogy 21
Nietzschean ontology 50
nominalism 29, 165n. 16
normal 21, 23, 31
normality/abnormality 18–19, 23, 28, 31–2, 84
normalization 10, 19, 21, 25–6, 31–2, 36, 39, 84, 161
Northcott, Michael 199n. 21
Nussbaum, Martha 17

Oksala, Johanna 183n. 30, 196n. 151
oppression 9, 11, 20, 23, 36, 111, 194n. 136
ordinary language (philosophy) 2, 126–30, 155, 181n. 11
Owen, David 181n. 11

panopticon/panopticism 24, 26–32, 36, 144, 167n. 68, 190n. 99
parrhesia 90–1, 141
patience 91–2, 168n. 75
Paul Veyne 9, 76, 92, 167n. 54, 182n. 15, 182n. 20, 183n. 29

209

Index

Peters, Michael 86
Philo 119
Pinto, Henrique 163n. 2
Plato/Platonism/Platonic 52, 104, 106, 123, 139, 179n. 73, 186n. 70, 186n. 72, 191n. 109, 195n. 137, 199n. 21
Plutarch 138
politics
  of immanence 38, 50–1
  political liberalism 61–2, 123
  political realism 60
post-structuralism 79
power *see also* biopower
  agential 24, 45
  and body/bodies 23–38, 60–1, 89, 116–17, 139, 151, 167n. 68, 184n. 45, 202n. 45, 203n. 53
  capillary 24, 27, 30, 34, 38–9, 58, 101, 111, 193n. 128
  centralized 23–5, 54, 98
  Christian 122
  classic liberal conceptions of 22
  double agency of 45, 49
  effects of 10, 22, 27, 98–9
  Foucault as theorist of 20, 45
  Foucault's restatement of 22, 196n. 147
  and intent 24–5
  Juridical account of 23, 46, 54
  and knowledge 77, 121
  Marxist forms of 46
  mechanisms of 30, 33, 37
  panoptic nature of 36, 167n. 68
  positive technologies of 18
  as relation 164n. 7
  relationships of 20, 164n. 7, 165n. 16, 169n. 88, 180n. 8, 184n. 39, 190n. 99
  resistance to 11, 25, 38, 173n. 40
  and the state 25
  technologies of 18, 165n. 18, 166n. 43, 184n. 45, 200n. 22
  ubiquity of 2, 22, 25, 34, 38, 43, 50, 62–3, 96–9, 112, 121–4, 133
Pseudo-Dionysius 82

Quash, Ben 156, 205n. 75

Rabinow, Paul 163n. 1
repressive hypothesis, the 8–12, 35–9, 57, 94, 111–12, 115, 126
Rhees, Rush 205n. 75
Rodrick, Dani 170n. 1
Rogers, Eugene 181n. 14, 202n. 45
Rorty, Richard 51, 74, 175n. 21
Rosenweig, Franz 53
Rousseau, Jean–Jacques 153

Safran Foer, Jonathan 125–6, 130–9, 142–3, 149–51, 155, 200n. 22
Salmagundi 73–8
Sartre, Jean-Paul 102–3
Schuld, J. Joyce 163n. 2
Scott, Charles E. 190n. 96, 201n. 37
self, the
  emergence of 107, 193n. 128
  modern conceptions of 115
  self-care (care for the self) 2, 13, 18, 21, 93–4, 96–7, 113, 115, 118–19, 125–59, 194n. 137, 200n. 25
  self-constitution 18–19, 21, 41, 43
  self-creation 72
  self-deception 36
  self-distancing 43
  self-governance 96
  self-knowledge 93, 117, 123
  self-sacrifice 93–4
  self-writing 2, 59, 65–92, 96, 120, 138
  selfhood 18, 22, 34, 37, 89, 93, 104, 112–13, 128, 130, 161, 163n. 2
  technologies/techniques of 119
Seneca 97, 112
sex/sexuality
  perversion 18
  sexual freedom 35
  sexual repression 9, 36, 95

Index

sin 6, 48, 120
Singer, Peter 136, 151, 198n. 13, 203n. 55
Socrates/Socratic 132, 138, 179n. 73
Sorabji, Richard 155
speech, habits of 10, 19, 32, 110
Spinoza, Baruch 51, 171n. 8
state of emergency 26
state of exception 27–8
state of plague 28
stoicism 138
Stout, Jeffrey 196n. 147, 171n. 6
subjectivity 2, 18, 34, 41–3, 46, 52, 57, 59, 70, 79, 84, 94, 96, 102–4, 108, 111, 125–6, 138, 160–1, 176n. 46, 180n. 3, 183n. 30, 186n. 72, 190n. 100
inter-subjectivity 94–104
suicide 20, 125–6, 138, 188n. 76
surveillance 19, 22, 26–30, 37, 71, 82, 96, 127, 180n. 8

Taylor, Charles 39–44, 47, 101, 168n. 88, 169n. 91, 170n. 96
Taylor, Chloe 100, 193n. 128
Taylor, Mark Lewis 171n. 4
tertullian 113
Thoreau, Henry David 153, 197n. 6
Tolstoy, Leo 153

transcendence/immanence 38, 42–3, 50–4, 58, 73, 79, 81–2, 104–6, 108, 112, 127–8, 186n. 72, 195n. 137
Turner, Denys 157

universals 19, 52, 153
utilitarianism (preference) 136, 151, 203n. 55

vegetarianism 126, 130–45, 152–3, 155, 157–8
biblical arguments for 198n.17
and moral conviction 140–5
Velázquez, Diego
(*Las Meninas*) 78–84
violence 5, 50, 55, 60, 63, 75, 95, 122, 145, 174n. 60
Visker, Rudy 183n. 28

Webb, Stephen H. 157, 205n. 74
Wells, Samuel 183n. 36, 198n. 16, 205n. 75
West, Cornel 171n. 6, 197n. 1
Williams, Rowan 204n. 65
Wittgenstein, Ludwig 86, 93, 126, 146–7, 150, 153, 155, 167n. 54, 181n. 11, 201n. 39
Wolfe, Cary 145, 147
Wolin, Sheldon 53, 171n. 16
worship 4, 6, 123, 205n. 75

www.ingramcontent.com/pod-product-compliance
Lightning Source LLC
Chambersburg PA
CBHW050138240426
43673CB00043B/1717